Kristen Nehemiah Horst (Ed.)

Lidia Yusupova

Kristen Nehemiah Horst (Ed.)

Lidia Yusupova

Coordinator, Human rights, Memorial (society), First Chechen War

Dign Press

Imprint

Publisher:
Dign Press is a trademark of
International Book Market Service Ltd., 17 Rue Meldrum, Beau Bassin, 1713-01 Mauritius
Email: info@bookmarketservice.com
Website: www.bookmarketservice.com

Published in 2011

Printed in: U.S.A., U.K., Germany. This book was not produced in Mauritius.

ISBN: 978-613-7-70372-4

Contents

Articles

References

Lidia Yusupova

Lidia Muhtarovna Yusupova (*Лидия Мухтаровна Юсупова*) (born September 15, 1961 in Grozny, Soviet Union) is the Coordinator of the law office of the Moscow-based human rights organization Memorial. Formerly, Yusupova was the director of the Grozny office of Memorial. Currently, Yusupova is completing a two year law fellowship in Moscow.

Yusupova was born to Chechen father and Russian mother in the city of Grozny. She studied Russian Literature at the Karachaevo-Cherkeski Intstitute. Later she studied law at the Chechen University in the city of Grozny, and served as a professor in that field. During the First Chechen War, she witnessed the tragedy of war, and suffered the loss of several friends, neighbors, colleagues, and family members. In 2000, during the Second Chechen War, she decided to devote her life to human rights, using her legal expertise and personal experience during both wars to help others that were entangled in the bloody conflict.

Yusupova gathers testimony from victims of human rights abuses, and presses their cases with law enforcement and military agencies. Not only does she, to the extent possible, provide the victims with legal assistance, but she also informs the rest of the world on violations of human rights, committed by Russian armed forces and Chechen rebels alike. Yusupova has been described by the BBC News service as "the bravest woman in Europe"[1], and representatives of Amnesty International have similarly declared her "one of the most courageous women in Europe".[2] Both Yusupova and her organization have been nominated for the Nobel Peace Prize.[3][4]

Yusupova has been awarded the 2004 Martin Ennals Award for Human Rights Defenders and the 2005 Professor Thorolf Rafto Memorial Prize.

The International Federation of Human Rights reported that Yusupova faced death threats for her work on October 12, 2006.[5]

Quotes

- "Mass-scale human-rights violations and state-level terror still are the order of the day...Everyone now is endangered, not only those who live in Chechnya, but those who live in Russia as well... Society will respond. Some counterweight to this lunacy must emerge, be it in the shape of a new dissident movement, or other forms we don't yet discern. The authorities will as inevitably seek to suppress this movement cruelly and brutally. But suppression will only promote its growth, all the fears notwithstanding." [6]
- "...we should not give up and say that the situation is hopeless. There is still our conscience, there is still the memory of the victims of this war, there is still our duty to try and prevent further bloodshed. We have to prosecute all the perpetrators of war crimes and crimes against humanity."[7]

External links

- First Post article [8]
- Reuters report [9]
- Time Europe: Dissident Voices [6]
- 2004 Martin Ennals Award Press Release [10]
- 2005 Rafto Prize Press Release [11]
- International Federation of Human Rights report on death threats [5]
- "Nobel candidacy spurred threat" - Aftenposten [12]
- Universal Declaration of Human Rights Heroes [13]
- Lida Yusupova - World People's Blog [14]
- Interview with Lida Yusupova - Ministry of Foreign Affairs of the Chechen Republic of Ichkeria (in French) [15]

References

[1] http://news.bbc.co.uk/2/shared/spl/hi/picture_gallery/04/europe_chechnya0s_bright_side/html/10.stm
[2] http://www.amnesty.org.uk/news_details.asp?NewsID=15041
[3] http://www.iht.com/articles/ap/2006/09/11/europe/EU_GEN_Norway_Nobel_Odds.php
[4] http://www.rferl.org/featuresarticle/2007/03/cec9aab7-5df5-4cc4-8dec-ca138c3cbdc7.html
[5] http://www.fidh.org/article.php3?id_article=3722
[6] http://www.time.com/time/europe/magazine/article/0,13005,901061204-1562922,00.html
[7] http://www.betterworld.net/heroes/yusupova.htm
[8] http://www.thefirstpost.co.uk/index.php?storyID=8236.html
[9] http://www.alertnet.org/thenews/newsdesk/L09657731.htm
[10] http://www.martinennalsaward.org/en/press/2003-12-05.html
[11] http://www.rafto.no/DesktopModules/ViewAnnouncement.aspx?ItemID=183&Mid=42
[12] http://www.aftenposten.no/english/local/article1493896.ece
[13] http://www.universalrights.net/heroes/display.php3?id=79
[14] http://word.world-citizenship.org/word/index.php/wp-archive/354
[15] http://www.chechnya-mfa.info/print_press.php?func=detail&par=12985

Coordinator

Coordinator may refer to:

- In academics: one who administers the research and teaching activities of the other professors.
- Coordinators (Gundam SEED), genetically engineered humans in the *Gundam SEED* series
- Coordinating conjunction or grammatical conjunction
- Coordinator Sprocket, a fictional character in *Viewtiful Joe*
- Parenting coordinator, a mental health professional assigned by the Court to manage on-going issues in child custody
- In the corporate world, "coordinator" can also be another name for an administrative assistant, or sometimes an employee slightly higher-ranking than an admin assistant. However, the term "Coordinator" can refer to a position within an organization or business with significant responsibilities for acting as a liaison between departments, stakeholders and information sources, which requires many non-administrative competencies. See facilitator.

Human rights

Human rights are "basic rights and freedoms that all people are entitled to regardless of nationality, sex, national or ethnic origin, race, religion, language, or other status."[1] Human rights are conceived as universal and egalitarian, with all people having equal rights by virtue of being human.[1] [2] These rights may exist as natural rights or as legal rights, in both national and international law.[3] The doctrine of human rights in international practice, within international law, global and regional institutions, in the policies of states and the activities of non-governmental organizations has been a cornerstone of public policy around the world. It has been said that: "if the public discourse of peacetime global society can be said to have a common moral language, it is that of human rights."[4] Despite this, the strong claims made by the doctrine of human rights continue to provoke considerable skepticism, debates about the content, nature and justifications of human rights continue to this day.

Many of the basic ideas that animated the movement developed in the aftermath of the Second World War and the atrocities of the Holocaust, culminating in the adoption of the *Universal Declaration of Human Rights* in Paris by the United Nations General Assembly in 1948. The ancient world did not possess the concept of universal human rights.[5] Ancient societies had "elaborate systems of duties... conceptions of justice, political legitimacy, and human flourishing that sought to realize human dignity, flourishing, or well-being entirely independent of human rights".[6] The modern concept of human rights developed during the early Modern period, alongside the European secularization of Judeo-Christian ethics.[7] The true forerunner of human rights discourse was the concept of natural rights which appeared as part of the medieval Natural law tradition, became prominent during the Enlightenment with such philosophers as John Locke, Francis Hutcheson, and Jean-Jacques Burlamaqui, and featured prominently in the political discourse of the American Revolution and the French Revolution.

From this foundation, the modern human rights movement emerged over the latter half of the twentieth century. Gelling as social activism and political rhetoric in many nations put it high on the world agenda.[8] By the 21st century, Moyn has argued, the human rights movement expanded beyond its original anti-totalitarianism to include numerous causes involving humanitarianism and social and economic development in the Third World.[9]

> "All human beings are born free and equal in dignity and rights. They are endowed with reason and conscience and should act towards one another in a spirit of brotherhood."
>
> —Article 1 of the United Nations Universal Declaration of Human Rights (UDHR)[2]

Theory

History

The Bill of Rights

The Bill of Rights (1688 or 1689)

Created	1689
Ratified	16 December 1689
Location	National Archives of the United Kingdom
Authors	Parliament of England
Purpose	Ensure certain freedoms and ensure a Protestant political supremacy.

The modern sense of human rights can be traced to Renaissance Europe and the Protestant Reformation, alongside the disappearance of the feudal authoritarianism and religious conservativism that dominated the Middle Ages. Human rights were defined as a result of European scholars attempting to form a "secularized version of Judeo-Christian ethics".[10] Although ideas of rights and liberty have existed in some form for much of human history, they do not resemble the modern conception of human rights. According to Jack Donnelly, in the ancient world, "traditional societies typically have had elaborate systems of duties... conceptions of justice, political legitimacy, and human flourishing that sought to realize human dignity, flourishing, or well-being entirely independent of human rights. These institutions and practices are alternative to, rather than different formulations of, human rights".[11] The concept of universal human rights was not known in the ancient world, not in Ancient Greece and Rome, Ancient India, Ancient China, nor among the Hebrews; slavery, for instance, was justified in ancient times as a natural condition.[5] Medieval charters of liberty such as the English Magna Carta were not charters of human rights, let alone general charters of rights: they instead constituted a form of limited political and legal agreement to address specific political circumstances, in the case of Magna Carta later being mythologized in the course of early modern debates about rights.[12]

The basis of most modern legal interpretations of human rights can be traced back to recent European history. The Twelve Articles (1525) are considered to be the first record of human rights in Europe. They were part of the peasants' demands raised towards the Swabian League in the German Peasants' War in Germany. In Spain in 1542 Bartolomé de Las Casas argued against Juan Ginés de Sepúlveda in the famous Valladolid debate, Sepúlveda mainted an Aristotelian view of humanity as divided into classes of different worth, while Las Casas argued in favor of equal rights to freedom of slavery for all humans regardless of race or religion. In Britain in 1683, the English Bill of Rights (or "An Act Declaring the Rights and Liberties of the Subject and Settling the Succession of the Crown") and the Scottish Claim of Right each made illegal a range of oppressive governmental actions. Two major revolutions occurred during the 18th century, in the United States (1776) and in France (1789), leading to the adoption of the United States Declaration of Independence and the French Declaration of the Rights of Man and of the Citizen respectively, both of which established certain legal rights. Additionally, the Virginia Declaration of Rights of 1776 encoded into law a number of fundamental civil rights and civil freedoms.

> We hold these truths to be self-evident, that all men are created equal, that they are endowed by their Creator with certain unalienable Rights, that among these are Life, Liberty and the pursuit of Happiness.
>
> —United States Declaration of Independence, 1776

Declaration of the Rights of Man and of the Citizen approved by the National Assembly of France, August 26, 1789.

These were followed by developments in philosophy of human rights by philosophers such as Thomas Paine, John Stuart Mill and G.W.F. Hegel during the 18th and 19th centuries. The term *human rights* probably came into use some time between Paine's *The Rights of Man* and William Lloyd Garrison's 1831 writings in *The Liberator*, in which he stated that he was trying to enlist his readers in "the great cause of human rights".[13]

In the 19th century, human rights became a central concern over the issue of slavery. A number of reformers, such as William Wilberforce in Britain, worked towards the abolition of slavery. This was achieved in the British Empire by the Slave Trade Act 1807 and the Slavery Abolition Act 1833. In the United States, all the northern states had abolished the institution of slavery between 1777 and 1804, although southern states clung tightly to the "peculiar institution". Conflict and debates over the expansion of slavery to new territories culminated in the southern states' secession and the American Civil War. During the reconstruction period immediately following the war, several amendments to the United States Constitution were made. These included the 13th amendment, banning slavery, the 14th amendment, assuring full citizenship and civil rights to all people born in the United States, and the 15th amendment, guaranteeing African Americans the right to vote.[14]

Many groups and movements have achieved profound social changes over the course of the 20th century in the name of human rights. In Western Europe and North America, labour unions brought about laws granting workers the right to strike, establishing minimum work conditions and forbidding or regulating child labor. The women's rights movement succeeded in gaining for many women the right to vote. National liberation movements in many countries succeeded in driving out colonial powers. One of the most influential was Mahatma Gandhi's movement to free his native India from British rule. Movements by long-oppressed racial and religious minorities succeeded in many parts of the world, among them the African American Civil Rights Movement, and more recent diverse identity politics movements, on behalf of women and minorities in the United States.

The establishment of the International Committee of the Red Cross, the 1864 Lieber Code and the first of the Geneva Conventions in 1864 laid the foundations of International humanitarian law, to be further developed following the two World Wars.

The World Wars, and the huge losses of life and gross abuses of human rights that took place during them, were a driving force behind the development of modern human rights instruments. The League of Nations was established in 1919 at the negotiations over the Treaty of Versailles following the end of World War I. The League's goals included disarmament, preventing war through collective security, settling disputes between countries through negotiation and diplomacy, and improving global welfare. Enshrined in its charter was a mandate to promote many of the rights later included in the Universal Declaration of Human Rights.

At the 1945 Yalta Conference, the Allied Powers agreed to create a new body to supplant the League's role; this was to be the United Nations. The United Nations has played an important role in international human-rights law since its creation. Following the World Wars, the United Nations and its members developed much of the discourse and the bodies of law that now make up international humanitarian law and international human rights law.

Philosophy

The philosophy of human rights attempts to examine the underlying basis of the concept of human rights and critically looks at its content and justification. Several theoretical approaches have been advanced to explain how and why human rights become part of social expectations.

One of the oldest Western philosophies on human rights is that they are a product of a natural law, stemming from different philosophical or religious grounds. Other theories hold that human rights codify moral behavior which is a human social product developed by a process of biological and social evolution (associated with Hume). Human rights are also described as a sociological pattern of rule setting (as in the sociological theory of law and the work of Weber). These approaches include the notion that individuals in a society accept rules from legitimate authority in exchange for security and economic advantage (as in Rawls) – a social contract. The two theories that dominate contemporary human rights discussion are the interest theory and the will theory. Interest theory argues that the principal function of human rights is to protect and promote certain essential human interests, while will theory attempts to establish the validity of human rights based on the unique human capacity for freedom.[15] The strong claims made by human rights to universality have led to persistent criticism. Philosophers who have criticized the concept of human rights include Jeremy Bentham, Edmund Burke, Friedrich Nietzsche and Karl Marx.

Classification of human rights

Human rights can be classified and organized in a number of different ways, at an international level the most common categorisation of human rights has been to split them into civil and political rights, and economic, social and cultural rights.

Civil and political rights are enshrined in articles 3 to 21 of the Universal Declaration of Human Rights (UDHR) and in the International Covenant on Civil and Political Rights (ICCPR). Economic, social and cultural rights are enshrined in articles 22 to 28 of the Universal Declaration of Human Rights (UDHR) and in the International Covenant on Economic, Social and Cultural Rights (ICESCR).

Indivisibility

The UDHR included both economic, social and cultural rights and civil and political rights because it was based on the principle that the different rights could only successfully exist in combination:

> The ideal of free human beings enjoying civil and political freedom and freedom from fear and want can only be achieved if conditions are created whereby everyone may enjoy his civil and political rights, as well as his social, economic and cultural rights.
>
> —International Covenant on Civil and Political Rights and the International Covenant on Economic Social and Cultural Rights, 1966

This is held to be true because without civil and political rights the public cannot assert their economic, social and cultural rights. Similarly, without livelihoods and a working society, the public cannot assert or make use of civil or political rights (known as the *full belly thesis*).

The indivisibility and interdependence of all human rights has been confirmed by the 1993 Vienna Declaration and Programme of Action:

> All human rights are universal, indivisible and interdependent and related. The international community must treat human rights globally in a fair and equal manner, on the same footing, and with the same emphasis.
>
> —Vienna Declaration and Programme of Action, World Conference on Human Rights, 1993

This statement was again endorsed at the 2005 World Summit in New York (paragraph 121).

Although accepted by the signatories to the UDHR, most do not in practice give equal weight to the different types of rights. Some Western cultures have often given priority to civil and political rights, sometimes at the expense of economic and social rights such as the right to work, to education, health and housing. For example, in the United

States there is no universal access to healthcare free at the point of use.[16] That is not to say that Western cultures have overlooked these rights entirely (the welfare states that exist in Western Europe are evidence of this). Similarly the ex Soviet bloc countries and Asian countries have tended to give priority to economic, social and cultural rights, but have often failed to provide civil and political rights.

Categorization

Opponents of the indivisibility of human rights argue that economic, social and cultural rights are fundamentally different from civil and political rights and require completely different approaches. Economic, social and cultural rights are argued to be:[17]

- *positive*, meaning that they require active provision of entitlements by the state (as opposed to the state being required only to prevent the breach of rights)
- *resource-intensive*, meaning that they are expensive and difficult to provide
- *progressive*, meaning that they will take significant time to implement
- *vague*, meaning they cannot be quantitatively measured, and whether they are adequately provided or not is difficult to judge
- *ideologically divisive/political*, meaning that there is no consensus on what should and shouldn't be provided as a right
- *socialist*, as opposed to capitalist
- *non-justiciable*, meaning that their provision, or the breach of them, cannot be judged in a court of law
- *aspirations or goals*, as opposed to real 'legal' rights

Similarly civil and political rights are categorized as:

- *negative*, meaning the state can protect them simply by taking no action
- *cost-free*
- *immediate*, meaning they can be immediately provided if the state decides to
- *precise*, meaning their provision is easy to judge and measure
- *non-ideological/non-political*
- *capitalist*
- *justiciable*
- *real 'legal' rights*

In *The No-Nonsense Guide to Human Rights,* Olivia Ball and Paul Gready argue that for both civil and political rights and economic, social and cultural rights, it is easy to find examples which do not fit into the above categorisation. Among several others, they highlight the fact that maintaining a judicial system, a fundamental requirement of the civil right to due process before the law and other rights relating to judicial process, is positive, resource-intensive, progressive and vague, while the social right to housing is precise, justiciable and can be a real 'legal' right.[18]

Three generations

Another categorization, offered by Karel Vasak, is that there are *three generations of human rights*: first-generation civil and political rights (right to life and political participation), second-generation economic, social and cultural rights (right to subsistence) and third-generation solidarity rights (right to peace, right to clean environment). Out of these generations, the third generation is the most debated and lacks both legal and political recognition. This categorisation is at odds with the indivisibility of rights, as it implicitly states that some rights can exist without others. Prioritisation of rights for pragmatic reasons is however a widely accepted necessity. Human rights expert Philip Alston argues:

> If every possible human rights element is deemed to be essential or necessary, then nothing will be treated as though it is truly important.[19]

He, and others, urge caution with prioritisation of rights:

> [T]he call for prioritizing is not to suggest that any obvious violations of rights can be ignored.
>
> —Philip Alston[19]
>
> Priorities, where necessary, should adhere to core concepts (such as reasonable attempts at progressive realization) and principles (such as non-discrimination, equality and participation.
>
> —Olivia Ball, Paul Gready[20]

Some human rights are said to be "inalienable rights". The term inalienable rights (or unalienable rights) refers to "a set of human rights that are fundamental, are not awarded by human power, and cannot be surrendered."

International protection

In the aftermath of the atrocities of World War II there was increased concern in the social and legal protection of human rights as fundamental freedoms. The foundation of the United Nations and the provisions of the United Nations Charter would provide a basis for a comprehensive system of international law and practise for the protection of human rights. The term "international human rights law" is often used as a category of reference to describe these systems, but this can be a source of confusion as there is no separate entity as "international human rights law" but an interlocking system of non-binding conventions, international treaties, domestic law, international organisations and political bodies .[21] .

United Nations Charter

The provisions of the United Nations charter provided a basis for the development of international human rights protection.[21] The preamble of the charter provides that the members "reaffirm faith in fundamental human rights, in the equal rights of men and women" and Article 1(3) of the United Nations charter states that one of the purposes of the UN is: "to achieve international cooperation in solving international problems of an economic, social, cultural, or humanitarian character, and in promoting and encouraging respect for human rights and for fundamental freedoms for all without distinction as to race, sex, language, or religion".[22] Article 55 provides that:

> The United Nations shall promote: a) higher standards of living, full employment, and conditions of economic and social progress and development; b) solutions of international economic, social, health, and related problems; c) international cultural and educational cooperation; d)universal respect for, and observance of, human rights and fundamental freedoms for all without distinction as to race, sex, language, or religion.

Of particular importance is Article 56 of the charter:"All Members pledge themselves to take joint and separate action in co-operation with the Organization for the achievement of the purposes set forth in Article 55." This is a binding treaty provision applicable to both the Organisation and its members and has been taken to constitute a legal obligation for the members of the United Nations.[21] Overall, the references to human rights in the Charter are general and vague. The Charter does not contain specific legal rights, nor does it mandate any enforcement procedures to protect these rights.[23] Despite this, the significance of the espousal of human rights within the UN charter must not be understated. The importance of human rights on the global stage can be traced to the importance of human rights within the United Nations framework and the UN Charter can be seen as the starting point for the development of a broad array of declarations, treaties, implementation and enforcement mechanisms, UN organs, committees and reports on the protection of human rights. [23] The rights espoused in the UN charter would be codified and defined in the International Bill of Human Rights, composing the Universal Declaration of Human Rights, the International Covenant on Civil and Political Rights and the International Covenant on Economic, Social and Cultural Rights.

Universal Declaration of Human Rights

The **Universal Declaration of Human Rights (UDHR)** was adopted by the United Nations General Assembly[25] in 1948, partly in response to the atrocities of World War II. Although the UDHR was a non-binding resolution, it is now considered by some to have acquired the force of international customary law which may be invoked in appropriate circumstances by national and other judiciaries.[26] The UDHR urges member nations to promote a number of human, civil, economic and social rights, asserting these rights as part of the "foundation of freedom, justice and peace in the world." The declaration was the first international legal effort to limit the behaviour of states and press upon them duties to their citizens following the model of the rights-duty duality.

"It is not a treaty...[In the future, it] may well become the international Magna Carta."[24] Eleanor Roosevelt with the Spanish text of the Universal Declaration in 1949.

> ...recognition of the inherent dignity and of the equal and inalienable rights of all members of the human family is the foundation of freedom, justice and peace in the world.
>
> —Preamble to the Universal Declaration of Human Rights, 1948

The UDHR was framed by members of the Human Rights Commission, with former First Lady Eleanor Roosevelt as Chair, who began to discuss an *International Bill of Rights* in 1947. The members of the Commission did not immediately agree on the form of such a bill of rights, and whether, or how, it should be enforced. The Commission proceeded to frame the UDHR and accompanying treaties, but the UDHR quickly became the priority.[27] Canadian law professor John Humphrey and French lawyer René Cassin were responsible for much of the cross-national research and the structure of the document respectively, where the articles of the declaration were interpretative of the general principle of the preamble. The document was structured by Cassin to include the basic principles of dignity, liberty, equality and brotherhood in the first two articles, followed successively by rights pertaining to individuals; rights of individuals in relation to each other and to groups; spiritual, public and political rights; and economic, social and cultural rights. The final three articles place, according to Cassin, rights in the context of limits, duties and the social and political order in which they are to be realized.[27] Humphrey and Cassin intended the rights in the UDHR to be legally enforceable through some means, as is reflected in the third clause of the preamble:[27]

> Whereas it is essential, if man is not to be compelled to have recourse, as a last resort, to rebellion against tyranny and oppression, that human rights should be protected by the rule of law.
>
> —Preamble to the Universal Declaration of Human Rights, 1948

Some of the UDHR was researched and written by a committee of international experts on human rights, including representatives from all continents and all major religions, and drawing on consultation with leaders such as Mahatma Gandhi.[28] [29] The inclusion of civil, political, economic, social and cultural rights[27] [30] was predicated on the assumption that all human rights are indivisible and that the different types of rights listed are inextricably linked. This principle was not then opposed by any member states (the declaration was adopted unanimously, Byelorussian SSR, Czechoslovakia, Poland, Saudi Arabia, Ukrainian SSR, Union of South Africa, USSR, Yugoslavia.); however, this principle was later subject to significant challenges.[30]

The Universal Declaration was bifurcated into treaties, a Covenant on Civil and Political Rights and another on social, economic, and cultural rights, due to questions about the relevance and propriety of economic and social provisions in covenants on human rights. Both covenants begin with the right of people to self-determination and to sovereignty over their natural resources. This debate over whether human rights are more fundamental than economic rights has continued to the present day.[31]

The drafters of the Covenants initially intended only one instrument. The original drafts included only political and civil rights, but economic and social rights were also proposed. The disagreement over which rights were basic human rights resulted in there being two covenants. The debate was whether economic and social rights are aspirational, as contrasted with basic human rights which all people possess purely by being human, because economic and social rights depend on wealth and the availability of resources. In addition, which social and economic rights should be recognised depends on ideology or economic theories, in contrast to basic human rights, which are defined purely by the nature (mental and physical abilities) of human beings. It was debated whether economic rights were appropriate subjects for binding obligations and whether the lack of consensus over such rights would dilute the strength of political-civil rights. There was wide agreement and clear recognition that the means required to enforce or induce compliance with socio-economic undertakings were different from the means required for civil-political rights.[32]

This debate and the desire for the greatest number of signatories to human-rights law led to the two covenants. The Soviet bloc and a number of developing countries had argued for the inclusion of all rights in a so-called *Unity Resolution*. Both covenants allowed states to derogate some rights. Those in favor of a single treaty could not gain sufficient consensus.[33] [34]

Treaties

In 1966, the International Covenant on Civil and Political Rights (**ICCPR**) and the International Covenant on Economic, Social and Cultural Rights (**ICESCR**) were adopted by the United Nations, between them making the rights contained in the UDHR binding on all states that have signed this treaty, creating human-rights law.

Since then numerous other treaties (pieces of legislation) have been offered at the international level. They are generally known as *human rights instruments*. Some of the most significant, referred to (with ICCPR and ICESCR) as "the seven core treaties", are:

- Convention on the Elimination of All Forms of Racial Discrimination (**CERD**) (adopted 1966, entry into force: 1969)
- Convention on the Elimination of All Forms of Discrimination Against Women (**CEDAW**) (adopted 1979, entry into force: 1981)
- United Nations Convention Against Torture (**CAT**) (adopted 1984, entry into force: 1984)
- Convention on the Rights of the Child (**CRC**) (adopted 1989, entry into force: 1989)
- Convention on the Rights of Persons with Disabilities (**CRPD**) (adopted 2006, entry into force: 2008)
- International Convention on the Protection of the Rights of All Migrant Workers and Members of their Families (**ICRMW** or more often **MWC**) (adopted 1990, entry into force: 2003)

International Humanitarian Law

The **Geneva Conventions** came into being between 1864 and 1949 as a result of efforts by Henry Dunant, the founder of the International Committee of the Red Cross. The conventions safeguard the human rights of individuals involved in armed conflict, and build on the 1899 and 1907 Hague Conventions, the international community's first attempt to formalize the laws of war and war crimes in the nascent body of secular international law. The conventions were revised as a result of World War II and readopted by the international community in 1949.

Original Geneva Convention in 1864.

United Nations

The UN General Assembly

The United Nations (UN) as an intergovernmental body seeks to apply international jurisdiction for universal human-rights legislation.[35] Within the UN machinery, human-rights issues are primarily the concern of the United Nations Security Council and the United Nations Human Rights Council, and there are numerous committees within the UN with responsibilities for safeguarding different human-rights treaties. The most senior body of the UN in the sphere of human rights is the Office of the High Commissioner for Human Rights. The United Nations has an international mandate to:

> achieve international co-operation in solving international problems of an economic, social, cultural, or humanitarian character, and in promoting and encouraging respect for human rights and for fundamental freedoms for all without distinction as to race, gender, language, or religion.
>
> —Article 1–3 of the United Nations Charter

Human Rights Council

United Nations Human Rights Council logo.

The United Nations **Human Rights Council**, created at the 2005 World Summit to replace the United Nations Commission on Human Rights, has a mandate to investigate violations of human rights.[36] The Human Rights Council is a subsidiary body of the General Assembly[37] and reports directly to it. It ranks below the Security Council, which is the final authority for the interpretation of the United Nations Charter.[38] Forty-seven of the one hundred ninety-one member states sit on the council, elected by simple majority in a secret ballot of the United Nations General Assembly. Members serve a maximum of six years and may have their membership suspended for gross human rights abuses. The Council is based in Geneva, and meets three times a year; with additional meetings to respond to urgent situations.[39]

Independent experts (*rapporteurs*) are retained by the Council to investigate alleged human rights abuses and to provide the Council with reports.

The Human Rights Council may request that the Security Council take action when human rights violations occur. This action may be direct actions, may involve sanctions, and the Security Council may also refer cases to the International Criminal Court (ICC) even if the issue being referred is outside the normal jurisdiction of the ICC.[40]

The United Nations Security Council has the primary responsibility for maintaining international peace and security and is the only body of the UN that can authorize the use of force. It has been criticised for failing to take action to prevent human rights abuses, including the Darfur crisis, the Srebrenica massacre and the Rwandan Genocide.[41] For example, critics blamed the presence of non-democracies on the Security Council for its failure regarding.[42]

On April 28, 2006 the Security Council adopted resolution 1674 that reaffirmed the responsibility to protect populations from genocide, war crimes, ethnic cleansing and crimes against humanity" and committed the Security Council to action to protect civilians in armed conflict.[43]

Other UN Treaty Bodies

A modern interpretation of the original Declaration of Human Rights was made in the Vienna Declaration and Programme of Action adopted by the World Conference on Human Rights in 1993. The degree of unanimity over these conventions, in terms of how many and which countries have ratified them varies, as does the degree to which they are respected by various states. The UN has set up a number of *treaty-based* bodies to monitor and study human rights, to be supported by the UN High Commissioner for Human Rights (UNHCHR). The bodies are committees of independent experts that monitor implementation of the core international human rights treaties. They are created by the treaty that they monitor, except CESCR.

- The *Human Rights Committee* promotes participation with the standards of the ICCPR. The eighteen members of the committee express opinions on member countries and make judgments on individual complaints against countries which have ratified an Optional Protocol to the treaty. The judgments, termed "views", are not legally binding.
- The *Committee on Economic, Social and Cultural Rights* monitors the ICESCR and makes general comments on ratifying countries performance. It will have the power to receive complaints against the countries that opted into the Optional Protocol once it has come into force.
- The *Committee on the Elimination of Racial Discrimination* monitors the CERD and conducts regular reviews of countries' performance. It can make judgments on complaints against member states allowing it, but these are not legally binding. It issues warnings to attempt to prevent serious contraventions of the convention.
- The *Committee on the Elimination of Discrimination against Women* monitors the CEDAW. It receives states' reports on their performance and comments on them, and can make judgments on complaints against countries which have opted into the 1999 Optional Protocol.
- The *Committee Against Torture* monitors the CAT and receives states' reports on their performance every four years and comments on them. Its subcommittee may visit and inspect countries which have opted into the Optional Protocol.
- The *Committee on the Rights of the Child* monitors the CRC and makes comments on reports submitted by states every five years. It does not have the power to receive complaints.
- The *Committee on Migrant Workers* was established in 2004 and monitors the ICRMW and makes comments on reports submitted by states every five years. It will have the power to receive complaints of specific violations only once ten member states allow it.
- The *Committee on the Rights of Persons with Disabilities* was established in 2008 to monitor the Convention on the Rights of Persons with Disabilities. It has the power to receive complaints against the countries which have opted into the Optional Protocol to the Convention on the Rights of Persons with Disabilities.

Each treaty body receives secretariat support from the Human Rights Council and Treaties Division of Office of the High Commissioner on Human Rights (OHCHR) in Geneva except CEDAW, which is supported by the Division for the Advancement of Women (DAW). CEDAW formerly held all its sessions at United Nations headquarters in New York but now frequently meets at the United Nations Office in Geneva; the other treaty bodies meet in Geneva. The Human Rights Committee usually holds its March session in New York City.

Regional human rights regimes

International human rights regime's are in several cases "nested" within more comprehensive and overlapping regional agreements. These regional regimes can be seen as relatively independently coherent human rights sub-regimes.[44] Three principle regional human rights instruments can be identified, the African Charter on Human and Peoples' Rights, the American Convention on Human Rights (the Americas) and the European Convention on Human Rights. The European Convention on Human Rights has since 1950 defined and guaranteed human rights and fundamental freedoms in Europe.[45] All 47 member states of the Council of Europe have signed the Convention and are therefore under the jurisdiction of the European Court of Human Rights in Strasbourg.[45]

Non-Governmental Actors

Non-governmental Organizations

International non-governmental human rights organizations such as Amnesty International, Human Rights Watch, International Service for Human Rights and FIDH monitor what they see as human rights issues around the world and promote their views on the subject. Human rights organizations have been said to ""translate complex international issues into activities to be undertaken by concerned citizens in their own community".[46] Human rights organizations frequently engage in lobbying and advocacy in an effort to convince the United Nations, supranational bodies and national governments to adopt their policies on human rights. Many human-rights organizations have observer status at the various UN bodies tasked with protecting human rights. A new (in 2009) nongovernmental human-rights conference is the Oslo Freedom Forum, a gathering described by The Economist as "on its way to becoming a human-rights equivalent of the Davos economic forum." The same article noted that human-rights advocates are more and more divided amongst themselves over how violations of human rights are to be defined, notably as regards the Middle East.[47]

There is criticism of human-rights organisations who use their status but allegedly move away from their stated goals. For example, Gerald M. Steinberg, an Israel-based academic, maintains that NGOs take advantage of a "halo effect" and are "given the status of impartial moral watchdogs" by governments and the media.[48] Such critics claim that this may be seen at various governmental levels, including when human-rights groups testify before investigation committees.[49]

Human Rights Defenders

Human rights defender is a term used to describe people who, individually or with others, act to promote or protect human rights. Human rights defenders (HRDs) are those men and women who act peacefully for the promotion and protection of those rights.

Corporations

Multinational companies play an increasingly large role in the world, and have been responsible for numerous human rights abuses.[50] Although the legal and moral environment surrounding the actions of governments is reasonably well developed, that surrounding multinational companies is both controversial and ill-defined. Multinational companies' primary responsibility is to their shareholders, not to those affected by their actions. Such companies may be larger than the economies of some the states within which they operate, and can wield significant economic and political power. No international treaties exist to specifically cover the behavior of companies with regard to human rights, and national legislation is very variable. Jean Ziegler, Special Rapporteur of the UN Commission on Human Rights on the right to food stated in a report in 2003:

> [T]he growing power of transnational corporations and their extension of power through privatization, deregulation and the rolling back of the State also mean that it is now time to develop binding legal norms that hold corporations to human rights standards and circumscribe potential abuses of their position of power.
>
> —Jean Ziegler[51]

In August 2003 the Human Rights Commission's Sub-Commission on the Promotion and Protection of Human Rights produced draft *Norms on the responsibilities of transnational corporations and other business enterprises with regard to human rights*.[52] These were considered by the Human Rights Commission in 2004, but have no binding status on corporations and are not monitored.[53]

Human rights violations

Human rights violations occur when actions by state (or non-state) actors abuse, ignore, or deny basic human rights (including civil, political, cultural, social, and economic rights). Furthermore, violations of human rights can occur when any state or non-state actor breaches any part of the UDHR treaty or other international human rights or humanitarian law. In regard to human rights violations of United Nations laws, Article 39 of the United Nations Charter designates the UN Security Council (or an appointed authority) as the only tribunal that may determine UN human rights violations.

Human rights abuses are monitored by United Nations committees, national institutions and governments and by many independent non-governmental organizations, such as Amnesty International, International Federation of Human Rights, Human Rights Watch, World Organisation Against Torture, Freedom House, International Freedom of Expression Exchange and Anti-Slavery International. These organisations collect evidence and documentation of alleged human rights abuses and apply pressure to enforce human rights laws.

There are a wide variety of databases available which attempt to measure, in a rigorous fashion, exactly what violations governments commit against those within their territorial jurisdiction. An example of this is the list created and maintained by Prof. Christian Davenport at the Kroc Institute – University of Notre Dame.[54]

Wars of aggression, war crimes and crimes against humanity, including genocide, are breaches of International humanitarian law and represent the most serious of human rights violations.

In efforts to eliminate violations of human rights, building awareness and protesting inhumane treatment has often led to calls for action and sometimes improved conditions. The UN Security Council has interceded with peace keeping forces, and other states and treaties (NATO) have intervened in situations to protect human rights.

Substantive Rights

Right to life

> “Every human being has the inherent right to life. This right shall be protected by law. No one shall be arbitrarily deprived of his life.”
>
> —Article 6.1 of the International Covenant on Civil and Political Rights

The right to life describes the essential right to live, particularly that a human being has the right not to be killed by another human being. The concept of a right to life is central to debates on the issues of abortion, capital punishment, euthanasia, self defense and war. According to many human rights activists, the death penalty violates this right.[55] The United Nations has called on retentionist states to establish a moratorium on capital punishment with a view to its abolition.[56] States which do not do so face considerable moral and political pressure.

Freedom from torture

Throughout history, torture has often been used as a method of political re-education, interrogation, punishment, and coercion. In addition to state-sponsored torture, individuals or groups may be motivated to inflict torture on others for similar reasons to those of a state; however, the motive for torture can also be for the sadistic gratification of the torturer, as in the Moors murders.

Torture is prohibited under international law and the domestic laws of most countries in the 21st century. It is considered to be a violation of human rights, and is declared to be unacceptable by Article 5 of the UN Universal Declaration of Human Rights. Signatories of the Third Geneva Convention and Fourth Geneva Convention officially agree not to torture prisoners in armed conflicts. Torture is also prohibited by the United Nations Convention Against Torture, which has been ratified by 147 states.[57]

National and international legal prohibitions on torture derive from a consensus that torture and similar ill-treatment are immoral, as well as impractical.[58] Despite these international conventions, organizations that monitor abuses of human rights (e.g. Amnesty International, the International Rehabilitation Council for Torture Victims) report widespread use condoned by states in many regions of the world.[59] Amnesty International estimates that at least 81 world governments currently practice torture, some of them openly.[60]

Freedom from slavery

Freedom from slavery is an internationally recognized human right. Article 4 of the Universal Declaration of Human Rights states:

> No one shall be held in slavery or servitude; slavery and the slave trade shall be prohibited in all their forms.[61]

Despite this, the number of slaves today is higher than at any point in history,[62] remaining as high as 12 million[63] to 27 million,[64] [65] [66] Most are debt slaves, largely in South Asia, who are under debt bondage incurred by lenders, sometimes even for generations.[67] Human trafficking is primarily for prostituting women and children into sex industries.[68]

Groups such as the American Anti-Slavery Group, Anti-Slavery International, Free the Slaves, the Anti-Slavery Society, and the Norwegian Anti-Slavery Society continue to campaign to rid the world of slavery.

Right to a fair trial

> Everyone is entitled in full equality to a fair and public hearing by an independent and impartial tribunal, in the determination of his rights and obligations and of any criminal charge against him.[69]

The right to a fair trial has been defined in numerous regional and international human rights instruments. It is one of the most extensive human rights and all international human rights instruments enshrine it in more than one article.[70] The right to a fair trial is one of the most litigated human rights and substantial case law has been established on the interpretation of this human right.[71] Despite variations in wording and placement of the various fair trial rights, international human rights instrument define the right to a fair trial in broadly the same terms.[72] The aim of the right is to ensure the proper administration of justice. As a minimum the right to fair trial includes the following fair trial rights in civil and criminal proceedings:[73]

- the right to be heard by a competent, independent and impartial tribunal
- the right to a public hearing
- the right to be heard within a reasonable time
- the right to counsel hi
- the right to interpretation[74]

Freedom of speech

Freedom of speech is the freedom to speak freely without censorship. The term freedom of expression is sometimes used synonymously, but includes any act of seeking, receiving and imparting information or ideas, regardless of the medium used. In practice, the right to freedom of speech is not absolute in any country and the right is commonly subject to limitations, such as on libel, slander, obscenity, incitement to commit a crime, etc. The right to freedom of expression is recognized as a human right under Article 19 of the Universal Declaration of Human Rights and recognized in international human rights law in the International Covenant on Civil and Political Rights (ICCPR). Article 19 of the ICCPR states that "[e]veryone shall have the right to hold opinions without interference" and "everyone shall have the right to freedom of expression; this right shall include freedom to seek, receive and impart information and ideas of all kinds, regardless of frontiers, either orally, in writing or in print, in the form of art, or through any other media of his choice".

Freedom of thought, conscience and religion

> "Everyone has the right to freedom of thought, conscience and religion; this right includes freedom to change his religion or belief, and freedom, either alone or in community with others and in public or private, to manifest his religion or belief in teaching, practice, worship and observance."
>
> —Article 18 of the International Covenant on Civil and Political Rights

Freedom of thought, conscience and religion are closely related rights that protect the freedom of an individual or community, in public or private, to think and freely hold conscientious beliefs and to manifest religion or belief in teaching, practice, worship, and observance; the concept is generally recognized also to include the freedom to change religion or not to follow any religion.[75] The freedom to *leave* or discontinue membership in a religion or religious group —in religious terms called "apostasy" —is also a fundamental part of religious freedom, covered by Article 18 of the Universal Declaration of Human Rights.[76]

Human rights groups such as Amnesty International organises campaigns to protect those arrested and or incarcerated as a prisoner of conscience because of their conscientious beliefs, particularly concerning intellectual, political and artistic freedom of expression and association.[77] In legislation, a conscience clause is a provision in a statute that excuses a health professional from complying with the law (for example legalising surgical or pharmaceutical abortion) if it is incompatible with religious or conscientious beliefs.[78]

Rights debates

Events and new possibilities can affect existing rights or require new ones. Advances of technology, medicine, and philosophy constantly challenge the status quo of human rights thinking.

Future generations

In 1997 UNESCO adopted the Declaration on the Responsibilities of the Present Generation Towards the Future Generation. The Declaration opens with the words:

> Mindful of the will of the peoples, set out solemnly in the Charter of the United Nations, to 'save succeeding generations from the scourge of war' and to safeguard the values and principles enshrined in the Universal Declaration of Human Rights, and all other relevant instruments of international law.
>
> —Declaration on the Responsibilities of the Present Generation Towards the Future Generation

Article 1 of the declaration states "the present generations have the responsibility of ensuring that the needs and interests of present and future generations are fully safeguarded." The preamble to the declaration states that "at this point in history, the very existence of humankind and its environment are threatened" and the declaration covers a variety of issues including protection of the environment, the human genome, biodiversity, cultural heritage, peace, development, and education. The preamble recalls that the responsibilities of the present generations towards future generations has been referred to in various international instruments, including the Convention for the Protection of the World Cultural and Natural Heritage (UNESCO 1972), the United Nations Framework Convention on Climate Change and the Convention on Biological Diversity (Rio de Janeiro, 1992), the Rio Declaration on Environment and Development (UN Conference on Environment and Development, 1992), the Vienna Declaration and Programme of Action (World Conference on Human Rights, 1993) and a number of UN General Assembly resolutions relating to the protection of the global climate for present and future generations adopted since 1990.[79]

Lesbian, Gay, Bisexual, Transgender (LGBT) rights

LGBT rights are rights that relate to sexual orientation, gender identity, and gender expression based on the right to respect for private life and the right not to be discriminated against on the ground of "other status" as defined in various human rights conventions, such as article 17 and 26 in the United Nations International Covenant on Civil and Political Rights and article 8 and article 14 in the European Convention on Human Rights.

Through the way many because of their religious beliefs claim that they support human rights in general while denying that LGBT rights are human rights, LGBT rights stand prominent in the very defense of the universal principle of the human rights. If human rights are understood in a way that makes it possible to exclude the basic rights of certain groups only because of certain religious and cultural prejudices, we find that the principle of universality is taken right out of the human rights, and human rights are transformed to a set of rules only reflecting certain historically values.[80]

In 77 countries, homosexuality remains a criminal offense, punishable by execution in seven countries.[81] The decriminalization of private, consensual, adult sexual relations, especially in countries where corporal or capital punishment is involved, remains one of the primary concerns of LGBT human rights advocates.[82]

Other issues include but are not limited to: government recognition of same-sex relationships, LGBT adoption, sexual orientation and military service, immigration equality, anti-discrimination laws, hate crime laws regarding violence against LGBT people, sodomy laws, anti-lesbianism laws, and equal age of consent for same-sex activity.[83] [84] [85] [86] [87] [88]

A global charter for LGBT rights has been proposed in the form of the 'Yogyakarta Principles', a set of 29 principles whose authors say they apply International Human Rights Law statutes and precedent to situations relevant to LGBT people's experience.[89] The principles were presented at a United Nations event in New York on November 7, 2007, co-sponsored by Argentina, Brazil and Uruguay.

The principles have been acknowledged with influencing the French proposed UN declaration on sexual orientation and gender identity, which focuses on ending violence, criminalization and capital punishment and does not include dialogue about same-sex marriage or right to start a family.[90] [91] The proposal was supported by 67 of the then 192 member countries of the United Nations, including all EU nations and the United States. An alternative statement opposing the proposal was initiated by Syria and signed by 57 member nations, including all 27 nations of the Arab League as well as Iran and North Korea.[92] [93]

Trade

Although both the Universal Declaration of Human Rights and the International Covenant on Economic, Social and Cultural Rights emphasize the importance of a right to work, neither of these documents explicitly mention trade as a mechanism for ensuring this fundamental right. And yet trade plays a key role in providing jobs.[94]

Some experts argue that trade is inherent to human nature and that when governments inhibit international trade they directly inhibit the right to work and the other indirect benefits, like the right to education, that increased work and investment help accrue.[95] Others have argued that the ability to trade does not affect everyone equally—often groups like the rural poor, indigenous groups and women are less likely to access the benefits of increased trade.[96]

On the other hand, others think that it is no longer primarily individuals but companies that trade, and therefore it cannot be guaranteed as a human right. Additionally, trying to fit too many concepts under the umbrella of what qualifies as a human right has the potential to dilute their importance. Finally, it is difficult to define a right to trade as either "fair"[97] or "just" in that the current trade regime produces winners and losers but its reform is likely to produce (different) winners and losers.[98]

See also: The Recognition of Labour Standards within the World Trade Organisation and Investor state dispute settlement

Water

In November 2002, the United Nations Committee on Economic, Social and Cultural Rights issued a non-binding comment affirming that access to water was a human right:

> the human right to water is indispensable for leading a life in human dignity. It is a prerequisite for the realization of other human rights.
>
> —United Nations Committee on Economic, Social and Cultural Rights

This principle was reaffirmed at the 3rd and 4th World Water Councils in 2003 and 2006. This marks a departure from the conclusions of the 2nd World Water Forum in The Hague in 2000, which stated that water was a commodity to be bought and sold, not a right.[99] There are calls from many NGOs and politicians to enshrine access to water as a binding human right, and not as a commodity.[100] [101] According to the United Nations, nearly 900 million people lack access to clean water and more than 2.6 billion people lack access to basic sanitation. On July 28, 2010, the UN declared water and sanitation as human rights. By declaring safe and clean drinking water and sanitation as a human right, the U.N. General Assembly made a step towards the Millennium Development Goal to ensure environmental sustainability, which in part aims to "halve, by 2015, the proportion of the population without sustainable access to safe drinking water and basic sanitation".

Reproductive rights

Reproductive rights are rights relating to reproduction and reproductive health.[102] The World Health Organisation defines reproductive rights as follows:

> Reproductive rights rest on the recognition of the basic right of all couples and individuals to decide freely and responsibly the number, spacing and timing of their children and to have the information and means to do so, and the right to attain the highest standard of sexual and reproductive health. They also include the right of all to make decisions concerning reproduction free of discrimination, coercion and violence.
>
> —World Health Organisation[103]

Reproductive rights were first established as a subset of human rights at the United Nation's 1968 International Conference on Human Rights.[104] The sixteenth article of the resulting Proclamation of Teheran states, "Parents have a basic human right to determine freely and responsibly the number and the spacing of their children."[104] [105]

Reproductive rights may include some or all of the following rights: the right to legal or safe abortion, the right to control one's reproductive functions, the right to quality reproductive healthcare, and the right to education and access in order to make reproductive choices free from coercion, discrimination, and violence.[106]

Reproductive rights may also be understood to include education about contraception and sexually transmitted infections, and freedom from coerced sterilization and contraception, protection from gender-based practices such as female genital cutting (FGC) and male genital mutilation (MGM).[102] [104] [106] [107]

Information and communication technologies

In 2009, Finland was the first country to make 1-megabit broadband Web access a legal right.[108]

In a survey conducted by the BBC in 2010, nearly four out of five people around the world believe that access to the internet is a fundamental right.[109]

Relationship with other topics

Human rights and the environment

There are two basic conceptions of environmental human rights in the current human rights system. The first is that the right to a healthy or adequate environment is itself a human right (as seen in both Article 24 of the African Charter on Human and Peoples' Rights, and Article 11 of the San Salvador Protocol to the American Convention on

Human Rights).[110] [111] The second conception is the idea that environmental human rights can be derived from other human rights, usually – the right to life, the right to health, the right to private family life and the right to property (among many others). This second theory enjoys much more widespread use in human rights courts around the world, as those rights are contained in many human rights documents.

The onset of various environmental issues, especially climate change, has created potential conflicts between different human rights. Human rights ultimately require a working ecosystem and healthy environment, but the granting of certain rights to individuals may damage these. Such as the conflict between right to decide number of offspring and the common need for a healthy environment, as noted in the tragedy of the commons.[112] In the area of environmental rights, the responsibilities of multinational corporations, so far relatively unaddressed by human rights legislation, is of paramount consideration.

Environmental Rights revolve largely around the idea of a right to a livable environment both for the present and the future generations.

National security

With the exception of non-derogable human rights (international conventions class the right to life, the right to be free from slavery, the right to be free from torture and the right to be free from retroactive application of penal laws as non-derogable),[113] the UN recognises that human rights can be limited or even pushed aside during times of national emergency – although

> the emergency must be actual, affect the whole population and the threat must be to the very existence of the nation. The declaration of emergency must also be a last resort and a temporary measure.
>
> —United Nations. *The Resource*[113]

Rights that cannot be derogated for reasons of national security in any circumstances are known as peremptory norms or *jus cogens*. Such United Nations Charter obligations are binding on all states and cannot be modified by treaty.

Examples of national security being used to justify human rights violations include the Japanese American internment during World War II,[114] Stalin's Great Purge,[115] and the modern-day abuses of terror suspects rights by some countries, often in the name of the War on Terror.[116] [117]

Relativism and universalism

Relativists argue that human rights must avoid pushing the values of a single culture at the expense of others. "The White Man's Burden" is seen as an example of the West using the spread of Western culture as a justification for colonization.

The UDHR enshrines universal rights that apply to all humans equally, whichever geographical location, state, race or culture they belong to. However, in academia there is a dispute between scholars that advocate moral relativism and scholars that advocate moral universalism. Relativists do not argue against human rights, but concede that human rights are social constructed and are shaped by cultural and environmental contexts. Universalists argue that human rights have always existed, and apply to all people regardless of culture, race, sex, or religion.

More specifically, proponents of cultural relativism argue for acceptance of different cultures, which may have practices conflicting with human rights. Relativists caution that universalism could be used as a form of cultural, economic or political imperialism. The White Man's Burden is used as an example of imperialism and the destruction of local cultures justified by the desire to spread Eurocentric values.[118] In particular, the concept of human rights is often claimed to be fundamentally rooted in a politically liberal outlook which, although generally accepted in Europe, Japan or North America, is not necessarily taken as standard elsewhere.

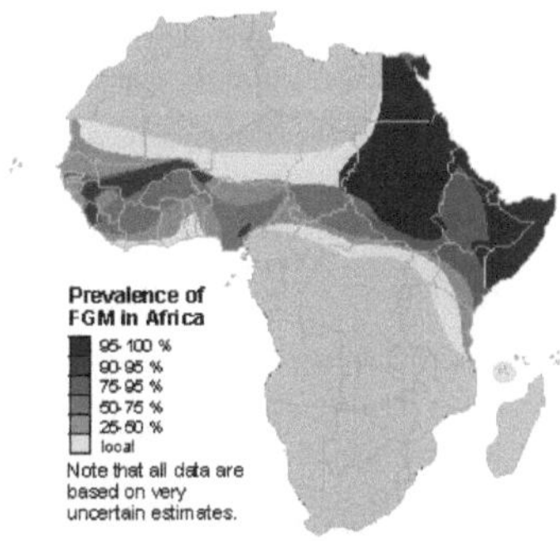

Universalists argue that some practices violate the norms of all human cultures. They point out that although Female Genital Cutting is prevalent in Africa, no religion supports the practice, and the tradition is in violation of women's rights.

Opponents of relativism argue that some practices exist that violate the norms of all human cultures. A common example is female genital mutilation, which occurs in different cultures in Africa, Asia and South America. It is not mandated by any religion, but has become a tradition in many cultures. It is considered a violation of women's and girl's rights by much of the international community, and is outlawed in some countries.

The former Prime Ministers of Singapore, Lee Kuan Yew, and of Malaysia, Mahathir bin Mohamad both claimed in the 1990s that *Asian values* were significantly different from western values and included a sense of loyalty and foregoing personal freedoms for the sake of social stability and prosperity, and therefore authoritarian government is more appropriate in Asia than democracy. Lee Kuan Yew argued that:

> What Asians value may not necessarily be what Americans or Europeans value. Westerners value the freedoms and liberties of the individual. As an Asian of Chinese cultural background, my values are for a government which is honest, effective, and efficient.
>
> —Lee Kuan Yew, 'Democracy, Human Rights and the Realities', Tokyo, Nov 10, 1992[119]

In response, critics have pointed out that cultural relativism could be used as a justification for authoritarianism. An example is in 1981, when the Iranian representative to the United Nations, Said Rajaie-Khorassani, articulated the position of his country regarding the Universal Declaration of Human Rights by saying that the UDHR was "a secular understanding of the Judeo-Christian tradition", which could not be implemented by Muslims without trespassing the Islamic law.[120] The Asian Values argument was criticized by Mahathir's former deputy:

> To say that freedom is Western or unAsian is to offend our traditions as well as our forefathers, who gave their lives in the struggle against tyranny and injustices.
>
> —A. Ibrabim in his keynote speech to the Asian Press Forum title *Media and Society in Asia*, December 2, 1994

and by Singapore's opposition leader Chee Soon Juan, who states that it is racist to assert that Asians do not want human rights.[121] [122]

An appeal is often made to the fact that influential human-rights thinkers, such as John Locke and John Stuart Mill, have all been Western and indeed that some were involved in the running of Empires themselves.[123] [124]

Defenders of moral universalism argue that relativistic arguments neglect the fact that modern human rights are new to all cultures, dating back no further than the UDHR in 1948. They argue that the UDHR was drafted by people from many different cultures and traditions, including a US Roman Catholic, a Chinese Confucian philosopher, a French zionist and a representative from the Arab League, amongst others, and drew upon advice from thinkers such as Mahatma Gandhi.[30] Michael Ignatieff has argued that cultural relativism is almost exclusively an argument used by those who wield power in cultures which commit human rights abuses, and that those whose human rights are compromised are the powerless.[125] This reflects the fact that the difficulty in judging universalism versus relativism lies in who is claiming to represent a particular culture.

Although the argument between universalism and relativism is far from complete, it is an academic discussion in that all international human rights instruments adhere to the principle that human rights are universally applicable. The 2005 World Summit reaffirmed the international community's adherence to this principle:

> The universal nature of human rights and freedoms is beyond question.
>
> —2005 World Summit, paragraph 121

See also

- International human rights instruments
- Customary international law
- Human responsibilities
- List of human rights organisations
- Rule of law
- Human security
- Rule According to Higher Law

References

[1] "Amnesty Basic Definition of Human Rights" (http://www.amnestyusa.org/research/human-rights-basics). Amnesty International. . Retrieved 19 June 2011.

[2] "Universal Declaration of Human Rights adopted by General Assembly resolution 217 A (III) of December 10, 1948" (http://www.un.org/en/documents/udhr/index.shtml#a1). .

[3] Nickel, James (July 29, 2006). "Human Rights" (http://plato.stanford.edu/archives/spr2009/entries/rights-human/). *Stanford Encyclopedia of Philosophy*. Stanford University. .

[4] Beitz (2001) p.1

[5] Freeman (2002) p.15-17

[6] Biletzki, Anat. "The Sacred and the Humane" (http://opinionator.blogs.nytimes.com/2011/07/17/the-sacred-and-the-humane/). *New York Times*. .

[7] Ishay, Michael (2008). *The History of Human Rights: From Ancient Times to the Globalization Era*. Cambridge, UK; Malden, MA: University of California Press. pp. 64.

[8] Moyn, Samuel (2010). *The Last Utopia: Human Rights in History*. Harvard University Press. ISBN 9780674048720

[9] McLemee, Scott (Decenber 8, 2010). "The Last Utopia" (http://www.insidehighered.com/views/mclemee/mclemee317). *Inside Higher Ed* (Washington DC).

[10] Ishay, Micheline (2008). *The History of Human Rights: From Ancient Times to the Globalization Era*. Cambridge, UK; Malden, MA: University of California Press. pp. 64.

[11] Biletzki, Anat. "The Sacred and the Humane" (http://opinionator.blogs.nytimes.com/2011/07/17/the-sacred-and-the-humane/). *New York Times*. .

[12] Freeman (2002) p18–19.

[13] Mayer (2000) p110.

[14] Seymour Drescher, *Abolition: A History of Slavery and Antislavery* (2009)

[15] Fagan, Andrew. "Human Rights" (http://www.iep.utm.edu/hum-rts/#SH4b). Internet Encyclopedia of Philosophy. . Retrieved November 20, 2010.

[16] Light (2002)

[17] Scott (1989

[18] Ball, Gready (2007) p.37

[19] Alston (2005)

[20] Ball, Gready. (2007) p.42

[21] Brownlie, Ian. *Principles of Public International Law*. OUP. ISBN 0199556830.

[22] (http://www1.umn.edu/humanrts/instree/chapter1.html) United Nations Charter Article 1(3).

[23] Shaw, Malcom (2008). *International Law*. Cambridge University Press. pp. 277. ISBN 9780521899291.

[24] Eleanor Roosevelt: Address to the United Nations General Assembly (http://www.americanrhetoric.com/speeches/eleanorrooseveltdeclarationhumanrights.htm), December 10, 1948 in Paris.

[25] (A/RES/217, December 10, 1948 at Palais de Chaillot, Paris)

[26] Ball, Gready.

[27] Glendon, Mary Ann (July 2004). "The Rule of Law in The Universal Declaration of Human Rights" (http://www.law.northwestern.edu/journals/jihr/v2/5/). *Northwestern University Journal of International Human Rights* **2** (5). .
[28] Glendon (2001).
[29] "'Mrs R' and the human rights scripture" (http://www.atimes.com/atimes/Front_Page/DK02Aa02.html). *Asia Times* (Hong Kong). November 2, 2002. . Retrieved August 29, 2010.
[30] Ball, Gready (2007) p.34.
[31] Henkin, Louis. The International Bill of Rights: The Universal Declaration and the Covenants, in International Enforcement of Human Rights 6–9, Bernhardt and Jolowicz, eds, (1987).
[32] Henkin, Louis. Introduction, The International Bill of Rights 9–10 (1981).
[33] Ball, Gready (2007) p.35.
[34] Littman, David G. (January 19, 2003). "Human Rights and Human Wrongs" (http://www.nationalreview.com/comment/comment-littman011903.asp). *National Review* (New York). . "The principal aim of the 1948 Universal Declaration of Human Rights (UDHR) was to create a framework for a universal code based on mutual consent. The early years of the United Nations were overshadowed by the division between the democratic and communist conceptions of human rights, although neither side called into question the concept of universality. The debate centered on which "rights" — political, economic, and social — were to be included among the Universal Instruments."
[35] Ball, Gready (2007) p.92
[36] "United Nations Rights Council Page" (http://www.un.org/apps/news/infocusRel.asp?infocusID=114&Body=human rights council&Body1=). United Nations News Page. .
[37] "The United Nations System" (http://www.un.org/aboutun/chart_en.pdf) (PDF). .
[38] UN Charter, Article 39
[39] Ball, Gready (2007) p.95
[40] The Security Council referred the human rights situation in Darfur in Sudan to the ICC despite the fact that Sudan has a functioning legal system
[41] Fred Grünfeld and Anke Huijboom, *The failure to prevent genocide in Rwanda: the role of bystanders* (2007) p. 199
[42] Lee Feinstein, *Darfur and beyond: what is needed to prevent mass atrocities* (2007) p. 46
[43] Security Council passes landmark resolution – world has responsibility to protect people from genocide (http://www.oxfam.org/en/news/pressreleases2006/pr060428_un) Oxfam Press Release - April 28, 2006
[44] Donnelly, Jack (2003). *Universal human rights in theory and practice* (2nd ed. ed.). Ithaca: Cornell University Press. pp. 138. ISBN 9780801487767.
[45] "Historical Background to the European Court of Human Rights" (http://web.archive.org/web/20071222001646/http://www.echr.coe.int/ECHR/EN/Header/The+Court/The+Court/History+of+the+Court/). European Court of Human Rights. Archived from the original (http://www.echr.coe.int/ECHR/EN/Header/The+Court/The+Court/History+of+the+Court/) on December 22, 2007. . Retrieved January 4, 2008.
[46] Durham, H. (2004). ""We the People: The Position of NGOs in Gathering Evidence and Giving Witness in International Criminal Trials". In Thakur, R, Malcontent, P. *From Sovereign Impunity to International Accountability*. New York: United Nations University Press.
[47] "Human rights: A crowded field" (http://www.economist.com/node/16219707?story_id=16219707). *The Economist* (London). May 27, 2010. . Retrieved August 9, 2010.
[48] Jeffay, Nathan (June 24, 2010). "Academic hits out at politicised charities" (http://www.thejc.com/news/uk-news/33415/interview-gerald-steinberg). *The Jewish Chronicle*. .
[49] Edelstein, Jason (October 12, 2010). "The Search for the Truth" (http://www.jpost.com/Opinion/Op-EdContributors/Article.aspx?id=191025). *The Jerusalem Post*. .
[50] "Corporations and Human Rights" (http://web.archive.org/web/20071215000427/http://hrw.org/worldreport99/special/corporations.html). Human Rights Watch. Archived from the original (http://www.hrw.org/worldreport99/special/corporations.html) on December 15, 2007. . Retrieved January 3, 2008.
[51] "Transnational corporations should be held to human rights standards – UN expert" (http://www.un.org/apps/news/story.asp?NewsID=8536&Cr=right&Cr1=food). UN News Centre. October 13, 2003. . Retrieved January 3, 2008.
[52] "Norms on the responsibilities of transnational corporations and other business enterprises with regard to human rights" (http://www.unhchr.ch/huridocda/huridoca.nsf/(Symbol)/E.CN.4.Sub.2.2003.12.Rev.2.En.). UN Sub-Commission on the Promotion and Protection of Human Rights. . Retrieved January 3, 2008.
[53] "Report to the Economic and Social Council on the sixtieth session of the commission (E/CN.4/2004/L.11/Add.7)" (http://www.unhchr.ch/huridocda/huridoca.nsf/e06a5300f90fa0238025668700518ca4/169143c3c1009015c1256e830058c441/$FILE/G0413976.pdf) (PDF). United Nations Commission on Human Rights. p. 81. . Retrieved January 3, 2008.
[54] Davenport, Christian. "Stop Our States (SOS): Analyzing and Ending State Repression" (http://web.mac.com/christiandavenport/iWeb/Christian Davenport/Stop Our States (SOS).html). . Retrieved January 19, 2008.
[55] "Amnesty International" (http://www.amnesty.org/en/death-penalty). Amnesty.org. . Retrieved August 29, 2010.
[56] United Nations resolution 62/149.
[57] "United Nations Treaty Collection" (http://treaties.un.org/pages/ViewDetails.aspx?src=TREATY&mtdsg_no=IV-9&chapter=4&lang=en). UN. . Retrieved 7 October 2010.

[58] "Torture and Ill-Treatment in the 'War on Terror'" (http://www.amnesty.org/en/library/info/ACT40/014/2005/en). Amnesty International. 2005-11-01. . Retrieved 2008-10-22.
[59] Amnesty International Report 2005 (http://web.amnesty.org/library/index/engPOL100012005) Report 2006 (http://web.archive.org/web/20070317170847/http://web.amnesty.org/report2006/2af-summary-eng)
[60] "Report 08: At a Glance" (http://web.archive.org/web/20080708202906/http://thereport.amnesty.org/eng/report-08-at-a-glance). Amnesty International. 2008. Archived from the original (http://thereport.amnesty.org/eng/report-08-at-a-glance) on July 8, 2008. . Retrieved 2008-10-22.
[61] "The law against slavery" (http://www.bbc.co.uk/ethics/slavery/modern/law.shtml). *Religion & Ethics – Ethical issues*. British Broadcasting Corporation. . Retrieved 2008-10-05.
[62] By E. Benjamin Skinner Monday, Jan. 18, 2010 (2010-01-18). "sex trafficking in South Africa: World Cup slavery fear" (http://www.time.com/time/magazine/article/0,9171,1952335,00.html). Time.com. . Retrieved 2010-08-29.
[63] "Forced labour – Themes" (http://www.ilo.org/global/Themes/Forced_Labour/lang--en/index.htm). Ilo.org. . Retrieved 2010-03-14.
[64] Bales, Kevin (1999). "1". *Disposable People: New Slavery in the Global Economy*. University of California Press. p. 9. ISBN 0-520-21797-7.
[65] "UN Chronicle | Slavery in the Twenty-First Century" (http://www.smfcdn.com/assets/pubs/un_chronicle.pdf). Un.org. . Retrieved 2010-08-29.
[66] "BBC Millions 'forced into slavery'" (http://news.bbc.co.uk/2/hi/2010401.stm). BBC News. 2002-05-27. . Retrieved 2010-08-29.
[67] UK. "Slavery in the 21st century" (http://www.newint.org/issue337/facts.htm). Newint.org. . Retrieved 2010-08-29.
[68] "Experts encourage action against sex trafficking" (http://www1.voanews.com/english/news/a-13-2009-05-15-voa30-68815957.html?rss=human+rights+and+law). .voanews.com. 2009-05-15. . Retrieved 2010-08-29.
[69] "Article 10 UDHR".
[70] Doebbler, Curtis (2006). *Introduction to International Human Rights Law* (http://books.google.com/books?id=mQ61oCPJ1GEC&pg=PA108&dq=right+to+fair+trial#v=onepage&q=right to fair trial&f=false). CD Publishing. pp. 107–108. ISBN 9780974357027. .
[71] Doebbler, Curtis (2006). *Introduction to International Human Rights Law* (http://books.google.com/books?id=mQ61oCPJ1GEC&pg=PA108&dq=right+to+fair+trial#v=onepage&q=right to fair trial&f=false). CD Publishing. pp. 110. ISBN 9780974357027. .
[72] Alfredsson, Gudmundur; Eide, Asbjorn (1999). *The Universal Declaration of Human Rights: a common standard of achievement* (http://books.google.com/books?id=FmuoB-BlMvEC&dq="right+to+property"). Martinus Nijhoff Publishers. pp. 225. ISBN 9789041111685. .
[73] Doebbler, Curtis (2006). *Introduction to International Human Rights Law* (http://books.google.com/books?id=mQ61oCPJ1GEC&pg=PA108&dq=right+to+fair+trial#v=onepage&q=right to fair trial&f=false). CD Publishing. pp. 108. ISBN 9780974357027. .
[74] Doebbler, Curtis (2006). *Introduction to International Human Rights Law* (http://books.google.com/books?id=mQ61oCPJ1GEC&pg=PA108&dq=right+to+fair+trial#v=onepage&q=right to fair trial&f=false). CD Publishing. pp. 108. ISBN 9780974357027. .
[75] Universal Declaration of Human Rights, Article 18.
[76] "The Universal Declaration of Human Rights" (http://www.un.org/en/documents/udhr/index.shtml). The United Nations (http://www.un.org). .
[77] For example see Jan Brabec, Václav Havel, Ivan Lamper, David Nemec, Petr Placak, Joska Skalnik *et al.* "Prisoners of Conscience" (http://www.nybooks.com/articles/4151). *New York Review of Books*. 1989; 36 (1) February 2. Accessed 18 October 2009.
[78] Katherine White. *Crisis of Conscience: Reconciling Religious Health Care Providers' Beliefs and Patients' Rights*. Stanford Law Review 1999; 51: 1703–1724.
[79] "Declaration on the Responsibilities of the Present Generation Towards the Future Generation" (http://portal.unesco.org/en/ev.php-URL_ID=13178&URL_DO=DO_PRINTPAGE&URL_SECTION=201.html). Portal.unesco.org. . Retrieved August 29, 2010.
[80] Dag Øistein Endsjø. "The queer periphery. Sexual deviancy and the cultural understanding of space" (http://www.informaworld.com/smpp/content~content=a903701414&db=all) in *Journal of Homosexuality*, vol. 54, 2008: 9-20..
[81] "World Day against Death Penalty" (http://ilga.org/ilga/en/article/1111). ILGA. . Retrieved August 29, 2010.
[82] "The Role of the Yogyakarta Principles" (http://www.iglhrc.org/cgi-bin/iowa/article/takeaction/partners/22.html). International Gay & Lesbian Human Rights Commission. April 8, 2008. .
[83] "Interactive Map of Legal Status of LGBT People" (http://www.amnestyusa.org/lgbt-human-rights/country-information/page.do?id=1106576). Amnestyusa.org. . Retrieved August 29, 2010.
[84] "About LGBT Human Rights" (http://www.amnestyusa.org/lgbt-human-rights/about-lgbt-human-rights/page.do?id=1106573). Amnestyusa.org. March 3, 2010. . Retrieved August 29, 2010.
[85] http://www.barackobama.com/pdf/lgbt.pdf
[86] "2000 CCAR Resolution" (http://www.shamash.org/lists/scj-faq/HTML/faq/18-03-08.html). March 18, 2008. . Retrieved October 12, 2008.
[87] "2003 URJ Resolution" (http://urj.org/Articles/index.cfm?id=13462&pge_prg_id=57308&pge_id=1607). . Retrieved October 12, 2008.
[88] "*John Geddes Lawrence and Tyron Garner v. State of Texas*" (http://supreme.lp.findlaw.com/supreme_court/briefs/02-102/02-102.mer.ami.aob.pdf). . Retrieved October 12, 2008.
[89] "The Application of International Human Rights Law in relation to Sexual Orientation and Gender Identity" (http://www.yogyakartaprinciples.org/). The Yogyakarta Principles. . Retrieved August 29, 2010.
[90] http://www.franceonu.org/spip.php?article4092

[91] "Human Rights: Statement on Human Rights, Sexual Orientation and Gender Identity at High Level Meeting" (http://www.netherlandsmission.org/article.asp?articleref=AR00000530EN). Mission of the Netherlands to the UN. June 3, 2008. . Retrieved August 29, 2010.

[92] Worsnip, Patrick (December 18, 2008). "U.N. divided over gay rights declaration" (http://www.reuters.com/article/idUSTRE4BH7EW20081218). Reuters. . Retrieved August 29, 2010.

[93] Macfarquhar, Neil (December 19, 2008). "In a First, Gay Rights Are Pressed at the U.N" (http://www.nytimes.com/2008/12/19/world/19nations.html?_r=1). *The New York Times*. .

[94] "Should trade be considered a human right?" (http://www.cop-la.net/en/node/523). COPLA. December 9, 2008. .

[95] Fernandez, Soraya (December 9, 2008). "Protecting access to markets" (http://www.cop-la.net/en/node/526). COPLA. .

[96] Jones, Nicola and Hayley Baker (March 2008). "Untangling links between trade, poverty and gender" (http://www.odi.org.uk/resources/details.asp?id=1011&title=untangling-links-trade-poverty-gender). Overseas Development Institute. .

[97] Ellis, Karen and Jodie Keane (November 2008). "Do we need a new 'Good for Development' label?" (http://www.odi.org.uk/resources/details.asp?id=532&title=time-ripe-good-development-product-label). Overseas Development Institute. .

[98] Mareike Meyn (December 9, 2008). "Beyond rights: Trading to win" (http://www.cop-la.net/en/node/524). COPLA. .

[99] Sutherland, Ben (March 17, 2003). "Water forum no 'talking shop'" (http://news.bbc.co.uk/2/hi/science/nature/2856755.stm). *BBC News*. .

[100] "2003 International Year of Water website press kit" (http://www.wateryear2003.org/en/ev.php-URL_ID=2915&URL_DO=DO_TOPIC&URL_SECTION=201.html). United Nations Department of Public Information. . Retrieved December 28, 2007.

[101] Water Justice (http://www.tni.org/work-area/water-justice).

[102] Cook, Rebecca J.; Fathalla, Mahmoud F. (September 1996). "Advancing Reproductive Rights Beyond Cairo and Beijing". *International Family Planning Perspectives* (Guttmacher Institute) **22** (3): 115–121. doi:10.2307/2950752. JSTOR 2950752.

[103] "Gender and reproductive rights" (http://who.int/reproductive-health/gender/index.html). World Health Organisation. . Retrieved August 29, 2010.

[104] Freedman, Lynn P.; Isaacs, Stephen L. (Jan.– Feb. 1993). "Human Rights and Reproductive Choice". *Studies in Family Planning* (Population Council) **24** (1): 18–30. doi:10.2307/2939211. JSTOR 2939211.

[105] "Proclamation of Teheran" (http://web.archive.org/web/20071017025912/http://www.unhchr.ch/html/menu3/b/b_tehern.htm). International Conference on Human Rights. 1968. Archived from the original (http://www.unhchr.ch/html/menu3/b/b_tehern.htm) on October 17, 2007. . Retrieved November 8, 2007.

[106] "Stop Violence Against Women: Reproductive rights" (http://www.amnestyusa.org/Stop_Violence_Against_Women_SVAW/Reproductive_Rights/page.do?id=1108242&n1=3&n2=39&n3=1101). Amnesty International USA. 2007. . Retrieved December 8, 2007. "Reproductive rights – access to sexual and reproductive healthcare and autonomy in sexual and reproductive decision-making – are human rights; they are universal, indivisible, and undeniable. These rights are founded upon principles of human dignity and equality, and have been enshrined in international human rights documents."

[107] Zavales, Anastasios (December 10, 1993). "Genital mutilation and the United Nations" (http://www.nocirc.org/symposia/fourth/zavales4.html). National Organization of Circumcision Information Resource Centers. . Retrieved August 29, 2010.

[108] "Finland makes 1Mb broadband access a legal right" (http://news.cnet.com/8301-17939_109-10374831-2.html). *cnet.com*. October 14, 2009. . Retrieved January 1, 2011.

[109] "Internet access is 'a fundamental right'" (http://news.bbc.co.uk/2/hi/8548190.stm). *BBC News Online* (London). February 8, 2010. . Retrieved January 1, 2011.

[110] "African Commission on Human and Peoples' Rights" (http://www.achpr.org/english/_info/charter_en.html). Achpr.org. July 20, 1979. . Retrieved August 29, 2010.

[111] "OAS – Organization of American States: Democracy for peace, security, and development" (http://www.oas.org/juridico/english/sigs/a-52.html). Oas.org. . Retrieved August 29, 2010.

[112] Garrett Hardin, "The Tragedy of the Commons" (http://www.sciencemag.org/cgi/content/full/162/3859/1243), *Science*, Vol. 162, No. 3859 (December 13, 1968), pp. 1243–1248. Also available here (http://www.sciencemag.org/cgi/reprint/162/3859/1243.pdf) and here. (http://www.garretthardinsociety.org/articles/art_tragedy_of_the_commons.html)

[113] "The Resource Part II: Human Rights in Times of Emergencies" (http://www.un.org/esa/socdev/enable/comp210.htm#10.2). United Nations. . Retrieved December 31, 2007.

[114] "Children of the Camps | Internment Timeline" (http://www.pbs.org/childofcamp/history/timeline.html). Pbs.org. . Retrieved August 29, 2010.

[115] "The Great Purge" (http://www.cusd.chico.k12.ca.us/~bsilva/projects/russia/stalin/great_purge.htm). Cusd.chico.k12.ca.us. . Retrieved August 29, 2010.

[116] "Fox News Report" (http://www.foxnews.com/story/0,2933,316382,00.html). Fox News. December 10, 2007. .

[117] "UK Law Lords Rule Indefinite Detention Breaches Human Rights" (http://www.hrw.org/english/docs/2004/12/16/uk9890.htm). Human Rights Watch. .

[118] "Eurocentrism". In *Encyclopedia of the Developing World*. Ed. Thomas M. Leonard, Taylor & Francis, 2006, ISBN 0415976626, p. 636.

[119] Halper, Stefan. *The Beijing consensus*. p 133

[120] Littman (1999)

[121] Ball, Gready (2007) p.25

[122] Chee, S.J. (July 3, 2003). *Human Rights: Dirty Words in Singapore*. Activating Human Rights and Diversity Conference (Byron Bay, Australia).
[123] Tunick (2006)
[124] Beate (2005)
[125] Ignatief, M. (2001) p.68

Bibliography

- Beitz, Charles R. (2009). *The idea of human rights*. Oxford: Oxford University Press. ISBN 9780199572458.
- Moyn, Samuel (2010). *The last utopia: human rights in history*. Cambridge, Mass.: Belknap Press of Harvard University Press. ISBN 9780674048720.
- Donnelly, Jack (2003). *Universal human rights in theory and practice* (2nd ed.). Ithaca: Cornell University Press. ISBN 9780801487767.
- Ball, Olivia; Gready, Paul (2006). *The no-nonsense guide to human rights*. Oxford: New Internationalist. ISBN 978-1-904456-45-2.
- Freeman, Michael (2002). *Human rights : an interdisciplinary approach*. Cambridge: Polity Press. ISBN 9780745623559.
- *Introduction to international human rights law.*. [S.l.]: Cd Publishing. 2006. ISBN 9780974357027.

Further reading

- Abouharb, R. and D. Cingranelli (2007). "Human Rights and Structural Adjustment". New York: Cambridge University Press.
- Ankerl, Guy (2011) Relativity of human rights (Sacha Journal of Human Rights, Sept. 2011, 14-36.)
- Anstis, Sebastian and Zacher, Mark (June 2010). "The Normative Bases of the Global Territorial Order." Diplomacy and Statecraft 21: 306-323.
- Barsh, R. (1993). "Measuring Human Rights: Problems of Methodology and Purpose." Human Rights Quarterly 15: 87-121.
- Chauhan, O.P. (2004). *Human Rights: Promotion and Protection*. Anmol Publications PVT. LTD. ISBN 812612119X
- Forsythe, David P. (2000). *Human Rights in International Relations*. Cambridge: Cambridge University Press. International Progress Organization. ISBN 3-900704-08-2
- Forsythe, Frederick P.(2009, *Encyclopedia of Human Rights* (New York: Oxford University Press)
- Glendon, Mary Ann (2001). *A World Made New: Eleanor Roosevelt and the Universal Declaration of Human Rights*. Random House of Canada Ltd. ISBN 0375506926
- Ignatieff, Michael (2001). *Human Rights as Politics and Idolatry*. Princeton & Oxford: Princeton University Press. ISBN 0691088934
- Landman, Todd (2006). *Studying Human Rights*. Oxford and London: Routledge ISBN 0-415-32605-2
- Robertson, Arthur Henry; Merrills, John Graham (1996). *Human Rights in the World: An Introduction to the Study of the International Protection of Human Rights*. Manchester University Press. ISBN 0719049237.
- Steiner, J. & Alston, Philip. (1996). *International Human Rights in Context: Law, Politics, Morals*. Oxford: Clarendon Press. ISBN 019825427X
- Shute, Stephen & Hurley, Susan (eds.). (1993). *On Human Rights: The Oxford Amnesty Lectures*. New York: BasicBooks. ISBN 046505224X

External links

- United Nations: Human Rights (http://www.un.org/rights/)
- UN Practitioner's Portal on HRBA Programming (http://www.hrbaportal.org) UN centralised webportal on the Human Rights-Based Approach to Development Programming
- Simple Guide to the UN Treaty Bodies (http://www.ishr.ch/guides-to-the-un-system/simple-guide-to-treaty-bodies) (International Service for Human Rights)
- International Center for Transitional Justice (ICTJ) (http://ictj.org/)
- IHRLaw.org (http://www.ihrlaw.org) International Human Rights Law – comprehensive online resources and news
- The Chr. Michelsen Institute (http://www.cmi.no) Largest centre for development research in Scandinavia, with a focus on Rights and Legal Institutions (http://www.cmi.no/research/themes/?rights-and-legal-institutions).
- Human Rights Record of the United States, 2010 (http://www.sourcewatch.org/index.php?title=Human_Rights_Record_of_the_United_States) SourceWatch.org
- Human rights (http://www.dmoz.org/Society/Issues/Human_Rights_and_Liberties/) at the Open Directory Project

mrj:Эдемӹн праваlлäжӹ rue:Людьскы права

First Chechen War

North Caucasus region

The **First Chechen War**, also known as the **War in Chechnya**, was a conflict between the Russian Federation and the Chechen Republic of Ichkeria, fought from December 1994 to August 1996. After the initial campaign of 1994–1995, culminating in the devastating Battle of Grozny, Russian federal forces attempted to seize control of the mountainous area of Chechnya but were set back by Chechen guerrilla warfare and raids on the flatlands in spite of Russia's overwhelming manpower, weaponry, and air support. The resulting widespread demoralization of federal forces, and the almost universal opposition of the Russian public to the conflict, led Boris Yeltsin's government to declare a ceasefire in 1996 and sign a peace treaty a year later. The official figure for Russian military deaths is 5,500, while most estimates put the number between 3,500 and 7,500, or even as high as 14,000.[1] Although there are no accurate figures for the number of Chechen militants killed, various estimates put the number at about 3,000 to over 15,000 deaths. Various figures estimate the number of civilian deaths at between 30,000 and 100,000 killed and possibly over 200,000 injured, while more than 500,000 people were displaced by the conflict, which left cities and villages across the republic in ruins.[2]

Origins

Chechnya within Imperial Russia and the Soviet Union

Following long resistance during the 1817–1864 Caucasian War, Russia finally defeated Chechnya and annexed it in the 1870s. The Chechens' subsequent attempts at gaining independence after the fall of the Russian Empire failed and in 1922 Chechnya was incorporated into Bolshevist Russia and later into the Soviet Union (USSR). In 1936, Soviet leader Joseph Stalin created the Chechen-Ingush Autonomous Soviet Socialist Republic. In 1944, on the orders of NKVD chief Lavrenti Beria, more than 1 million Chechens, the Ingush, and several other North Caucasian peoples were deported to Siberia and Central Asia, officially as punishment for alleged collaboration with the invading German forces; the Chechen-Ingush Republic was abolished. Eventually, Soviet first secretary Nikita Khrushchev granted the Vainakh (Chechen and Ingush) peoples permission to return to their homeland and restored their republic in 1957.

The dissolution of the Soviet Union and the Russian Federation Treaty

Russia became an independent nation after the dissolution of the Soviet Union in December 1991. While Russia was widely accepted as the successor state to the USSR, it lost a significant amount of its military and economic power. While ethnic Russians made up more than 80% of the population of the Russian Soviet Federative Socialist Republic, significant ethnic and religious differences posed a threat of political disintegration in some regions. In the Soviet period, some of Russia's approximately 100 nationalities were granted ethnic enclaves that had various formal federal rights attached. Relations of these entities with the federal government and demands for autonomy erupted into a major political issue in the early 1990s. Boris Yeltsin incorporated these demands into his 1990 election campaign by claiming that their resolution was a high priority.

There was an urgent need for a law to clearly define the powers of each federal subject. Such a law was passed on March 31, 1992, when Yeltsin and Ruslan Khasbulatov, then chairman of the Russian Supreme Soviet and an ethnic Chechen himself, signed the Federation Treaty bilaterally with 86 out of 88 federal subjects. In almost all cases, demands for greater autonomy or independence were satisfied by concessions of regional autonomy and tax privileges. The treaty outlined three basic types of federal subjects and the powers that were reserved for local and federal government. The only federal subjects that did not sign the treaty were Chechnya and Tatarstan. Eventually, in the spring of 1994, President Yeltsin signed a special political accord with Mintimer Shaeymiev, the president of Tatarstan, granting many of its demands for greater autonomy for the republic within Russia; thus, Chechnya remained the only federal subject that did not sign the treaty. Neither Yeltsin nor the Chechen government attempted any serious negotiations and the situation deteriorated into a full-scale conflict.

Chechen declaration of independence

Chechnya (red) and the Russian Federation

Meanwhile, on September 6, 1991, militants of the All-National Congress of the Chechen People (NCChP) party, created by the former Soviet Air Force general Dzhokhar Dudayev, stormed a session of the Chechen-Ingush ASSR Supreme Soviet with the aim of asserting independence. It caused the death of the head of the Grozny's branch of the Communist Party of the Soviet Union Vitaly Kutsenko, who was thrown out of a window or fell trying to escape, and effectively dissolved the government of the Chechen-Ingush Autonomous Republic of the Soviet Union.[3] [4] [5] In the following month, Dudayev won overwhelming popular support (as evidenced by the later presidential elections with high turn out and a clear Dudayev victory) to oust the interim administration supported by central government. He was made president and declared independence from the Soviet Union.

In November 1991, Yeltsin dispatched Internal Troops to Grozny, but they were forced to withdraw when Dudayev's forces surrounded them at the airport. After Chechnya made its initial declaration of sovereignty, the Chechen-Ingush Autonomous Republic split in two in June 1992 amidst the Ingush armed conflict against another Russian republic, North Ossetia. The newly created republic of Ingushetia then joined the Russian Federation, while Chechnya declared full independence from Moscow in 1993 as the Chechen Republic of Ichkeria (ChRI).

Internal conflict in Chechnya and the Grozny-Moscow tensions

From 1991 to 1994 tens of thousands of people of non-Chechen ethnicity left the republic amidst reports of violence and discrimination against the non-Chechen population (mostly Russians, Ukrainians and Armenians).[6] [7] [8] Chechen industry began to fail as a result of many Russian engineers and workers leaving or being expelled from the republic combined with the Soviet era's crippling of the non-Russian/Armenian/Ukrainian populace (Chechens, some Ingush and Nogais, Jews) through Russian-only schooling, heavy discrimination in the public sector of the workforce, and other similar measures (even as late as 1989, Checheno-Ingushetia was ruled by a bureaucracy of ethnic Russians). During the undeclared Chechen civil war, factions both sympathetic and opposed to Dudayev fought for power, sometimes in pitched battles with the use of heavy weapons. In March 1992, the opposition attempted a coup d'état, but their attempt was crushed by force. A month later, Dudayev introduced direct presidential rule, and in June 1993, dissolved the Chechen parliament to avoid a referendum on a vote of non-confidence. In late October 1992, Russian forces dispatched to the zone of the Ossetian-Ingush conflict were ordered to move to the Chechen border; Dudayev, who perceived this as "an act of aggression against the Chechen Republic", declared a state of emergency and threatened general mobilization if the Russian troops did not withdraw from the Chechen border. To prevent invasion of Chechnya, he did not provoke the Russian troops.

After staging another coup attempt in December 1993, the opposition organized themselves into the Provisional Council of the Chechen Republic as a potential alternative government for Chechnya, calling on Moscow for assistance. In August 1994, the coalition of the opposition factions based in north Chechnya launched a large-scale armed campaign to remove Dudayev's government.

Dudayev's supporters pray in front of the Presidential Palace in Grozny, 1994

However, the issue of contention was not independence from Russia: even the opposition stated there was no alternative to an international boundary separating Chechnya from Russia. In 1992, Russian newspaper *Moscow News* made note that, just like the most other seceding republics except for Tatarstan, ethnic Chechens universally supported the establishment of an independent Chechen state.[9] Again, in 1995, during the heat of the First Chechen War, Khalid Delmayev, an anti-Dudayev belonging to an Ichkerian liberal coalition, stated that "Chechnya's statehood may be postponed... but cannot be avoided".[10] Opposition to Dudayev came mainly due to his domestic policy and personality: he once notoriously claimed that Russia intended to destabilize his nation by "artificially creating earthquakes" in Georgia and Armenia. This did not go off well with most Chechens, who came to view him as a national embarrassment at times (if still a patriot at others), but it did not, by any means, dismantle the determination for independence, as most Western commentators note.[11]

Moscow clandestinely supplied separatist forces with financial support, military equipment and mercenaries. Russia also suspended all civilian flights to Grozny while the aviation and border troops set up a military blockade of the republic and eventually unmarked Russian aircraft began combat operations over Chechnya. The opposition forces, who were joined by Russian troops, launched a clandestine but badly organized assault on Grozny in mid-October 1994, followed by the second, larger attack on November 26–27, 1994. Despite Russian support, both attempts were unsuccessful. In a major embarrassment for the Kremlin, Dudayev loyalists succeeded in capturing some 20 Russian Army regulars and about 50 other Russian citizens who were clandestinely hired by the Russian FSK state security organization to fight for the Provisional Council forces.[12] On November 29, President Boris Yeltsin issued an ultimatum to all warring factions in Chechnya ordering them to disarm and surrender. When the government in Grozny refused, Yeltsin ordered his army to "restore constitutional order" by force.

Since December 1, Russian forces were openly carrying out heavy aerial bombardments of Chechnya. On December 11, 1994, five days after Dudayev and Russian Minister of Defense Gen. Pavel Grachev of Russia had agreed to "avoid the further use of force", Russian forces entered the republic in order to "establish constitutional order in Chechnya and to preserve the territorial integrity of Russia." Grachev boasted he could topple Dudayev in a couple of hours with a single airborne regiment, and proclaimed that it will be "a bloodless blitzkrieg, that would not last any longer than December 20."

The Russian war in Chechnya

Initial stages

Chechen women pray for Russian troops not to advance towards the capital Grozny, December 1994.

On December 11, 1994, Russian forces launched a three-pronged ground attack towards Grozny. The main attack was temporarily halted by deputy commander of the Russian Ground Forces, Gen. Eduard Vorobyov, who then resigned in protest, stating that it is "a crime" to "send the army against its own people."[13] Many in the Russian military and government opposed the war as well. Yeltsin's adviser on nationality affairs, Emil Pain, and Russia's Deputy Minister of Defense Gen. Boris Gromov (esteemed commander of the Soviet-Afghan War), also resigned in protest of the invasion ("It will be a bloodbath, another Afghanistan", Gromov said on television), as did Gen. Borys Poliakov. More than 800 professional soldiers and officers refused to take part in the operation; of these, 83 were convicted by military courts and the rest were discharged. Later Gen. Lev Rokhlin also refused to be decorated as a Hero of Russia for his part in the war.

The Chechen Air Force (as well as the republic's civilian aircraft fleet) was completely destroyed in the air strikes of the very first few hours of the war, while around 500 people took advantage of the mid-December amnesty declared by Yeltsin for members of Dzhokhar Dudayev's armed groups. Nevertheless, Boris Yeltsin's cabinet's expectations of a quick surgical strike, quickly followed by Chechen capitulation and regime change, were misguided. Russia found itself in a quagmire practically instantly. The morale of the Russian troops, poorly prepared and not understanding why and even where they were sent, was low from the beginning. Some Russian units resisted the order to advance, and in some cases, the troops sabotaged their own equipment. In Ingushetia, civilian protesters stopped the western column and set 30 military vehicles on fire, while about 70 conscripts deserted their units. Advance of the northern column was halted by the unexpected Chechen resistance at Dolinskoye and the Russian forces suffered the first serious losses.[13] Deeper in Chechnya, a group of 50 Russian paratroopers surrendered to the local militia, after being deployed by helicopters behind enemy lines and then abandoned.

Yeltsin ordered the Russian Army to show restraint, but it was neither prepared nor trained for this. Civilian losses quickly mounted, alienating the Chechen population and raising hostility to the Russian forces, even among those who initially supported the attempts to unseat Dudayev. Other problems occurred as Yeltsin sent in freshly trained conscripts from neighboring regions rather than regular soldiers. Highly mobile units of Chechen fighters caused severe losses to Russia's ill-prepared, demoralized troops. The Russian military command then resorted to carpet bombing tactics and indiscriminate barrages of rocket artillery, causing enormous casualties among the Chechen and Russian civilian population.[14] On December 29, in a rare instance of a Russian outright victory, the Russian airborne forces seized the military airfield next to Grozny and repelled a Chechen armored counterattack in the battle of Khankala; the next objective was the city itself. With the Russians closing in on the capital, Chechens began to hastily set up defensive fighting positions and group their forces in the city.

Storming of Grozny

A Chechen fighter near the burned-out ruins of the Presidential Palace in Grozny, January 1995

When the Russians besieged the Chechen capital, thousands of civilians died from a week-long series of air raids and artillery bombardment in the heaviest bombing campaign in Europe since the destruction of Dresden.[15] The initial assault on the New Year's Eve of 1995 ended in a major Russian defeat, resulting in heavy casualties and at first nearly a complete breakdown of morale in the Russian forces. The disaster claimed lives of an estimated 1,000 to 2,000 Russian soldiers, mostly barely trained and disoriented conscripts; the worst losses were suffered by the 131st 'Maikop' Motor Rifle Brigade, completely destroyed in the fighting near the central railway station.[13] Despite the early Chechen defeat of the New Year assault and many further casualties, Grozny was eventually conquered by Russian forces amidst bitter urban warfare. After armored assaults failed, the Russian military set out to pulverize the sealed-off city into submission using air power and artillery, at the same time accusing their enemies of using civilians as human shields by preventing them from leaving the capital as it came under continued bombardment.[16] On January 7, 1995, Russia's Major-General Viktor Vorobyov was killed by mortar fire, becoming the first on a long list of generals to be killed in Chechnya. On January 19, despite heavy casualties, Russian forces seized the ruins of the Chechen presidential palace, which had been heavily contested for more than three weeks as Chechens finally abandoned their positions in the destroyed downtown area. The battle for the southern part of the city continued until the official end on March 6, 1995.

By the estimates of Yeltsin's human rights adviser Sergey Kovalev, about 27,000 civilians died in the first five weeks of fighting. Russian historian and general Dmitri Volkogonov said the Russian military's bombardment of Grozny killed around 35,000 civilians, including 5,000 children, and that the vast majority of those killed were ethnic Russians. While military casualties are not known, the Russian side admitted to having lost nearly 2,000 soldiers killed or missing.[17] The bloodbath of Grozny shocked Russia and the outside world, causing severe criticism of the war. International monitors from the OSCE described the scenes as nothing short of an "unimaginable catastrophe", while former Soviet leader Mikhail Gorbachev called the war a "disgraceful, bloody adventure" and German Chancellor Helmut Kohl called it "sheer madness".[18]

Continued Russian offensive

A boy stands near a house in Chechnya

Following the fall of Grozny, the Russians slowly but systematically expanded their control over the lowland areas and then into the mountains. In what was dubbed the worst massacre in the war, the OMON and other federal forces killed at least 103 civilians while seizing the border village of Samashki on April 7 (several hundred more were detained and beaten or otherwise tortured).[19] In the southern mountains, the Russians launched an offensive along the entire front on April 15, advancing in large columns of 200-300 vehicles.[20] The ChRI forces defended the city of Argun, moving their military headquarters first to completely surrounded Shali, then shortly after to Serzhen-Yurt as they were forced into the mountains, and finally to Shamil Basayev's ancestral stronghold of Vedeno. Chechnya's second-largest city of Gudermes was surrendered without a fight, but the village of Shatoy was fought for and defended by the men of Ruslan Gelayev. Eventually, the Chechen command withdrew from the area of Vedeno to the Chechen opposition-aligned village of Dargo, and from there to Benoy.[21] According to an estimate cited in a United States Army analysis report, between January and June 1995, when the Russian forces conquered most of the republic in the conventional campaign, their losses in Chechnya were approximately 2,800 killed, 10,000 wounded and more than 500 missing or captured.[22] However, some Chechen fighters infiltrated already pacified places hiding in crowds of returning refugees.[23]

As the war continued, separatists resorted to large hostage takings, attempting to influence the Russian public and leadership. In June 1995, a group led by the maverick field commander Shamil Basayev took more than 1,500 people hostage in southern Russia in the Budyonnovsk hospital hostage crisis; about 120 Russian civilians died before a ceasefire was signed after negotiations between Basayev and the Russian Prime Minister Viktor Chernomyrdin. The raid enforced a temporary stop in Russian military operations, allowing the Chechens the time to regroup during their greatest crisis and prepare for the national militant campaign. The full-scale Russian attack led many of Dudayev's opponents to side with his forces and thousands of volunteers to swell the ranks of mobile militant units. Many others formed local self-defence militia units to defend their settlements in the case of the federal offensive action, officially numbering 5,000–6,000 armed men in late 1995. Altogether, the ChRI forces fielded some 10,000–12,000 full-time and reserve fighters at a time, according to the Chechen command. According to the UN report, the Chechen separatist forces included a large number of child soldiers, some as young as 11 and including females.[24] As the territory controlled by them shrank the separatists increasingly resorted to the classic guerrilla warfare tactics, such as setting booby traps and mining roads in the enemy-held territory. The successful use of improvised explosive devices was particularly noteworthy; they also effectively exploited a combination of mines and ambushes.

In the fall of 1995, Gen. Anatoliy Romanov, the federal commander in Chechnya at the time, was critically injured and paralyzed in a bomb blast in Grozny. Suspicion of responsibility for the attack fell on rogue elements of the Russian military, as the attack destroyed hopes for a permanent ceasefire based on the developing trust between Gen. Romanov and the ChRI Chief of Staff Aslan Maskhadov, a former colonel in the Soviet Army;[25] in August, the two went to southern Chechnya in an effort to convince the local commanders to release Russian prisoners.[26] In February 1996, the federal and pro-Russian Chechen forces in Grozny opened fire on the massive pro-independence peace march involving tens of thousands of people, killing a number of demonstrators;[27] the ruins of the presidential palace, the symbol of the Chechen independence, were then demolished two days later.

Human rights and laws of war violations

Human rights organizations accused the federal forces of engaging in indiscriminate and disproportionate use of force whenever encountering resistance, resulting in numerous civilian deaths (for example, according to Human Rights Watch, Russian artillery and rocket attacks killed at least 267 civilians during the December 1995 separatist raid on Gudermes[19]). The dominant Russian strategy was to use heavy artillery and air strikes throughout the campaign, leading some Western and Chechen sources to call the air strikes deliberate terror bombing on the part of Russia.[28] Ironically, due to the fact that ethnic Chechens in Grozny were able to seek refuge among their respective *teips* in the surrounding villages of the countryside, a high proportion of initial civilian casualties were inflicted against ethnic Russians who were unable to procure viable escape routes. The villages, however, were also heavily targeted from the first weeks of the conflict (the Russian cluster bombs, for example, killed at least 55 civilians during the January 3, 1995 Shali cluster bomb attack). The Russian soldiers often prevented civilians from evacuating from areas of imminent danger and prevented humanitarian organizations from assisting civilians in need. It was widely alleged that Russian troops, especially those belonging to the MVD, committed numerous and in part systematic acts of torture and summary executions on separatist sympathizers; they were often linked to *zachistka* ("cleansing" raids, affecting entire town districts and villages suspected of harboring *boyeviki* - the separatist fighters). Humanitarian and aid groups chronicled persistent patterns of Russian soldiers killing, raping and looting civilians at random, often in disregard of their nationality. Separatist fighters took hostages on a massive scale, kidnapped or killed Chechens considered to be collaborators, and mistreated civilian captives and federal prisoners of war (especially pilots). Both separatist and federal sides of the conflict kidnapped hostages for ransom and used human shields for cover during the fighting and movement of troops (for example, a group of surrounded Russian troops took approximately 500 civilian hostages at Grozny's 9th Municipal Hospital[29]).

The violations by the members of the Russian forces were usually tolerated by their superiors and not punished even when investigated (story of Vladimir Glebov serving as an example of such policy). However, television and newspaper accounts widely reported largely uncensored images of the carnage to the Russian public. As a result, the Russian media coverage partially precipitated a loss of public confidence in the government and a steep decline in president Yeltsin's popularity. Chechnya was one of the heaviest burdens on Yeltsin's 1996 presidential election campaign. In addition, the protracted war in Chechnya, especially many reports of extreme violence against civilians, ignited fear and contempt of Russia among other ethnic groups in the federation.

Spread of the war

Chechen irregular fighter with a *Borz* submachine gun

Chechnya's Chief Mufti Akhmad Kadyrov's declaration that the ChRI was waging a *Jihad* (*struggle*) against Russia raised the spectre that Jihadis from other regions and even outside Russia would enter the war. By one estimate, up to 5,000 non-Chechens served as foreign volunteers, motivated by religious and/or nationalistic reasons.

Limited fighting occurred in the neighbouring small Russian republic of Ingushetia, mostly when Russian commanders sent troops over the border in pursuit of Chechen fighters, while as many as 200,000 refugees (from Chechnya and the conflict in North Ossetia) strained Ingushetia's already weak economy. On several occasions, Ingush president Ruslan Aushev protested incursions by Russian soldiers and even threatened to sue the Russian Ministry of Defence for damages inflicted, recalling how the federal forces previously assisted in the expulsion of Ingush population from North Ossetia.[30] Undisciplined Russian soldiers were also reported to be committing murders, rapes, and looting in Ingushetia (in an incident partially witnessed by visiting Russian Duma deputies, at least nine Ingush civilians and an ethnic Bashkir soldier were murdered by apparently drunk Russian soldiers; earlier, drunken Russian soldiers killed another Russian soldier, five Ingush villagers and even the Ingushetia's health minister).[31] Much larger and more deadly hostilities took place in the republic of Dagestan. In particular a border village of Pervomayskoye was completely destroyed by the Russian forces in January 1996 in reaction to the large-scale Chechen hostage taking in Kizlyar in Dagestan (more than 2,000 hostages), bringing strong criticism from this hitherto loyal republic and escalating domestic dissatisfaction. The Don Cossacks of southern Russia, originally sympathetic to the Chechen cause , turned hostile as a result of their Russian-esque culture and language and stronger affinity to Moscow than Grozny (their long history of conflict with indigenous peoples such as the Chechens should also be considered), and the Kuban Cossacks started organising themselves against the Chechens, including manning paramilitary roadblocks against infiltration of their territories.

Meanwhile, the war in Chechnya spawned new forms of separatist activities in the Russian Federation. Resistance to the conscription of men from minority ethnic groups to fight in Chechnya was widespread among other republics, many of which passed laws and decrees on the subject. For example, the government of Chuvashia passed a decree providing legal protection to soldiers from the republic who refused to participate in the Chechen war and imposed limits on the use of the federal army in ethnic or regional conflicts within Russia. Some regional and local legislative bodies called for a prohibition on the use of draftees in quelling internal conflicts, while others demanded a total ban on the use of the armed forces in such situations. Russian government officials feared that a move to end the war short of victory would create a cascade of secession attempts by other ethnic minorities.

On March 6, 1996, a Cypriot passenger jet was hijacked by Chechen sympathisers while flying toward Germany. On January 9, 1996, a Turkish passenger ship carrying 200 Russian passengers was taken over by the mostly Turkish gunmen seeking to publicize the Chechen cause. Both of these incidents were resolved through negotiations and the hijackers surrendered without fatalities.

Continued Russian offensive

On March 6, 1996, between 1,500 and 2,000 Chechen fighters infiltrated Grozny and launched a three-day surprise raid on the city, overrunning much of the city and capturing caches of weapons and ammunition. Also in March, the Chechen fighters attacked Samashki, where hundreds of villagers were killed. A month later, on April 16, forces of Arab commander Ibn al-Khattab destroyed a large Russian armored column in an ambush near Shatoy, killing at least 53 soldiers (some 100 according to most estimates); in another one, near Vedeno, at least 28 troops were killed.[32]

A group of the Chechen *boyeviki* (fighters)

As military defeats and growing casualties made the war more and more unpopular in Russia, and as the 1996 presidential elections neared, Yeltsin's government sought a way out of the conflict. Although a Russian guided missile attack assassinated the ChRI President Dzhokhar Dudayev on April 21, 1996, the separatists persisted. Yeltsin even officially declared "victory" in Grozny on May 28, 1996, after a new temporary ceasefire was signed with the ChRI Acting President Zelimkhan Yandarbiyev.[33] While the political leaders were talking about the ceasefires and peace negotiations, military forces continued to conduct combat operations. On August 6, 1996, three days before Yeltsin was to be inaugurated for his second term as president and when most of the Russian Army troops were moved south due to what was planned as their final offensive against remaining mountainous separatist strongholds, the Chechens launched another surprise attack on Grozny.

3rd Battle of Grozny and the Khasav-Yurt Accord

Despite Russian troops in and around Grozny numbering approximately 12,000, more than 1,500 Chechen guerrillas (whose numbers soon swelled) overran the key districts within hours in an operation prepared and led by Maskhadov (who named it Operation Zero option) and Basayev (who called it Operation Jihad). The separatists then laid siege to the Russian posts and bases and the government compound in the city centre, while a number of Chechens deemed to be Russian collaborators were rounded up, detained and, in some cases, executed.[34] At the same time, Russian troops in the cities of Argun and Gudermes were also surrounded in their garrisons. Several attempts by the armored columns to rescue the units trapped in Grozny were repelled with heavy Russian casualties (the 276th Motorized Regiment of 900 men suffered 50% casualties in a two-day attempt to reach the city centre). Russian military officials said that more than 200 soldiers had been killed and nearly 800 wounded in five days of fighting, and that an unknown number were missing; Chechens put the number of Russian dead at close to 1,000. Thousands of troops were either taken prisoner or surrounded and largely disarmed, their heavy weapons and ammunition commandeered by the separatists.

On August 19, despite the presence of 50,000 to 200,000 Chechen and Russian civilians and thousands of federal servicemen in Grozny, the Russian commander Konstantin Pulikovsky gave an ultimatum for Chechen fighters to leave the city within 48 hours, or else it would be leveled in a massive aerial and artillery bombardment, including by strategic bombers (not used in Chechnya up to this point) and ballistic missiles. This announcement was followed by chaotic scenes of panic as civilians tried to flee before the army carried out its threat, with parts of the city ablaze and falling shells scattering refugee columns.[35] The bombardment was however soon halted by the ceasefire brokered by Gen. Alexander Lebed, Yeltsin's national security adviser, on August 22. Gen. Lebed called the ultimatum, issued by Gen. Pulikovsky (now replaced), a "bad joke".[36]

During eight hours of subsequent talks, Lebed and Maskhadov drafted and signed the Khasav-Yurt Accord on August 31, 1996. It included: technical aspects of demilitarization, the withdrawal of both sides' forces from Grozny, the creation of joint headquarters to preclude looting in the city, the withdrawal of all federal forces from Chechnya by December 31, 1996, and a stipulation that any agreement on the relations between the Chechen Republic of Ichkeria and the Russian federal government need not be signed until late 2001.

Aftermath

Casualties

According to the General Staff of the Russian Armed Forces, 3,826 troops were killed, 17,892 were wounded, and 1,906 are missing in action.[37] According to *NVO*, the authoritative Russian independent military weekly, at least 5,362 Russian soldiers died during the war, 52,000 got wounded or sick, and some 3,000 more remained missing by 2005.[38] The estimate of the Committee of Soldiers' Mothers of Russia, however, put the number of the Russian military dead at 14,000,[1] based on information from wounded troops and soldiers' relatives (counting only regular troops, i.e. not the *kontraktniki* and special service forces).[39] In 2009 the official Russian number of troops still missing from the two wars in Chechnya and presumed dead was some 700, while about 400 remains of the missing servicemen were said to be recovered up to this point.[40]

Dead bodies on a truck in Grozny

Chechen casualties are estimated at up to 100,000 dead or more, of which most were civilians.[41] Various estimates put the number of Chechens dead or missing between 50,000 and 100,000.[] Russian Interior Minister Anatoly Kulikov claimed that fewer than 20,000 civilians were killed. Sergey Kovalyov's team could offer their conservative, documented estimate of more than 50,000 civilian deaths. Aleksander Lebed asserted that 80,000 to 100,000 had been killed and 240,000 had been injured. The number given by the ChRI authorities was about 100,000 killed.[] According to Russian newspaper *Gazeta*, approximately 35,000 ethnic Russian civilians were killed by Russian forces operating in Chechnya, most of them during the bombardment of Grozny.[42]

The ChRI separatists estimated their combat deaths at about 3,000 (including some 800 in the first three months of the war and said to be mostly killed by mortar fire[43]), although this number is almost certainly too low. Tony Wood, a journalist and author who has written extensively about Chechnya, estimated about 4,000 Chechen combatant losses.[44] It is impossible to know exactly how many Chechen separatists were killed, however, because many fought independently and were not under the control of Dudayev (as such, their deaths were not counted among official Chechen losses). The Russian estimate is much higher; Russia's Federal Forces Command estimated that 15,000 Chechen fighters had been killed by the end of the war.[45]

Prisoners and missing persons

In the Khasav-Yurt Accord, both sides agreed to an "all for all" exchange of prisoners to be carried out at the end of the war. However, despite this commitment, many persons remained forcibly detained. A partial analysis of the list of 1,432 reported missing found that, as of October 30, 1996, at least 139 Chechens were still being forcibly detained by the Russian side; it was entirely unclear how many of these men were alive.[46] As of mid-January 1997, the Chechens still held between 700 and 1,000 Russian soldiers and officers as prisoners of war, according to Human Rights Watch.[46] According to Amnesty International that same month, 1,058 Russian soldiers and officers were being detained by Chechen fighters who were willing to release them in exchange for members of Chechen armed groups.[47] American freelance journalist Andrew Shumack has been missing from the Chechen capital, Grozny since July 1995 and is presumed dead.

The Moscow peace treaty

The Khasav-Yurt Accord paved the way for the signing of two further agreements between Russia and Chechnya. In mid-November 1996, Yeltsin and Maskhadov signed an agreement on economic relations and reparations to Chechens who had been "affected" by the 1994–96 war. In February 1997, Russia also approved an amnesty for Russian soldiers and Chechen separatists alike who committed illegal acts in connection with the war in Chechnya between December 1994 and September 1996.[48]

Street of the ruined capital Grozny after war

Six months after the Khasav-Yurt Accord, on May 12, 1997, Chechen-elected president Aslan Maskhadov traveled to Moscow where he and Yeltsin signed a formal treaty "on peace and the principles of Russian-Chechen relations" that Maskhadov predicted would demolish "any basis to create ill-feelings between Moscow and Grozny."[49] Maskhadov's optimism, however, proved misplaced. Little more than two years later, some of Maskhadov's former comrades-in-arms, led by radical field commanders Shamil Basayev and Ibn al-Khattab, launched an invasion of Dagestan in the summer of 1999 – and soon Russia invaded Chechnya again, marking beginning of the Second Chechen War.

See also

- Second Chechen War
- History of post-Soviet Russia
- Islam in Russia

Notes

[1] Casualty Figures (http://www.cdi.org/russia/245-14.cfm) Jamestown Foundation

[2] First Chechnya War - 1994-1996 (http://www.globalsecurity.org/military/world/war/chechnya1.htm) Globalsecurity.org

[3] *The Chechen Wars: Will Russia Go the Way of the Soviet Union? by Matthew Evangelista* Page 18.

[4] *Russia's Chechen war by Tracey C. German* Page 176

[5] *Chechnya: Calamity in the Caucasus by Carlotta Gall and Thomas De Waal* Page 96; *Vitaly Kutsenko, the elderly First Secretary of the town soviet either was pushed out of a first-floor window or tried to clamber out to escape the crowd.*

[6] O.P. Orlov; V.P. Cherkassov. "Россия — Чечня: Цепь ошибок и преступлений" (http://www.memo.ru/hr/hotpoints/chechen/itogi/preface.htm#_VPID_2) (in Russian). Memorial. .

[7] Unity Or Separation: Center-periphery Relations in the Former Soviet Union By Daniel R. Kempton, Terry D. Clark p.122

[8] *Allah's Mountains: Politics and War in the Russian Caucasus* By Sebastian Smith p.134

[9] *Moscow News*. November 22–29, 1992
[10] *Moscow News*. September 1–7, 1995
[11] For example, see Wood, Tony. *Chechnya: the Case for Independence*. Page 61, or alternatively, works by Anatol Lieven on the issue.
[12] The battle(s) of Grozny (http://www.bdcol.ee/fileadmin/docs/bdreview/07bdr299.pdf)
[13] Gall, Carlotta; Thomas de Waal (1998). *Chechnya: Calamity in the Caucasus*. New York University Press. ISBN 0-8147-2963-0.: pp. 177-181.
[14] Cluster Munitions Use by Russian Federation Forces in Chechnya (http://mcc.org/clusterbombs/resources/research/death/chapter3.html#4B1A) Mennonite Central Committee
[15] Williams, Bryan Glyn (2001). The Russo-Chechen War: A Threat to Stability in the Middle East and Eurasia? (http://www.blackwell-synergy.com/doi/pdf/10.1111/1475-4967.00012). *Middle East Policy* 8.1.
[16] Chechens 'using human shields' (http://news.bbc.co.uk/1/hi/world/europe/545672.stm) BBC News
[17] Faurby, Ib; Märta-Lisa Magnusson (1999). "The Battle(s) of Grozny" (http://www.caucasus.dk/publication1.htm). *Baltic Defence Review* (2): 75–87. .
[18] "The First Bloody Battle" (http://news.bbc.co.uk/2/hi/europe/482323.stm). *The Chechen Conflict* (BBC News). 2000-03-16. .
[19] The Russian Federation Human Rights Developments (http://www.hrw.org/reports/1996/WR96/Helsinki-16.htm) Human Rights Watch
[20] Alikhadzhiev interview (http://smallwarsjournal.com/documents/alikhadzhievinterview.pdf)
[21] Iskhanov interview (http://smallwarsjournal.com/documents/iskhanovinterview.pdf)
[22] Lessons Learned from Modern Urban Combat (http://www.inetres.com/gp/military/FM3-06_11H.html) U.S. Army
[23] Foreign Military Studies Office Publications - Combat Stress in Chechnya: "The Equal Opportunity Disorder" (http://leav-www.army.mil/fmso/documents/stress.htm)
[24] The situation of human rights in the Republic of Chechnya of the Russian Federation (http://www1.umn.edu/humanrts/commission/country52/1996_13.htm) United Nations
[25] Honoring a General Who is Silenced (http://www.sptimes.ru/index.php?action_id=2&story_id=11071) *The St. Petersburg Times*
[26] Chechnya: Election Date Postponed, Prisoner Exchange in Trouble. (http://www.jamestown.org/publications_details.php?volume_id=14&&issue_id=740) The Jamestown Foundation
[27] Mass protests in Grozny end in bloodshed (http://www.hartford-hwp.com/archives/63/080.html)
[28] Russia's Invasion of Chechnya: A Preliminary Assessment (http://www.dtic.mil/doctrine/jel/research_pubs/chechna.pdf)
[29] Grozny, August 1996. Occupation of Municipal Hospital No. 9 (http://www.memo.ru/hr/hotpoints/chechen/szczyt/eng/Chapter7.htm) Memorial
[30] July archive (http://psi.ece.jhu.edu/~kaplan/IRUSS/ARCHIVE/2.94.html)
[31] Army demoralized (http://www.nupi.no/cgi-win/Russland/krono.exe?3271)
[32] Russian fighting ceases in Chechnya; Skeptical troops comply with Yeltsin order (http://edition.cnn.com/WORLD/9604/01/russia_chechnya/) CNN
[33] Yeltsin declares Russian victory over Chechnya (http://www.cnn.com/WORLD/9605/28/russia.chechnya/) CNN
[34] The Violation of Human Rights and Norms of Humanitarian Law in the Course of the Armed Conflict in the Chechen Republic (http://www.memo.ru/hr/hotpoints/chechen/checheng/fin_rep.htm) Memorial
[35] Lebed calls off assault on Grozny (http://www.telegraph.co.uk/htmlContent.jhtml?html=/archive/1996/08/22/wrus22.html) *The Daily Telegraph*
[36] Lebed promises peace in Grozny and no Russian assault (http://www.cnn.com/WORLD/9608/21/chechnya.final/) CNN
[37] "The War in Chechnya" (http://mosnews.com/mn-files/chechnya.shtml). *MN-Files*. Mosnews.com. 2007-02-07. .
[38] Saradzhyan, Simon (2005-03-09). "Army Learned Few Lessons From Chechnya" (http://www.worldpress.org/Europe/2043.cfm). Moscow Times. .
[39] Civil and military casualties of the wars in Chechnya (http://www.hrvc.net/htmls/references.htm)
[40] [700 Russian servicemen missing in Chechnya - officer], Interfax
[41] The Russian Army in Chechnya (http://www.crimesofwar.org/chechnya-mag/chech-felgenhauer.html) by Pavel Felgenhauer
[42] Do Ethnic Russians Support Putin's War in Chechnya? (http://jamestown.org/chechnya_weekly/article.php?articleid=2371378) The Jamestown Foundation
[43] Khozhev interview (http://smallwarsjournal.com/documents/khozhevinterview.pdf)
[44] New Left Review - Tony Wood: The Case for Chechnya (http://newleftreview.org/A2533)
[45] Knezys, Stasys, and Romaras Sedlickas. *The War in Chechnya*. 1st ed. College Station: Texas A&M University Press, 1999. 303-304
[46] Missing Persons, Those Forcibly Detained, and Exchanges (http://www.hrw.org/reports/1997/russia2/Russia-03.htm) Human Rights Watch
[47] AI Report 1998: Russian Federation (http://www.amnesty.org/ailib/aireport/ar98/eur46.htm) Amnesty International
[48] First Chechnya War - 1994-1996 (http://www.worldaffairsboard.com/showthread.php?t=1965)
[49] Yeltshin, Maskhadov Sign Peace Agreement (http://www.friends-partners.org/friends/news/omri/1997/05/970512I.html(opt,mozilla,unix,english,,new)). RFE/RL

Further Reading

- Bennett, Vanora. *Crying Wolf.* Picador (1998). ISBN 0-330-35170-2
- *A Military History of Russia: From Ivan the Terrible to the War in Chechnya* (http://books.google.com/books?id=DbR62llvLh0C&printsec=frontcover) Author: David R. Stone (preview available)
- *A Small Corner of Hell: Dispatches from Chechnya* (http://books.google.com/books?id=M0NgDHDnpqgC&printsec=frontcover) Author: Anna Politkovskaya (preview available)
- *Allah's Mountains: The Battle for Chechnya* (http://books.google.com/books?id=NPkH-7BCB6AC&printsec=frontcover) Author: Sebastian Smith (preview available)
- *Angel of Grozny* (http://books.google.com/books?id=iljEKQAACAAJ&dq) Author: Asne Seierstad
- *Chechnya: Calamity in the Caucasus* (http://books.google.com/books?id=AEjQHgAACAAJ&dq) Author: Carlotta Gall, Thomas De Waal
- *Chechnya: From Nationalism to Jihad* (http://books.google.com/books?id=VhtNIDj6evUC&printsec=frontcover) Author: James Hughes (preview available)
- *Chechnya: From Past To Future* (http://books.google.com/books?id=mPZeN5Wh1e4C&printsec=frontcover) Author: Richard Sakwa and others (preview available)
- *Chechnya: Life in a War-Torn Society* (http://books.google.com/books?id=BbYP8pOVv-AC&printsec=frontcover) Author: Valery Tishkov (preview available)
- *Chechnya: The Case for Independence* (http://books.google.com/books?id=5z4hAAAACAAJ&dq) Author: Tony Wood
- *Chechnya: Tombstone of Russian Power* (http://books.google.com/books?id=0Q98IQAACAAJ&dq) Author: Anatol Lieven
- *Landscapes of War: From Sarajevo to Chechnya* (http://books.google.com/books?id=q_aVaqdZhQwC&printsec=frontcover) Author: Juan Goytisolo (preview available)
- *My Jihad* (http://books.google.com/books?id=NukGAAAACAAJ&dq) Author: Aukai Collins
- *Open Wound: Chechnya 1994-2003* (http://books.google.com/books?id=taoIAAAACAAJ&dq) Author: Stanley Greene
- *Russia Confronts Chechnya: Roots of a Separatist Conflict* (http://books.google.com/books?id=IMlcz5bhkqUC&printsec=frontcover) Author: John B. Dunlop (preview available)
- *Russia in Afghanistan and Chechnya* (http://books.google.com/books?id=7D1ou91YCi8C&printsec=frontcover) Author: Robert M. Cassidy (preview available)
- *Russia's Chechen War* (http://books.google.com/books?id=0zW8V-8YcBAC&printsec=frontcover) Author: Tracey C. German (preview available)
- *Russia's Restless Frontier: The Chechnya Factor in Post-Soviet Russia* (http://books.google.com/books?id=Tcab0VXTqnQC&printsec=frontcover) Author: Dmitri Trenin, Anatol Lieven (preview available)
- *Russia's Wars with Chechnya 1994-2003* (http://books.google.com/books?id=zPgeAQAACAAJ&dq) Author: Michael Orr
- *Russian Military Reform, 1992-2002* (http://books.google.com/books?id=7JLYiPmzD5oC&pg=PA160&dq) Author: Anne Aldis, Roger N. McDermott
- *The Chechen Wars: Will Russia Go the Way of the Soviet Union?* (http://books.google.com/books?id=inc4KfEHymYC&printsec=frontcover) Author: Matthew Evangelista (preview available)
- *The Lone Wolf and the Bear: Three Centuries of Chechen Defiance of Russian Rule* (http://books.google.com/books?id=OuzqrrzVspEC&printsec=frontcover) Author: Moshe Gammer (preview available)
- *The Russian Army in a Time of Troubles* (http://books.google.com/books?id=7JPQyDDFC-8C&printsec=frontcover) Author: Pavel K. Baev (preview available)
- *The Oath: A Surgeon Under Fire* (http://books.google.com/books?id=vcMMAAAACAAJ&dq) Author: Khassan Baiev

- *The Wolves of Islam: Russia and the Faces of Chechen Terror* (http://books.google.com/books?id=_LXfR7wNWTUC&printsec=frontcover) Author: Paul J. Murphy (preview available)

External links

- YouTubeDon't Ever ForgetYoung Russian Conscripts Beheaded by Chechen Terrorists 1999 (http://www.youtube.com/watch?v=YN8wSBklQ6Q)
- Chechen War 1994-96 (http://www.boyntonweb.net/Policy/Chechnya.htm) The World Regional Conflicts Project
- Chechnya (http://www.crimesofwar.org/thebook/chechnya.html) Crimes of War Project
- Chechnya Reference Library (http://smallwarsjournal.com/reference/chechnya.php) A collection of analyses and interviews of Chechen commanders conducted by the United States Marine Corps
- Chechnya: Two Federal Interventions (http://www.da.mod.uk/colleges/csrc/document-listings/caucasus/P29) Conflict Studies Research Centre
- *Damned and forgotten* (http://russianremote.com/1241.html) Documentary by Sergey Govorukhin
- First Chechnya War - 1994-1996 (http://www.globalsecurity.org/military/world/war/chechnya1.htm) Foreign Military Studies Office
- The Chechen Campaign (http://www.ccc.nps.navy.mil/people/tsypkinConf/Felgenhauer 95_.doc) by Pavel Felgenhauer
- War and Human Rights (http://www.hro.org/war/source_e.htm) Memorial human rights group
- Why It All Went So Very Wrong (http://www.time.com/time/magazine/article/0,9171,982351,00.html) *TIME*
- Why the Russian Military Failed in Chechnya (http://www.amina.com/article/whyrus_failed.html) U.S. Foreign Studies
- Wounded Bear (http://www.globalsecurity.org/military/library/report/1996/wounded.htm) GlobalSecurity.org
- Vyacheslav Mironov. *I was at that war.* Translation available online* (http://artofwar.ru/a/abramow_o_b/)

Second Chechen War

The **Second Chechen War**, in a later phase better known as the **War in the North Caucasus**,[1] was launched by the Russian Federation starting 26 August 1999, in response to the Invasion of Dagestan by the Islamic International Peacekeeping Brigade (IIPB).

On 1 October Russian troops entered Chechnya.[2] [3] The campaign ended the de facto independence of Chechen Republic of Ichkeria and restored Russian federal control over the territory. Although it is regarded by many as an internal conflict within the Russian Federation, the war attracted a large number of foreign fighters.

During the initial campaign, Russian military and pro-Russian Chechen paramilitary forces faced Chechen separatists in open combat, and seized the Chechen capital Grozny after a winter siege that lasted from late 1999 to the following February 2000. Russia established direct rule of Chechnya in May 2000 and after the full-scale offensive, Chechen militant resistance throughout the North Caucasus region continued to inflict heavy Russian casualties and challenge Russian political control over Chechnya for several more years. Some Chechen separatists also carried out terrorist attacks against civilians in Russia. These terrorist attacks, as well as widespread human rights violations by Russian and separatist forces, drew international condemnation.

As of 2009, Russia has severely disabled the Chechen separatist movement and large-scale fighting has ceased. Russian army and interior ministry troops no longer occupy the streets. The once leveled city of Grozny has recently undergone massive reconstruction efforts and much of the city and surrounding areas have been rebuilt at a quick pace. However sporadic violence still exists throughout the North Caucasus; occasional bombings and ambushes targeting federal troops and forces of the regional governments in the area still occur.[4] [5]

On 16 April 2009, the counter-terrorism operation in Chechnya was officially ended.[6] As the main bulk of the army was withdrawn, the burden of dealing with the ongoing low-level insurgency mainly fell on the shoulders of the local police force. Three months later, the exiled leader of the separatist government, Akhmed Zakayev, called for a halt to armed resistance against the Chechen police force starting on 1 August, and said he hoped that "starting with this day Chechens will never shoot at each other".[7]

The exact death toll from this conflict is unknown. Unofficial estimates range from 25,000 to 50,000 dead or missing, mostly civilians in Chechnya. Russian casualties are over 5,200 (official Russian casualty figures)[8] and are about 11,000 according to the Committee of Soldiers' Mothers.[9]

Historical basis of the conflict

Russian Empire

Chechnya is a region in the Northern Caucasus which has constantly fought against foreign rule, including the Ottoman Turks in the 15th century. The Russian Terek Cossack Host was established in lowland Chechnya in 1577 by free Cossacks who were resettled from the Volga to the Terek River. In 1783 Russia and the Georgian kingdom of Kartl-Kakheti signed the Treaty of Georgievsk, under which Kartl-Kakheti became a Russian

Chechnya and the Caucasus region

protectorate. To secure communications with Georgia and other regions of the Transcaucasia, the Russian Empire began spreading its influence into the Caucasus region, starting the Caucasus War in 1817. Russian forces first moved into highland Chechnya in 1830, and the conflict in the area lasted until 1859, when a 250,000 strong army under General Baryatinsky broke down the mountaineers' resistance. However, frequent uprisings in the Caucasus also occurred during the Russo-Turkish War, 1877-78.

Soviet Union

Following the Russian Revolution of 1917, Chechens established a short-lived Caucasian Imamate which included parts of Chechnya, Dagestan and Ingushetia; there was also secular pan-Caucasian Mountainous Republic of the Northern Caucasus.[10] The Chechen states were opposed by both sides of the Russian Civil War and most of the resistance was crushed by Bolshevik troops by 1922. Then, months before the creation of the Soviet Union, the Chechen Autonomous Oblast of Russian SFSR was established. It annexed a part of territory of the former Terek Cossack Host. Chechnya and neighbouring Ingushetia formed the Chechen-Ingush Autonomous Soviet Socialist Republic in 1936. In 1941, during World War II, a Chechen revolt broke out, led by Khasan Israilov. Chechens were accused by Joseph Stalin of aiding Nazi forces. In February 1944 Stalin deported all the Chechens and Ingush to Kazakh and Kirghiz SSRs. Up to a quarter of these people died during the "resettlement."[11] [12] [13] In 1957, after the death of Stalin, Nikita Khrushchev allowed the Chechens to return and the Chechen republic was reinstated in 1958, the authority of the Soviet government gradually eroded.

The First Chechen War

A Russian helicopter downed by Chechen militants near the capital Grozny, during the First Chechen War

During the dissolution of the Soviet Union in 1991, Chechnya declared independence. In 1992, Chechen and Ingush leaders signed an agreement splitting the joint Chechen-Ingush republic in two, with Ingushetia joining the Russian Federation and Chechnya remaining independent. The debate over independence ultimately led to a small-scale civil war since 1992, in which the Russians supported the opposition forces against Dzhokhar Dudayev. Thousands of people of non-Chechen ethnicity (mostly Russians) fled the Chechen Republic and Chechnya's industrial production began failing after Russian engineers and workers fled or were expelled. The First Chechen War began in 1994, when Russian forces entered Chechnya to "restore constitutional order". Following nearly two years of brutal fighting, in which an estimated tens of thousands to more than 100,000 people died, and the 1996 Khasavyurt ceasefire agreement, the Russian troops were withdrawn from the republic.

Prelude to the Second Chechen War

Chaos in Chechnya

Following the first war, the separatist government's grip on the chaotic republic was weak, especially outside the ruined capital Grozny. The areas controlled by separatist groups grew larger and the country became increasingly lawless.[14] The war ravages and lack of economic opportunities left large numbers of heavily armed and brutalized former militants with no occupation but further violence. The authority of the government in Grozny was opposed by extremist warlords like Arbi Barayev and Salman Raduyev. Abductions and raids into other parts of the Northern Caucasus by various Chechen warlords had been steadily increasing.[15] In lieu of the devastated economic structure, kidnapping emerged as the principal source of income countrywide, procuring over $200 million during the three year independence of the chaotic fledgling state.[16] It has been estimated that up to 1,300 people were kidnapped in

Chechnya between 1996 and 1999,[14] and in 1998 a group of four Western hostages were executed. Political violence and religious extremism, in the form of islamist Wahhabism, was rife as well. In 1998, a state of emergency was declared by the authorities in Grozny. Tensions led to the open clashes like the July 1998 confrontation in Gudermes in which some 50 people died in the fight between Chechen National Guard and the Islamist militias.

Russian-Chechen relations 1996–1999

The 1997 election brought to power the separatist president Aslan Maskhadov. In 1998 and 1999 President Maskhadov survived several assassination attempts, blamed on the Russian intelligence services. In March 1999, General Gennady Shpigun, the Kremlin's envoy to Chechnya, was kidnapped at the airport in Grozny, and ultimately found dead in 2000 during the war.

The political tensions were fueled in part by allegedly Chechen or pro-Chechen terrorist and criminal activity in Russia, as well as border clashes.

Russian plans for the war

On 7 March 1999 interior minister Sergei Stepashin called for an invasion of Chechnya, in response to the abduction of MVD General Gennady Shpigun. However, Stepashin's plan was overridden by the prime minister Yevgeny Primakov.[17] Stepashin later said:[18]

> The decision to invade Chechnya was made in March 1999... I was prepared for an active intervention. We were planning to be on the north side of the Terek River by August–September [of 1999] This [the war] would happen regardless to the bombings in Moscow... Putin did not discover anything new. You can ask him about this. He was the director of FSB at this time and had all information.[19] [20]

According to Robert Bruce Ware, these plans should be regarded as contingency plans.[21]

Terrorist incidents and border clashes

On 16 November 1996, in Kaspiysk (Dagestan) a bomb destroyed an apartment building housing Russian border guards; 68 people died. The cause of the blast was never determined, but many in Russia blamed it on Chechen separatists.[22] Three people died on 23 April 1997, when a bomb exploded in the Russian railway station of Armavir (Krasnodar Krai), and two on 28 May 1997, when another bomb exploded in the Russian railway station of Pyatigorsk (Stavropol Krai).

On 22 December 1997, forces of Dagestani militants and Chechnya-based Arab warlord Ibn al-Khattab raided the base of the 136th Motor Rifle Brigade of the Russian Army in Buynaksk, Dagestan, inflicting severe losses on the men[23] and equipment of the unit. In late May Russia announced that it was closing the Russian-Chechnya border in an attempt to combat terrorist and criminal activity; border guards were ordered to shoot suspects on sight. On 18 June 1999, seven servicemen were killed when Russian border guard posts were attacked in Dagestan. On 29 July 1999, the Russian Interior Ministry troops destroyed a Chechen border post and captured a 800 meter-section of strategic road. On 22 August 1999, 10 Russian policemen were killed by an anti-tank mine blast in North Ossetia, and on 9 August 1999 six servicemen were kidnapped in the Ossetian capital Vladikavkaz.

Invasion of Dagestan

The Invasion of Dagestan was the trigger for the Second Chechen War. In August and September 1999, Shamil Basayev (in association with the Saudi-born Ibn al-Khattab, Commander of the Mujahedeen) led two armies of up to 2,000 Chechen, Dagestani, Arab and international mujahideen and Wahhabist militants from Chechnya into the neighboring Republic of Dagestan. This war saw the first use of aerial-delivered fuel air explosives (FAE) in populated areas, notably in the village of Tando. By mid-September 1999, the militants were routed from the villages and pushed back into Chechnya. At least several hundred militants were killed in the fighting; the Federal side reported 279 servicemen killed and approximately 900 wounded.[3]

Bombings in Russia

Before the wake of the Dagestani invasion had settled, a series of bombings took place in Russia (in Moscow and in Volgodonsk) and in the Dagestani town of Buynaksk. On 4 September 1999, 62 people died in an apartment building housing members of families of Russian soldiers. Over the next two weeks, the bombs targeted three other apartment buildings and a mall; in total nearly 300 people were killed. Khattab initially claimed responsibility for the bombings, but later denied responsibility. This was followed by an anonymous caller, who said he belonged to a group called the Liberation Army of Dagestan.[24] There were no other calls or acts by the Liberation Army of Dagestan.

A criminal investigation of the bombings was completed in 2002. The results of the investigation, and the court ruling that followed, concluded that they were organized by Achemez Gochiyaev, who remains at large, and ordered by Khattab and Abu Omar al-Saif (both of whom were later killed), in retaliation for the Russian counteroffensive against their incursion into Dagestan. Six other suspects have been convicted by Russian courts. However, many observers, including State Duma deputies Yuri Shchekochikhin, Sergei Kovalev and Sergei Yushenkov, cast doubts on the official version and sought an independent investigation. Some others, including David Satter, Yury Felshtinsky, Vladimir Pribylovsky and Alexander Litvinenko, as well as the secessionist Chechen authorities, claimed that the 1999 bombings were a false flag attack coordinated by the FSB in order to win public support for a new full-scale war in Chechnya, which boosted Prime Minister and former FSB Director Vladimir Putin's popularity, brought the pro-war Unity Party to the State Duma and him to the presidency within a few months.[19] [25] [26] [27] [28] [29] [30] [31] [32] [33] The theories' strongest proponents have links with each other as well as with Boris Berezovsky, an exiled oil-tycoon who advocates the forcible overthrowing of the Russian Government.[34] For example, Berezovsky sponsored Litivinenko's book.[35] [36] [37] [38] [39]

Other researchers have criticized the theory, stating that it is a conspiracy theory. The researchers pointed out that the theory's proponents have provided little or no evidence to support the theory.[40] [41] [42] [43] Gordon Bennett also points out that the decision to send troops to Chechnya was taken by Boris Yeltsin – not Vladimir Putin – with the wholehearted support of all power structures after the Invasion of Dagestan.[41]

1999–2000 Russian offensive

Air war

In late August and September 1999, Russia mounted a massive air campaign over Chechnya, with the stated aim of wiping out militants who invaded Dagestan the previous month. On 26 August 1999 Russia acknowledged bombing raids in Chechnya.[44] The Russian air strikes were reported to have forced at least 100,000 Chechens to flee their homes to the safety; the neighbouring region of Ingushetia was reported to have appealed for United Nations aid to deal with tens of thousands of refugees.[45] On 2 October 1999, Russia's Ministry of Emergency Situations admitted that 78,000 people have fled the air strikes in Chechnya; most of them were heading for Ingushetia, where they were arriving at a rate of 5,000 to 6,000 a day.

As of 22 September 1999 Deputy Interior Minister Igor Zubov said that Russian troops had surrounded Chechnya and were prepared to retake the region, but the military planners were advising against a ground invasion because of the likelihood of heavy Russian casualties. By the end of September Russian forces made repeated incursions onto Chechen soil, and had captured some territory.

Land war

The Chechen conflict entered a new phase on 1 October 1999, when Russia's new Prime Minister Vladimir Putin declared the authority of Chechen President Aslan Maskhadov and his parliament illegitimate. At this time, Putin announced that Russian troops would initiate a land invasion but progress only as far as the Terek River, which cuts the northern third of Chechnya off from the rest of the republic. Putin's stated intention was to take control of Chechnya's northern plain and establish a *cordon sanitaire* against further Chechen aggression; however, later recalled that the cordon alone was "pointless and technically impossible," apparently because of Chechnya's rugged terrain. According to Russian accounts, Putin accelerated a plan for a major crackdown against Chechnya that had been drawn up months earlier.[46]

The Russian army moved with ease in the wide open spaces of northern Chechnya and on 5 October 1999, reached the Terek River. On this day, a bus filled with refugees was reportedly hit by a Russian tank shell, killing at least 11 civilians;[47] two days later, Russian Su-24 fighter bombers dropped cluster bombs on the village of Elistanzhi, killing some 35 people.[48] On 10 October 1999, Maskhadov outlined a peace plan offering a crackdown on renegade warlords;[48] the offer was rejected by the Russian side. He also appealed to NATO to help end fighting between his forces and Russian troops, without effect.[49]

On 12 October 1999, the Russian forces crossed the Terek and began a two-pronged advance on the capital Grozny to the south. Hoping to avoid the significant casualties which plagued the first Chechen War, the Russians advanced slowly and in force, making extensive use of artillery and air power in an attempt to soften Chechen defences. Many thousands of civilians fled the Russian advance, leaving Chechnya for neighbouring Russian republics. Their numbers were later estimated to reach 200,000 to 350,000, out of the approximately 800,000 residents of the Chechen Republic. The Russians appeared to be taking no chances with the Chechen population in its rear areas, setting up "filtration camps" in October in northern Chechnya for detaining suspected members of *bandformirovaniya* militant formations, literally: "bandit formations").

On 15 October 1999, Russian forces took control of a strategic ridge within artillery range of the Chechen capital Grozny after mounting an intense tank and artillery barrage against Chechen fighters. In response, President Maskhadov declared a *gazavat* (holy war) to confront the approaching Russian army. Martial law was declared in Ichkeria and reservists were called; but no martial law or state of emergency had been declared in Chechnya or Russia by the Russian government.[50] The next day, Russian forces captured strategic Tersky Heights within sight of Grozny, dislodging 200 entrenched Chechen fighters. After heavy fighting, Russia seized the Chechen base in the village of Goragorsky, west of the city.[51]

On 21 October 1999, a Russian short-range ballistic missile strike on the central Grozny killed more than 140 people, including many women and children, and left hundreds more wounded. A Russian spokesman said the busy market place was targeted because it was used by separatists as an arms bazaar.[52] Eight days later Russian aircraft carried out a rocket attack on a large convoy of refugees heading into Ingushetia, killing at least 25 civilians including Red Cross workers and journalists.[53] Two days later the Russian forces conducted a heavy artillery and rocket attack on Samashki. Some claimed that civilians were killed in Samashki in revenge for the heavy casualties suffered there by Russian forces during the first war.[54]

On 12 November 1999, the Russian flag was raised over Chechnya's second largest city, Gudermes, when the local Chechen commanders, the Yamadayev brothers, defected to the federal side; the Russians also entered the bombed-out former Cossack village of Asinovskaya. The fighting in and around Kulary continued until January 2000. On 17 November 1999, Russian soldiers dislodged separatists in Bamut, the symbolic separatist stronghold in the first war; dozens of Chechen fighters and many civilians were reported killed, and the village was levelled in the FAE bombing. Two days later, after a failed attempt five days earlier, Russian forces managed to capture the village of Achkhoy-Martan.

On 26 November 1999, Deputy Army Chief of Staff Valery Manilov said that phase two of the Chechnya campaign was just about complete, and a final third phase was about to begin. According to Manilov, the aim of the third phase was to destroy "bandit groups" in the mountains. A few days later Russia's Defense Minister Igor Sergeyev said Russian forces might need up to three more months to complete their military campaign in Chechnya, while some generals said the offensive could be over by New Year's Day. The next day the Chechens briefly recaptured the town of Novogroznensky.[55]

On 1 December 1999, after weeks of heavy fighting, Russian forces under Major General Vladimir Shamanov took control of Alkhan-Yurt, a village just south of Grozny. The Chechen and foreign fighters inflicted heavy losses on the Russian forces, reportedly killing more than 70 Russian soldiers before retreating,[56] suffering heavy losses of their own.[57] On the same day, Chechen separatist forces began carrying out a series of counter-attacks against federal troops in several villages as well as in the outskirts of Gudermes. Chechen fighters in Argun, a small town five kilometres east of Grozny, put up some of the strongest resistance to federal troops since the start of Moscow's military offensive. The separatists in the town of Urus-Martan also offered fierce resistance, employing guerilla tactics Russia had been anxious to avoid; by 9 December 1999, Russian forces were still bombarding Urus-Martan, although Chechen commanders said their fighters had already pulled out.

On 4 December 1999, the commander of Russian forces in the North Caucasus, General Viktor Kazantsev, claimed that Grozny was fully blockaded by Russian troops. The Russian military's next task was the seizure of the town of Shali, 20 kilometres south-east of the capital, one of the last remaining separatist-held towns apart from Grozny. Russian troops started by capturing two bridges that link Shali to the capital, and by 11 December 1999, Russian troops had encircled Shali and were slowly forcing separatist forces out. By mid-December the Russian military was concentrating attacks in southern parts of Chechnya and preparing to launch another offensive from Dagestan.

Siege of Grozny

Meanwhile, the assault on Grozny started in early December. The battle accompanied by the struggle for the neighbouring settlements ended when the Russian army seized the city on 2 February 2000.

According to the official Russian figures, at least 368 federal troops and an unknown number of pro-Russian militiamen died in Grozny. The separatist forces too suffered heavy losses, including losing several top commanders. Russian Defense Minister Igor Sergeyev said that 1,500 separatists were killed trying to leave Grozny. The separatists said they lost at least 400 fighters in the mine field at Alkhan-Kala.[58]

The siege and fighting left the capital devastated like no other European city since World War II; in 2003 the United Nations called Grozny the most destroyed city on Earth.[59]

The Russians suffered heavy losses also as they advanced elsewhere, and from the series of Chechen counter attacks and convoy ambushes. On 26 January 2000, the Russian government announced that 1,173 servicemen had been killed in Chechnya since October[60] – a more than double rise from 544 killed reported just 19 days earlier.[61]

Battle for the mountains

Heavy fighting accompanied by a massive shelling and bombing continued through the winter of 2000 in the mountainous south of Chechnya, particularly in the areas around Argun, Vedeno and Shatoy, where the fighting involving Russian paratroopers raged since 1999.

On 9 February 2000 a Russian tactical missile hit a crowd of people who had come to the local administration building in Shali, a town previously declared as one of the "safe areas", to collect their pensions. The attack was a response to a report that a group of fighters had entered the town. The missile is estimated to have killed some 150 civilians, and was followed by an attack by combat helicopters causing further casualties.[62] Human Rights Watch has called on the Russian military to stop using FAE, known in Russia as "vacuum bombs", in Chechnya, concerned about the large number of civilian casualties caused by what it calls "the widespread and often indiscriminate bombing and shelling by Russian forces".[63] On 18 February 2000, a Russian army transport helicopter was shot down in the south, killing 15 men aboard, Russian Interior Minister Vladimir Rushailo said in a rare admission by Moscow of losses in the war.[64]

On 29 February 2000, United Army Group commander Gennady Troshev said that "the counter-terrorism operation in Chechnya is over. It will take a couple of weeks longer to pick up splinter groups now." Russia's Defense Minister, Marshal of the Russian Federation Igor Sergeyev, evaluated numerical strength of the separatists at between 2,000 and 2,500 men, "scattered all over Chechnya." On the same day, a Russian VDV paratroop company from Pskov was attacked by Chechen and Arab fighters near the village of Ulus-Kert in Chechnya's southern lowlands; at least 84 Russian soldiers were killed in the especially heavy fighting. The official newspaper of the Russian Ministry of Defense reported that at least 400 separatists were killed, figures which they said were based on radio-intercept data, intelligence reports, eyewitnesses, local residents and captured Chechens.[65] On 2 March 2000, a unit of OMON from Podolsk opened fire in Grozny on another OMON unit from Sergiyev Posad; at least 24 Russian servicemen were killed in the incident.

In March a large group of more than 1,000 Chechen fighters led by field commander Ruslan Gelayev, pursued since their withdrawal from Grozny, entered the village of Komsomolskoye in the Chechen foothills; they held off a full-scale Russian attack on the town for over two weeks, but suffered hundreds of casualties in the process; the Russians also admitted more than 50 killed. On 29 March 2000, a total of about 52 Russian soldiers were killed as a result of the separatist ambush on the OMON convoy from Perm.

On 23 April 2000, a 22-vehicle convoy carrying ammunition and other supplies to the airborne unit was ambushed near Serzhen-Yurt in the Vedeno Gorge, by an estimated 80 to 100 "bandits" according to General Troshev; in the ensuing 4-hour battle the federal side lost 15 government soldiers, according to the Russian defence minister. General Troshev told the press that the bodies of four separatist fighters were found. The Russian Airborne Troops headquarters later stated that 20 separatists were killed and 2 taken prisoner.[66] Soon, the Russian forces seized last populated centres of the organized resistance. (Another offensive against the remaining mountain strongholds was launched by the Russian forces in December 2000.)

Restoration of federal government

Russian President Vladimir Putin established direct rule of Chechnya in May 2000. The following month, Putin appointed Akhmad Kadyrov interim head of the pro-Moscow government. This development met with early approval in the rest of Russia, but the continued deaths of Russian troops dampened public enthusiasm. On 23 March 2003, a new Chechen constitution was passed in a referendum. The 2003 Constitution granted the Chechen Republic a significant degree of autonomy, but still tied it firmly to Russia and Moscow's rule, and went into force on 2 April 2003. The referendum was strongly supported by the Russian government but met a harsh critical response from Chechen separatists; many citizens chose to boycott the ballot. Akhmad Kadyrov was assassinated by a bomb blast in 2004. Since December 2005, his son Ramzan Kadyrov, leader of the pro-Moscow militia leader known as *kadyrovites*, has been functioning as the Chechnya's *de facto* ruler. Kadyrov, whose irregular forces are accused of carrying out many of the abductions and atrocities, has become Chechnya's most powerful leader and on February 2007, with support from Putin, Ramzan Kadyrov replaced Alu Alkhanov as president.

Insurgency

Guerilla war in Chechnya

Guerrilla phase by year: 2000, 2001, 2002, 2003, 2004, 2005, 2006, 2007, 2008, 2009

Although large-scale fighting within Chechnya had ceased, daily attacks continued particularly in the southern portions of Chechnya, spilling into nearby territories of the Caucasus as well, especially since the Caucasus Front was established. Typically small separatist units target Russian and pro-Russian officials, security forces, and military and police convoys and vehicles. The separatist units employ IEDs and sometimes group up for larger raids. Russian forces then retaliate with artillery and air strikes, as well as counter-insurgency operations. Most soldiers in Chechnya are now *kontraktniki* (contract soldiers) as opposed to the earlier conscripts. While Russia continues to maintain military presence within Chechnya, Russia's federal forces play less of a direct role in Chechnya. Pro-Kremlin Chechen forces under the command of the local strongman Ramzan Kadyrov, known as the *kadyrovtsy* now dominate law enforcement and security operations, with many members (including Kadyrov himself) being former Chechen separatists who have defected since 1999. Since 2004, the Kadyrovtsy were partly incorporated into two Interior Ministry units *North* and *South* (*Sever* and *Yug*). Two other units of the Chechen pro-Moscow forces, *East* and *West* (*Vostok* and *Zapad*), are commanded by Sulim Yamadayev (*Vostok*) and Said-Magomed Kakiyev (*Zapad*) and their men.[67]

On 16 April 2009 the head of the Federal Security Service of Alexander Bortnikov announced that they "cancelled the decree imposing an anti-terror operation on the territory of, effective from midnight". According to Chechen President Ramzan Kadyrov the announcement means that the war is finished by their victory. Still while Chechnya has largely stabilised, there are clashes with militants in the nearby regions of Dagestan and Ingushetia.[68]

Suicide attacks

Between June 2000 and September 2004 Chechen insurgents added suicide attacks to their tactics. During this period there have been 23 Chechen related suicide attacks in and outside Chechnya. The profiles of the Chechen suicide bombers have varied just as much as the circumstances surrounding the bombings, most of which targeted military or government-related targets.

Assassinations

Both sides of the war carried out multiple assassinations. The most prominent of these included the 13 February 2004, killing of exiled former separatist Chechen President Zelimkhan Yandarbiyev in Qatar, and the 9 May 2004, killing of pro-Russian Chechen President Akhmad Kadyrov during the parade in Grozny.

Caucasus Front

While the anti-Russian local insurgencies in the North Caucasus started even before the war, in May 2005, two months after Maskahdov's death, the Chechen separatists officially announced that they had formed a Caucasus Front within the framework of "reforming the system of military-political power." Along with the Chechen, Dagestani and Ingush "sectors," the Stavropol, Kabardin-Balkar, Krasnodar, Karachai-Circassian, Ossetian and Adyghe *jamaats* were included in it. This, in essence, means that practically all the regions of the Russia's south are involved in the hostilities.

The Chechen separatist movement has taken on a new role as the official ideological, logistical and, probably, financial hub of the new insurgency in the North Caucasus.[69] Increasingly frequent clashes between federal forces and local militants continue in Dagestan, while sporadic fighting erupts in the other southern Russia regions, most notably in Ingushetia, but also elsewhere, notably in Nalchik on 13 October 2005.

Human rights and terrorism

Human rights and war crimes

Russian officials and Chechen separatists have regularly and repeatedly accused the opposing side of committing various war crimes including kidnapping, murder, hostage taking, looting, rape, and assorted other breaches of the laws of war. International and humanitarian organizations, including the Council of Europe and Amnesty International, have criticized both sides of the conflict for "blatant and sustained" violations of international humanitarian law.

A mass grave in Chechnya

Western European rights groups estimate there have been about 5,000 forced disappearances in Chechnya since 1999.[70]

Secretary of State Madeleine Albright noted in her 24 March 2000, speech to the United Nations Commission on Human Rights:

> We cannot ignore the fact that thousands of Chechen civilians have died and more than 200,000 have been driven from their homes. Together with other delegations, we have expressed our alarm at the persistent, credible reports of human rights violations by Russian forces in Chechnya, including extrajudicial killings. There are also reports that Chechen separatists have committed abuses, including the killing of civilians and prisoners.... The war in Chechnya has greatly damaged Russia's international standing and is isolating Russia from the international community. Russia's work to repair that damage, both at home and abroad, or its choice to risk further isolating itself, is the most immediate and momentous challenge that Russia faces.[71]

According to the 2001 annual report by Amnesty International:

> There were frequent reports that Russian forces indiscriminately bombed and shelled civilian areas. Chechen civilians, including medical personnel, continued to be the target of military attacks by Russian forces. Hundreds of Chechen civilians and prisoners of war were extra judicially executed. Journalists and independent monitors continued to be refused access to Chechnya. According to reports, Chechen fighters frequently threatened, and in some cases killed, members of the Russian-appointed civilian administration and executed Russian captured soldiers.[72]

In 2001 the United States Holocaust Memorial Museum has placed Chechnya on its Genocide Watch List:

> Chechnya was devastated, including the almost complete destruction of Grozny, the Chechen capital. Russian artillery and air indiscriminately pounded populated areas. Human rights organizations also documented several massacres of civilians by Russian units. Russian President Vladimir Putin proclaimed Chechnya pacified by Spring 2000. But peace has been elusive for Chechen civilians, victims of a continuing war of attrition. They are plagued by abuses committed by Russian forces – arbitrary arrest, extortion, torture, murder. Chechen civilians also suffer because there have been no sustained efforts to rebuild basic social services, such as public utilities or education. Chechen fighters also commit abuses against civilians, but neither on the same scale nor with the same intensity as Russian forces.[73]

The Russian government failed to pursue any accountability process for human rights abuses committed during the course of the conflict in Chechnya. Unable to secure justice domestically, hundreds of victims of abuse have filed applications with the European Court of Human Rights (ECHR). In March 2005 the court issued the first rulings on Chechnya, finding the Russian government guilty of violating the right to life and even if the prohibition of torture with respect to civilians who had died or forcibly disappeared at the hands of Russia's federal troops.[74] Many similar claims were ruled since against Russia.

Dozens of mass graves (created by the Russian side) containing hundreds of corpses have been uncovered since the beginning of the Chechen wars in 1994. As of June 2008, there were 57 registered locations of mass graves in Chechnya.[75] According to Amnesty International, thousands may be buried in unmarked graves including up to 5,000 civilians who disappeared since the beginning of the Second Chechen War in 1999.[76] In 2008, the largest mass grave found to date was uncovered in Grozny, containing some 800 bodies from the First Chechen War in 1995.[75] Russia's general policy to the Chechen mass graves is to not exhume them.[77]

Photos of the victims of the 2004 Beslan school hostage crisis

Terrorist attacks

Between May 2002 and September 2004, the Chechen and Chechen-led militants, mostly answering to Shamil Basayev, launched a campaign of terrorism directed against civilian targets in Russia. About 200 people were killed in a series of bombings (most of them suicide attacks), most of them in the 2003 Stavropol train bombing (46), the 2004 Moscow metro bombing (40), and the 2004 Russian aircraft bombings (89).

Two large-scale hostage takings, the 2002 Moscow theater hostage crisis (850 hostages) and the 2004 Beslan school siege (about 1,200), resulted in the deaths of hundreds of civilians. In the Moscow stand-off, FSB Spetsnaz forces stormed the buildings on the third day using a lethal chemical agent. In the Beslan hostage case, a grenade exploding inside the school triggered the storming of the school. Some 20 Beslan hostages had been executed by their captors before the storming.

Other issues

Pankisi crisis

Russian officials have accused the bordering republic of Georgia of allowing Chechen separatists to operate on Georgian territory and permitting the flow of militants and materiel across the Georgian border with Russia. In February 2002, the United States began offering assistance to Georgia in combating "criminal elements" as well as alleged Arab mujahideen activity in Pankisi Gorge as part of the War on Terrorism. Without resistance, Georgian troops have detained an Arab man and six criminals, and declared the region under control.[78] In August 2002, Georgia accused Russia of a series of secret air strikes on purported separatists havens in the Pankisi Gorge in which a Georgian civilian was reported killed.

On 8 October 2001, a UNOMIG helicopter was shot down in Georgia in Kodori Valley gorge near Abkhazia, amid fighting between Chechens and Abkhazians, killing nine including five UN observers.[79] Georgia denied having troops in the area, and the suspicion fell on the armed group headed by Chechen warlord Ruslan Gelayev, who was speculated to have been hired by the Georgian government to wage proxy war against separatist Abkhazia. On 2 March 2004, following a number of cross-border raids from Georgia into Chechnya, Ingushetia, and Dagestan, Gelayev was killed in a clash with Russian border guards while trying to get back from Dagestan into Georgia.

Unilateral ceasefire of 2005

On 2 February 2005, Chechen separatist president Aslan Maskhadov issued a call for a ceasefire lasting until at least 22 February (the day preceding the anniversary of Stalin's deportation of the Chechen population). The call was issued through a separatist website and addressed to President Putin, described as a gesture of goodwill. On 8 March 2005, Maskhadov was killed in an operation by Russian security forces in the Chechen community of Tolstoy-Yurt, northeast of Grozny.

Shortly following Maskhadov's death, the Chechen separatist council announced that Abdul-Khalim Sadulayev had assumed the leadership, a move that was quickly endorsed by Shamil Basayev (Basayev himself died in July 2006). On 2 February 2006, Sadulayev made large-scale changes in his government, ordering all its members to move into Chechen territory. Among other things, he removed First Vice-Premier Akhmed Zakayev from his post (although later Zakayev was appointed a Foreign Minister[80]). Sadulayev was killed in June 2006, after which he was succeeded as the separatist leader by the veteran terrorist commander Doku Umarov.

Amnesties

As of November 2007, there were at least seven amnesties for separatist militants, as well as federal servicemen who committed crimes, declared in Chechnya by Moscow since the start of the second war. The first one was announced in 1999 when about 400 Chechen switched sides. (However, according to Putin's advisor and aide Aslambek Aslakhanov most of them were since killed, both by their former comrades and by the Russians, who by then perceived them as a potential "fifth column".[81]) Some of the other amnesties included one during September 2003 in connection with the adoption of the republic's new constitution, and then another between mid-2006 and January 2007. According to Ramzan Kadyrov, himself former separatist, more than 7,000 separatist fighters defected to the federal side ("returned to the peaceful life") by 2005. In 2006 more than 600 militants in Chechnya and adjacent provinces reportedly surrendered their arms in response to a six-month amnesty "for those not involved in any serious crimes".[82] In 2007, the International Helsinki Federation for Human Rights published a report entitled Amnestied People as Targets for Persecution in Chechnya [83], which documents the fate of several persons who have been amnestied and subsequently abducted, tortured and killed.

Government censorship of the media coverage

The first war, with its extensive and largely unrestricted coverage (despite deaths of many journalists), convinced the Kremlin more than any other event that it needed to control national television channels, which most Russians rely on for news, to successfully undertake any major national policy. By the time the second war began, federal authorities had designed and introduced a comprehensive system to limit the access of journalists to Chechnya and shape their coverage.[84]

The Russian government's control of all Russian television stations and its use of repressive rules, harassment, censorship, intimidation[85] and attacks on journalists almost completely deprived the Russian public of the independent information on the conflict. Practically all the local Chechen media are under total control of the pro-Moscow government, Russian journalists in Chechnya face intense harassment and obstruction[86] leading to widespread self-censorship, while foreign journalists and media outlets too are pressured into censoring their reports on the conflict.[87] In some cases Russian journalists reporting on Chechnya were jailed (Boris Stomakhin) or kidnapped by the federal forces (Andrei Babitsky), and foreign media outlets (American Broadcasting Company) banned from Russia.[88] The Russian-Chechen Friendship Society was shut down on "extremism and national hatred" charges. According to a 2007 poll only 11 percent of Russians said they were happy with media coverage of Chechnya.[89]

Effects

Civilian losses

Civilian casualty estimates vary widely. According to the pro-Moscow government, 160,000 combatants and non-combatants died or have gone missing in the two wars, including 30,000–40,000 Chechens and about 100,000 Russians;[90] [91] while separatist leader Aslan Maskhadov (deceased) repeatedly claimed about 200,000 ethnic Chechens died as a consequence of the two conflicts.[92] As in the case of military losses, these claims can not be independently verified. According to a count by the Russian human rights group Memorial in 2007, up to 25,000 civilians have died or disappeared since 1999.[93] According to Amnesty International in 2007, the second war killed up to 25,000 civilians since 1999, with up to another 5,000 people missing.[94] However, the Russian-Chechen Friendship Society set their estimate of the total death toll in two wars at about 150,000 to 200,000 civilians.[95]

Environmental damage

Environmental agencies warn that the Russian republic of Chechnya, devastated by war, now faces ecological disaster. A former aide to Boris Yeltsin believes Russian bombing has rendered Chechnya an "environmental wasteland."[96] There is a special concern over widespread oil spills and pollution from sewers damaged by war (the water is polluted to a depth of 250 m[97]), and chemical and radioactive pollution, as a result of the bombardment of chemical facalities and storages during the conflict.[98] Chechnya's wildlife also sustained heavy damage during the hostilities, as animals that had once populated the Chechen forests have moved off to seek safer havens.[99] In 2004, Russian government has designated one-third of Chechnya a "zone of ecological disaster" and another 40% "a zone of extreme environmental distress".[100]

Land mines

Chechnya is the most land mine-affected region worldwide.[101] Since 1999 there have been widespread use of mines, by both sides (Russia is a party to the 1980 Convention on Conventional Weapons but not the 1996 protocol on land mines and other devices). The most heavily mined areas of Chechnya are those in which separatists continue to put up resistance, namely the southern regions, as well as the borders of the republic.[102] No humanitarian mine clearance has taken place since the HALO Trust was evicted by Russia in December 1999. In June 2002, Olara Otunnu, the UN official, estimated that there were 500,000 land mines placed in the region. UNICEF has recorded 2,340 civilian land mine and unexploded ordnance casualties occurring in Chechnya between 1999 and the end of 2003.

Military losses

Military casualty figures from both sides are impossible to verify and are generally believed to be higher. In September 2000, the National Endowment for Democracy compiled the list of casualties officially announced in the first year of the conflict [103], which, although incomplete and with little factual value, provide a minimum insight in the information war. According to the figures released by the Russian Ministry of Defence on in August 2005, at least 3,450 Russian Armed Forces soldiers have been killed in action 1999–2005.[104] This death toll did not include losses of Internal Troops, the FSB, police and local paramilitaries, all of whom at least 4,720 were killed by October 2003.[95] The independent Russian and Western estimates are much higher; the Union of the Committees of Soldiers' Mothers of Russia for instance estimated about 11,000 Russian Army servicemen have been killed between 1999 and 2003. In 2007, Memorial estimated about 15,000 Russian soldiers have died in two wars, while others estimate up to 40,000.[93]

Political radicalization of the separatist movement

The Chechens had become increasingly radicalized. Former Soviet Army officers Dzhokhar Dudayev and Aslan Maskhadov have been succeeded by people who rely more on religious ideology, rather than the nationalistic feelings of the population. While Dudayev and Maskhadov were seeking from Moscow recognition of the independence of the Chechen Republic Ichkeria, other leaders spoke out more about the need to expel Russia from the territory of the whole North Caucasus, an impoverished mountain region inhabited mostly by Muslim, non-Russian ethnic groups.

In April 2006, asked whether negotiations with Russians are possible, the top separatist commander and future president Doku Umarov answered: "We offered them many times. But it turned out that we constantly press for negotiations and it's as if we are always standing with an extended hand and this is taken as a sign of our weakness. Therefore we don't plan to do this any more." In the same month, the new separatist spokesman Movladi Udugov said that attacks should be expected anywhere in Russia: "Today, we have a different task on our hands – total war, war everywhere our enemy can be reached. (...) And this means mounting attacks at any place, not just in the Caucasus but in all Russia." Reflecting growing radicalization of the Chechen-led militants, Udugov said their goal was no longer Western-style democracy and independence, but the Islamist "North Caucasian Emirate".

This trend ultimately resulted in the October 2007 declaration of Caucasus Emirate by Doku Umarov where he also urged for a global Jihad, and the political schism between the moderates, and the radical Islamists fighting in Chechnya and the neighbouring regions with ties in the Middle East.[105] Some commanders, still fighting along with Doku Umarov, like Anzor Astemirov, have publicly denounced the idea of a global Jihad, but keep fighting for the independence of Caucasus states.[106]

The struggle has garnered support from Muslim sympathizers around the world nonetheless, and some of them have been willing to take up arms. Many commentators think it is likely that Chechen fighters have links with international Islamist separatist groups. The BBC said in an online Q&A on the conflict: "It has been known for years that Muslim volunteers have traveled to Chechnya to join the fight, reportedly after attending training camps in Afghanistan or Pakistan."[93]

Impact on the Chechen population

According to a 2006 report by Médecins Sans Frontières, "the majority of Chechens still struggle through lives burdened by fear, uncertainty and poverty." A survey conducted by MSF in September 2005 showed that 77% of the respondents were suffering from "discernible symptoms of psychological distress".[107]

As of 2008, the infant mortality rate stood at 17 per 1,000, the highest in Russia;[108] There are reports of growing a number of genetic disorders in babies and unexplained illnesses among school children.[98] One child in 10 is born with some kind of anomaly that requires treatment. Some children whose parents can afford it are sent to the neighbouring republic of Dagestan, where treatment is better; Chechnya lacks sufficient medical equipment in most of its medical facilities.[109] According to the United Nations Children's Fund (UNICEF), since 1994 to 2008 about 25,000 children in Chechnya have lost one or both parents.[110] A whole generation of Chechen children is showing symptoms of psychological trauma. In 2006, Chechnya's pro-Moscow deputy health minister, said the Chechen children had become "living specimens" of what it means to grow up with the constant threat of violence and chronic poverty.[111] In 2007, the Chechen interior ministry has identified 1,000 street children involved in vagrancy; the number was increasing.[112] [113]

According to official statistics, Chechnya's unemployment rate in August 2009 was 32.9%. Although the second highest among Russian regions, the unemployment rate has almost halved since 2007.[114] [115] Many people remain homeless because so much of Chechnya's housing was destroyed by the Russian federal forces and many people have not yet been given compensation.[116] Not only the social (such as housing and hospitals) and economic infrastructure but also the foundations of culture and education, including most of educational and cultural institutions, were destroyed over the course of the two wars in Chechnya.[117] However ongoing reconstruction efforts have been rebuilding the region at a quick pace over the past few years, including new housing, facilities, paved roads and traffic lights, a new mosque and restoration of electricity to much of the region.[118] Governmental, social and commercial life remain hobbled by bribery, kidnapping, extortion and other criminal activity; reports by the Russian government estimate that the organized crime sector is twice the Russian average and the government is widely perceived to be corrupt and unresponsive.[119]

Hundreds of thousands of Chechens were displaced by the conflict, including 300,000 at the height of the conflict in 2000.[93] Most of them were displaced internally in Chechnya and in neighbouring republic of Ingushetia, but thousands of refugees also went into exile, as of 2008 most of them residing in the European Union countries.

Impact on the Russian population

The start of the war bolstered the domestic popularity of Vladimir Putin as the campaign was started one month after he had become Russian prime minister. However, the war eventually became less popular; according to a March 2007 poll 70% of Russians believe there should be negotiations with the separatists, and only 16% believe the military campaign should continue.[89] The conflict greatly contributed to the deep changes in the Russian politics and society.[120]

Since the Chechen conflict began in 1994, cases of young veterans returning embittered and traumatized to their home towns have been reported all across Russia. Psychiatrists, law-enforcement officials and journalists have started calling the condition of psychologically scarred soldiers "Chechen syndrome" (CS), drawing a parallel with the post-traumatic stress disorders suffered by Soviet soldiers who fought in Afghanistan. According to Yuri Alexandrovsky, deputy director of the Moscow Serbsky Institute in 2003, at least 70% of the estimated 1.5 million Chechnya veterans suffered CS.[121] Many of the veterans came back alcoholic, unemployable and antisocial.[120] Thousands were also physically disabled for life and left with very limited help from the government.[122]

According to the 2007 study by Memorial and Demos human rights organisations, Russian policemen lose their qualifications and professional skills during their duty tours in Chechnya.[123] This conflict was linked to the rising brutality and general criminalisation of the Russian police forces. According to human rights activists and journalists, tens of thousands of police and security forces that have been to Chechnya learned patterns of brutality and impunity and brought them to their home regions, often returning with disciplinary and psychological problems. Reliable numbers on police brutality are hard to come by, but in a statement released in 2006, the internal affairs department of Russia's Interior Ministry said that the number of recorded crimes committed by police officers rose 46.8% in 2005. In one nationwide poll in 2005, 71% of respondents said they didn't trust their police at all; in another, 41% Russians said they lived in fear of police violence.[124] [125] According to Amnesty International, torture of detainees in Russia is now endemic.[120] Since 2007, police officers from outside Caucasus are now not only being sent to Chechnya, but to all the region's republics.[123]

The wars in Chechnya, and the associated Caucasian terrorism in Russia, were a major factor in the growth of intolerance, xenophobia and racist violence in Russia, directed in a great part against the people from Caucasus.[120] The Russian authorities were unlikely to label random attacks on people of non-Russian ethnicity as racist, preferring calling it "hooliganism". The number of murders officially classified as racist more than doubled in Russia between 2003 and 2004. The violence included an acts of terrorism such as the 2006 Moscow market bombing which killed 13 people.[126] [127] In 2007, 18-year old Artur Ryno claimed responsibility for 37 racially-motivated murders in the course of one year, saying that "since school [he] hated people from the Caucasus."[128] On 5 June 2007, an anti-Chechen riot involving hundreds of people took place in the town of Stavropol in southern Russia. Rioters demanded the eviction of ethnic Chechens following the murder of two young Russians who locals believed were killed by Chechens. The event revived memories of a recent clash between Chechens and local Russians in Kondopoga over an unpaid bill, when two Russians were killed.[129] The Caucasians also face ethnic-related violence in the ranks of Russian Army.[130]

Status

In 2005 there were about 60,000 Russian troops in Chechnya, but that number has since decreased significantly. Tony Wood, a journalist and author who has written extensively about Chechnya, estimated there were about 8,000 pro-Moscow security forces remaining in the region as of 2007. Independent analysts say there are no more than 2,000 armed separatist combatants still fighting, while Russia says only a few hundred remain. There is still some sporadic fighting in the mountains and south of the republic, but Russia has scaled down its presence significantly leaving the pro-Moscow government to stabilize things further.[93] In February 2008 the President of the separatist Chechen Republic of Ichkeria, Dokka Umarov, spoke of "thousands of fighters" when he addressed a speech to all his fighters in the mountains.[131]

Most of the more prominent past Chechen separatist leaders have died or have been killed, including former president Aslan Maskhadov and leading warlord and terrorist attack mastermind Shamil Basayev. Meanwhile, the fortunes of the Chechen independence movement sagged, plagued by the internal disunity between Chechen moderates and Islamist radicals and the changing global political climate after 11 September 2001, as well as the general war weariness of the Chechen population. Large-scale fighting has been replaced by guerrilla warfare and bombings targeting federal troops and forces of the regional government, with the violence often spilling over into adjacent regions. Since 2005, the insurgency has largely shifted out of Chechnya proper and into the nearby Russian territories, such as Ingushetia and Dagestan; the Russian government, for its part, has focused on the stabilization of the North Caucasus.

Throughout the years Russian officials have often announced that the war is over. In April 2002 President Vladimir Putin's declared that the war in Chechnya was over.[132] The Russian government maintains the conflict officially ended in April 2002,[132] [133] and since then has continued largely as a peacekeeping operation. In a 10 July 2006, interview with the BBC, Sergei Ivanov, Russia's then-prime minister and former minister of defense, said that "the war is over," and that "the military campaign lasted only 2 years,"[134] Ramzan Kadyrov, the current president of the Chechnya, has also stated the war is over.[135] Others believe the war ended in 2003 with the passage of a Moscow-backed constitutional referendum and the election of pro-Moscow president Akhmad Kadyrov, while some consider the conflict on-going.[136] Some independent observers, including Álvaro Gil-Robles, the human rights envoy for the Council of Europe, and Louise Arbour, the UN High Commissioner for Human Rights, have said that the war has largely concluded as of 2006.[137] [138]

The separatists, however, deny that the war is over, and guerrilla warfare continues throughout the entire North Caucasus. Colonel Sulim Yamadayev, Chechnya's second most powerful loyalist warlord after Kadyrov, also denies that the war is over. In March 2007, Yamadayev claimed there were well over 1,000 separatists and foreign Islamic militants entrenched in the mountains of Chechnya alone: "The war is not over, the war is far from being over. What we are facing now is basically a classic partisan war and my prognosis is that it will last two, three, maybe even five more years."[139] According to the Central Intelligence Agency factbook, Russia has severely disabled the Chechen separatist movement, although sporadic violence still occurs throughout the North Caucasus.[140] The overall security situation in Chechnya remains exceedingly difficult to accurately report due to the near monopoly the Russian government has on media covering the issue.[141] In May 2007 Amnesty International refuted claims by the government that the conflict has ended, stating "while large-scale military operations have been reduced, the conflict continues."[142] The strength of the separatists has for many years been unknown. Although Russia has killed a lot of separatists throughout the war, many young fighters have joined the separatists.[143]

An estimation, based on the war reports, shows that in the past three years Federal casualties are higher than the amount of coalition casualties of the War in Afghanistan (2001–present).[144] [145] [146] With the abolition of the Chechen Republic of Ichkeria and the proclamation of the Caucasus Emirate by the president of the separatist movement Dokka Umarov, the conflict in Chechnya and the rest of the North Caucasus is often referred to as the "War in the North Caucasus". The Russian government has given no new name to the conflict while most international observers still refer to it as a continuation of the Second Chechen War.[147]

Dmitry Medvedev meets with Alexander Bortnikov on 27 March 2009 to discuss the ending of counter-terrorism operations in Chechnya.

In late April, 2008, the Human Rights Commissioner for the Council of Europe, Thomas Hammarberg, visited Russia's Caucasian republics. After wrapping up the week long visit, he said he observed a number of positive developments in Chechnya, and that there was "obvious progress". He also noted that the judicial system in Chechnya was functioning properly. According to Hammarberg, missing people and the identification of missing bodies were still the two biggest human rights issues in the region, and he expressed his wish that further efforts be done to clarify the issue. President Putin responded to his comments, saying that the visit was of "great significance", and that Russia will take into account what the council had to say.[148] [149] [150]

Counter-insurgency operations have been conducted by Russian army in Chechnya since 1999. President of Chechnya, and former separatist, Ramzan Kadyrov declared this phase to end in March 2009.[151] On 27 March 2009, President of Russia Dmitry Medvedev met with Alexander Bortnikov, the Director of the Federal Security Service to discuss the official ending of counter-terrorism operations in Chechnya. Medvedev directed the National Anti-Terrorism Committee, which Bortnikov also heads, to report to the Russian government on this issue, which will then be decided by the Russian parliament.[152] However Medvedev asserted that situation in Chechnya must remain under direct control of the FSB. Close to 480 active insurgents are currently fighting in the mountains under leadership of field commander Doku Umarov according to official data.[153]

On 16 April 2009 the counter-terrorism operation in Chechnya was officially ended.[6]

People of the Second Chechen War

Russian political leaders and commanders

President of Russia

(in chronological order) Boris Yeltsin (died 2007), Vladimir Putin (Prime Minister from 2008)

Chiefs of the FSB, the GRU, and the General Staff of the Armed Forces

Nikolai Patrushev – Valentin Korabelnikov – Anatoly Kvashnin, Yuri Baluyevsky

Commander of the Joint Group of Forces in the North Caucasus

(in chronological order) Vladimir Moltenskoy, Sergey Makarov, Valery Baranov (maimed 2004), Yakov Nedobitko

Commander of the North Caucasus Military District

(in chronological order) Viktor Kazantsev, Gennady Troshev, Vladimir Boldyrev, Alexander Baranov

Defence Minister of the Russian Federation

(in chronological order) Igor Sergeyev, Sergei Ivanov, Anatoliy Serdyukov

Interior Minister of Russia

(in chronological order) Vladimir Rushailo, Boris Gryzlov, Rashid Nurgaliyev

Military commandant of Chechnya

Yevgeniy Abrashin, Ivan Babichev, Grigory Fomenko, Leonid Krivonos

President of the Chechen Republic

(in chronological order) Akhmad Kadyrov (assassinated 2004), Alu Alkhanov, Ramzan Kadyrov

Pro-Russian Chechen commanders and politicians

Salman Abuyev (assassinated 2001), Artur Akhmadov, Ruslan Alkhanov, Abu Arsanukayev, Aslambek Aslakhanov, Movladi Baisarov (assassinated 2006), Shamil Burayev, Zina Batyzheva, Odes Baysultanov, Alimbek Delimkhanov, Adam Demilkhanov, Adam Deniyev (assassinated 2000), Rudnik Dudayev †, Taus Dzhabrailov, Bislan Gantamirov, Musa Gazimagomadov (died 2003), Hussein Isayev (assassinated 2004), Idris Gaibov, Muslim Ilyasov, Zelimkhan Kadyrov (died 2004), Said-Magomed Kakiyev, Nusreda Khabuseyeva †, Magomed Khambiyev, Ibragim Khultygov, Rezvan Kutsuyev, Supyan Makhchayev, Malik Saidullayev, Sultan Satuyev, Movsar Temirbayev, Raybek Tovzayev (killed 2001), Ruslan Tsakayev (died 2003), Said-Selim Tsuyev, Dzhabrail Yamadayev (assassinated 2003), Khalid Yamadayev, Ruslan Yamadayev, Sulim Yamadayev, Alambek Yasayev, Aud Yusupov †, Akhmad Zavgayev (assassinated 2002), and others

Russian commanders and politicians

Sergei Abramov, Mukhu Aliyev, Aslambek Aslakhanov, Mikhail Babich, Viktor Barsukov, Aleksandr Bespalov, Yuri Budanov (imprisoned 2003–2009, assassinated 2011), Boris Fadeyev, Gaidar Gadzhiyev (assassinated 2001), Magomed Gazimagomedov, Nikolai Goridov (assassinated 2002), Aleksandr Kayak (assassinated 2005), Oleg Khotin, Alexander Kolmakov, Dzhabrail Kostoyev (assassinated 2006), Abukar Kostoyev (killed 2004), Anatoly Kyarov (assassinated 2008), Alexander Lentsov, Adilgerei Magomedtagirov, Magomedali Magomedov, Ibragim Malsagov, Mikhail Malofayev (killed 2000), Valery Manilov, Mark Metsayev †, Magomed Omarov (assassinated 2005), Boris Podoprigora, Aleksandr Potapov, Anatoly Pozdnyakov (assassinated 2001), Mikhail Rudchenko (assassinated 2002), Yan Sergunin (assassinated 2004), Vladimir Shamanov, Igor Shifrin (assassinated 2002), Georgy Shpak, German Ugryumov (died 2001), Pavel Varfolomeyev (assassinated 2001), Sergei Yastrzhembsky, Sergei Zveryev (assassinated 2000), Murat Zyazikov, and others

Separatist political leaders and commanders

President of Ichkeria

(in chronological order) Aslan Maskhadov (killed 2005), Sheikh Abdul Halim (killed 2006), Dokka Umarov

Chechen separatist commanders and politicians

Salman Abuyev (defected), Aslambek Abdulkhadzhiev (killed 2002), Artur Akhmadov (defected), Ilyas Akhmadov, Uvais Akhmadov, Ruslan Alikhadzhyev (forcibly disappeared 2000), Ruslan Alkhanov (defected), Vakha Arsanov (killed or murdered in captivity 2005), Turpal-Ali Atgeriev (died or murdered in captivity 2002), Akhmed Avtorkhanov (killed 2005), Arbi Barayev (killed 2001), Movsar Barayev (killed 2002), Shamil Basayev (killed 2006), Rizvan Chitigov (killed 2005), Lecha Dudayev (killed 2000), Suleiman Elmurzayev (killed 2007), Idris Gaibov (defected), Ruslan Gelayev (killed 2004), Sultan Geliskhanov (captured 2006), Lecha Islamov (died or murdered in captivity 2005), Aslambek Ismailov (killed 2000), Khunkarpasha Israpilov (killed 2000), Magomed Khambiyev (defected), Umar Khambiyev, Ibragim Khultygov (defected), Isa Munayev, Isa Muskiyev (killed 2006), Abu Movsayev (killed 2000), Khozh-Ahmed Noukhayev (unknown fate), Salman Raduyev (died or murdered in captivity 2002), Salautdin Temirbulatov (imprisoned), Movladi Udugov, Yamadayev brothers (defected), Zelimkhan Yandarbiyev (assassinated 2004), Akhmed Zakayev, and others

North Caucasian and foreign militant leaders

Anzor Astemirov (killed 2010), Muslim Atayev (killed 2005), Alan Digorsky, Ilias Gorchkhanov (killed 2005), Rappani Khalilov (killed 2007), Ibn al-Khattab (assassinated 2002), Abdul Madzhid (killed September 2008), Rasul Makasharipov (killed 2005), Muhannad, Abu Hafs al-Urduni (killed 2006), Abu al-Walid (killed 2004), Akhmed Yevloyev (captured 2010), and others

Other associated people

Journalists

Andrei Babitsky, Supian Ependiyev (killed 1999), Adlan Khasanov (killed 2004), Ramzan Mezhidov (killed 1999), Anna Politkovskaya (assassinated 2006), Roddy Scott (killed 2002), Fatima Tlisova, and others

Victims of human rights abuses

Ruslan Alikhadzhyev (kidnapped 2000, presumed dead), Shakhid Baysayev (kidnapped 2000, presumed dead), Zura Bitiyeva (murdered with her family 2003), Elza Kungayeva (kidnapped, raped and murdered 2000), Nura Luluyeva (kidnapped and murdered 2000), Zelimkhan Murdalov (forcibly disappeared 2001, presumed dead), Malika Umazheva (murdered 2002), Khadzhi-Murat Yandiyev (forcibly disappeared 2000, presumed dead), and others

Various

Ruslan Aushev, Shamil Beno, Aleksey Galkin, Nur-Pashi Kulayev (imprisoned 2006, unknown fate), Sergei Lapin (imprisoned 2005), Timur Mucuraev, Lidia Yusupova, and others

See also

- First Chechen War
- Chechen people
- International response to the Second Chechen War
- Islam in Russia
- Peoples of the Caucasus

References

[1] "War in the north Caucasus" (http://www.economist.com/world/europe/displaystory.cfm?story_id=2794465). *The Economist*. June 2004.
.

[2] Sakwa, Richard (2005). "Introduction: Why Chechnya?". In Richard Sakwa. *Chechnya: From Past to Future* (1st ed.). London: Anthem Press. pp. 1–42. ISBN 9781843311645.

[3] Pashin, Alexander. "Russian Army Operations and Weaponry During Second Military Campaign in Chechnya" (http://mdb.cast.ru/mdb/3-2002/ac/raowdsmcc/). *Moscow Defense Brief* (Centre for Analysis of Strategies and Technologies) (3/2002). . Retrieved 2009-05-29.

[4] "CIA – The World Factbook – Russia" (https://www.cia.gov/library/publications/the-world-factbook/geos/rs.html). Cia.gov. . Retrieved 17 October 2011.

[5] It's over, and Putin won (http://www.guardian.co.uk/commentisfree/2008/sep/30/russia.chechnya) The Guardian Retrieved on 23 February 2009

[6] "Russia 'ends Chechnya operation'" (http://news.bbc.co.uk/1/hi/world/europe/8001495.stm). *BBC News*. 16 April 2009. . Retrieved 2009-04-14.

[7] Chechen self-proclaimed government-in-exile lays down weapons (http://russiatoday.ru/Top_News/2009-07-27/chechen-self-proclaimed-government-in-exile-lays-down-weapons.html) Russia Today Retrieved on 29 July 2009

[8] (http://news.bbc.co.uk/hi/russian/news/newsid_2773000/2773997.stm) 4,572 servicemen of all security agencies killed by December 2002, 680 Russian Armed Forces soldiers killed in 2003–2007 (http://gzt.ru/society/2006/02/26/113846.html)

[9] Chechnya War (http://www.alertnet.org/db/crisisprofiles/RU_WAR.htm?v=in_detail), Reuters, 11 April 2007

[10] Armstrong, Patrick. "Conflict in Chechnya: A Background Perspective." *Journal of Conflict Studies*. November 1999; Evangelista, Matthew. *The Chechen Wars: Will Russia Go the Way of the Soviet Union?* Washington, D.C.: Brookings Institution Press, 2003. ISBN 0-8157-2498-5; Dunlop, John B. *Russia Confronts Chechnya: Roots of a Separatist Conflict*. Cambridge, Mass.: Cambridge University Press, 1998. ISBN 0-521-63184-X; Seely, Robert. *Russo-Chechen Conflict, 1800–2000: A Deadly Embrace*. Florence, Ky.: Routledge, 2000. ISBN 0-7146-4992-9.

[11] In one estimate, based on a report by Lavrenti Beria to Joseph Stalin, 150,000 of 478,479 deported Ingush and Chechen people (or 31.3 percent) died within the first four years of the resettlement. See: Kleveman, Lutz. *The New Great Game: Blood and Oil in Central Asia*. Jackson, Tenn.: Atlantic Monthly Press, 2003. ISBN 0-87113-906-5. Another scholar puts the number of deaths at 22.7 percent: Extrapolating from NKVD records, 113,000 Ingush and Chechens died (3,000 before deportation, 10,000 during deportation, and 100,000 after resettlement) in the first three years of the resettlement out of 496,460 total deportees. See: Naimark, Norman M. *Fires of Hatred: Ethnic Cleansing in*

Twentieth-Century Europe. Cambridge, Mass.: Harvard University Press, 2001. ISBN 0-674-00994-0. A third source says a quarter of the 650,000 deported Chechens, Ingush, Karachais and Kalmyks died within four years of resettlement. See: Mawdsley, Evan. *The Stalin Years: The Soviet Union 1929–1953*. Manchester, England: Manchester University Press, 2003. ISBN 0-7190-6377-9. However, estimates of the number of deportees sometimes varies widely. Two scholars estimated the number of Chechen and Ingush deportees at 700,000, which would have the percentage estimates of deaths. See: Fischer, Ruth and Leggett, John C. *Stalin and German Communism: A Study in the Origins of the State Party*. Edison, N.J.: Transaction Publishers, 2006. ISBN 0-87855-822-5

[12] Conquest, Robert. *The Nation Killers*. New York: Macmillan, 1970. ISBN 0-333-10575-3

[13] The European Parliament recognized this as an act of genocide on 26 February 2004. Campana, Aurélie. "Case Study: The Massive Deportation of the Chechen People: How and why Chechens were Deported." Online Encyclopedia of Mass Violence. November 2007. (http://www.massviolence.org/The-Massive-Deportation-of-the-Chechen-People-How-and-why?artpage=8#outil_sommaire_5) Accessed 11 August 2008; Nurbiyev, Aslan. "Relocation of Chechen 'Genocide' Memorial Opens Wounds." *Agence France Press*. 4 June 2008 (http://www.canada.com/topics/news/world/story.html?id=9f271375-e372-4ce9-acb0-64ce7bf80458); Jaimoukha, Amjad M. *The Chechens: A Handbook*. Florence, Ky.: Routledge, 2005. ISBN 0-415-32328-2.

[14] "Second Chechnya War – 1999–???" (http://www.globalsecurity.org/military/world/war/chechnya2.htm). GlobalSecurity.org. . Retrieved 2008-04-15.

[15] Lajos F. Szászdi, *Russian Civil-Military Relations and the Origins of the Second Chechen War*, page 155, University Press of America, 2008. ISBN 0-7618-4037-0

[16] Tishkov, Valery. *Chechnya: Life in a War-Torn Society*. Berkeley: University of California Press, 2004. Page 114.

[17] Russell, John (2005). "Chechnya, 11 September and the War Against Terrorism". In Richard Sakwa. *Chechnya: From Past to Future* (1st ed.). London: Anthem Press. pp. 239–265. ISBN 9781843311645.

[18] from the Russian original of interview given by Stepashin: В отношении Чечни могу сказать следующее. План активных действий в этой республике разрабатывался начиная с марта. И мы планировали выйти к Тереку в августе-сентябре. Так что это произошло бы, даже если бы не было взрывов в Москве. Я активно вел работу по укреплению границ с Чечней, готовясь к активному наступлению. Так что Владимир Путин здесь ничего нового не открыл. Об этом вы можете спросить его самого. Он был в то время директором ФСБ и владел всей информацией.

[19] Yuri Felshtinsky and Vladimir Pribylovsky *The Age of Assassins. The Rise and Rise of Vladimir Putin*, Gibson Square Books, London, 2008, ISBN 1-906142-07-6, page 105. The interview was given on 14 January 2000

[20] Sergey Pravosudov. Interview with Sergei Stepashin. (http://www.ng.ru/politics/2000-01-14/1_ovr.html) Nezavisimaya Gazeta, January 14, 2000(in Russian)

[21] Richard Sakwa, ed (2005). "Robert Bruce Ware: Mythology and Political Failure in Chechnya". *Chechnya: From Past to Future*. Anthem Press. pp. 79–115. ISBN 978-1-84331-164-5.

[22] "Deadly blast hits Russian parade" (http://news.bbc.co.uk/2/hi/europe/1976776.stm). *BBC News*. 9 May 2002. . Retrieved 23 May 2010.

[23] The Jamestown Foundation; CHECHEN GUNMEN ATTACK RUSSIAN ARMY UNIT IN DAGESTAN. (http://www.jamestown.org/publications_details.php?volume_id=2&issue_id=328&article_id=3598)

[24] "Russia's bombs: Who is to blame?" (http://news.bbc.co.uk/2/hi/europe/449325.stm). BBC News. 30 September 1999. . Retrieved 17 October 2011.

[25] "David Satter – House committee on Foreign Affairs" (http://www.hudson.org/files/publications/SatterHouseTestimony2007.pdf) (PDF). . Retrieved 17 October 2011.

[26] David Satter. *Darkness at Dawn: The Rise of the Russian Criminal State*. Yale University Press. 2003. ISBN 0-300-09892-8, pages 24–33 and 63–71.

[27] Video (http://www.youtube.com/watch?v=PnkYo9TuBIQ) on YouTube*In Memoriam Aleksander Litvinenko*, Jos de Putter, Tegenlicht documentary VPRO 2007, Moscow, 2004 Interview with Anna Politkovskaya.

[28] Russian Federation: Amnesty International's concerns and recommendations in the case of Mikhail Trepashkin – Amnesty International (http://asiapacific.amnesty.org/library/Index/ENGEUR460122006?open&of=ENG-2EU)

[29] **(Russian)** Litvinenko's details on apartment bombings in Moscow (http://echo.msk.ru/programs/beseda/19169/), an interview with Sergei Kovalev, radio Echo of Moscow, 25 July 2002, computer translation (http://translate.google.com/translate?sl=ru&tl=en&u=http://echo.msk.ru/programs/beseda/19169/)

[30] Bomb Blamed in Fatal Moscow Apartment Blast (http://articles.latimes.com/1999/sep/10/news/mn-8677), Richard C. Paddock, Los Angeles Times, 10 September 1999

[31] At least 90 dead in Moscow apartment blast (http://web.archive.org/web/2000/http://www.cnn.com/WORLD/europe/9909/10/russia.explosion.03/), from staff and wire reports, CNN, 10 September 1999

[32] *The Chechen Wars: Will Russia Go the Way of the Soviet Union?*, p. 81, Matthew Evangelista, pub. Brookings Institution Press, 2002, ISBN 0-8157-2499-3, ISBN 978-0-8157-2499-5

[33] Did Putin's Agents Plant the Bombs? (http://findarticles.com/p/articles/mi_m1571/is_14_16/ai_61892243/print), Jamie Dettmer, Insight on the News, 17 April 2000.

[34] Cobain, Ian (13 April 2007). "I am plotting a new Russian revolution" (http://www.guardian.co.uk/world/2007/apr/13/topstories3.russia). *The Guardian* (London). . Retrieved 23 May 2010.

[35] "Re: 7727 No. 11, Jeremy Putley's review of "Darkness at Dawn" by D. Satter" (http://www.cdi.org/russia/johnson/7284-11.cfm). Cdi.org. . Retrieved 17 October 2011.

[36] "The Shadow of Ryazan" (http://www.nationalreview.com/comment/comment-satter043002.asp). Nationalreview.com. . Retrieved 17 October 2011.

[37] Commentary: Litvinenko Under the Microscope (http://www.nationalinterest.org/Article.aspx?id=13140). The National Interest (2006-12-01). Retrieved on 2010-11-25.

[38] "Doom, gloom and boom" (http://www.economist.com/books/displaystory.cfm?story_id=11745535). *The Economist*. 17 July 2008. .

[39] "Alexander Litvinenko" (http://www.telegraph.co.uk/news/obituaries/1535094/Alexander-Litvinenko.html). *The Daily Telegraph* (London). 25 November 2006. . Retrieved 23 May 2010.

[40] [[Richard Sakwa Sakwa, Richard (2008). *Putin, Russia's choice* (2nd ed.). Routledge. pp. 333–334. ISBN 978-0-415-40765-6.

[41] Vladimir Putin & Russia's Special Services (http://www.da.mod.uk/colleges/arag/document-listings/russian/C108) Gordon Bennet, 2002

[42] Western treatment of Russia signifies erosion of reason (http://theivanovosti.typepad.com/the_ivanov_report/files/download_the_article.pdf) Dr. Vlad Sobell, 2007

[43] Russia Profile Weekly Experts Panel: Russian Presidential Election – Affirming Democracy or Confirming Autocracy? (http://www.russiaprofile.org/page.php?pageid=Experts'+Panel&articleid=a1204913239)

[44] Russia acknowledges bombing raids in Chechnya (http://web.archive.org/web/20000919000313/http://www.cnn.com/WORLD/europe/9908/26/russia.chechnya/), CNN, 26 August 1999

[45] Russia launches more air strikes against Chechnya (http://www.rte.ie/news/1999/0927/russia.html), RTÉ news, 27 September 1999

[46] David Hoffman Miscalculations Paved Path to Chechen War (http://www.hartford-hwp.com/archives/63/251.html) *Washington Post*, 20 March 2000

[47] Refugee bus reportedly shelled by Russian tank (http://www.cnn.com/WORLD/europe/9910/07/chechnya.bus/) CNN, 7 October 1999

[48] Russian warplanes kill dozens of villagers (http://www.findarticles.com/p/articles/mi_qn4158/is_19991011/ai_n14278495) The Independent, 11 Oct 1999

[49] Russia to 'display' truth on Chechnya (http://www.indianexpress.com/res/web/pIe/ie/daily/19991009/ige09005.html), Reuters, 9 October 1999

[50] CHAMBER JUDGMENTS IN SIX APPLICATIONS AGAINST RUSSIA (http://www.echr.coe.int/Eng/Press/2005/Feb/ChamberjudgmentsChechencases2422005.htm) European Court of Human Rights, 24.2.2005

[51] Europe: Russians 'within sight' of Grozny (http://news.bbc.co.uk/2/hi/europe/475791.stm) BBC News, 16 October 1999

[52] Phase Two – The Ground Campaign – October–November 1999 (http://www.globalsecurity.org/military/world/war/chechnya2-5.htm) Globalsecurity.org

[53] Crimes Of War Project > Expert Analysis (http://www.crimesofwar.org/expert/chech-lohman.html)

[54] http://www.parliament.uk/commons/lib/research/rp2000/rp00-014.pdf

[55] Can Russia win the Chechen war? (http://news.bbc.co.uk/2/hi/europe/597594.stm) BBC News, 10 January 2000

[56] "Russia/Chechnya: "No Happiness Remains": Civilian Killings, Pillage, And Rape In Alkhan-Yurt, Chechnya" (http://www.hrw.org/reports/2000/russia_chechnya2/index.htm#TopOfPage). Hrw.org. . Retrieved 17 October 2011.

[57] "A letter of Sgt. S.Durov" (http://www.army.lv/?s=79&id=658). Army.lv. . Retrieved 17 October 2011.

[58] Russia may withdraw some troops from Chechnya (http://archives.cnn.com/2000/WORLD/europe/02/04/russia.chechnya.01/index.html)

[59] Scars remain amid Chechen revival (http://news.bbc.co.uk/2/hi/programmes/from_our_own_correspondent/6414603.stm) BBC News, 3 March 2007

[60] "Russia admits heavy casualties" (http://news.bbc.co.uk/2/hi/europe/618971.stm). *BBC News*. 26 January 2000. . Retrieved 2006-06-10.

[61] "Russian army battered in Grozny" (http://news.bbc.co.uk/2/hi/europe/592919.stm). *BBC News*. 6 January 2000. . Retrieved 2006-06-10.

[62] Oleg Orlov War Crimes and Human Rights Violations in Chechnya (http://www.crimesofwar.org/expert/chech-oleg.html) 26 May 2000

[63] Russians urged to stop 'vacuum' bombings (http://news.bbc.co.uk/2/hi/europe/644087.stm) BBC News, 15 February 2000

[64] Chechens down Russian helicopter (http://news.bbc.co.uk/1/hi/world/europe/648895.stm) BBC News, 19 February 2000

[65] "Reassessing Strategy: A Historical Examination" (http://usacac.army.mil/CAC/milreview/English/JulAug01/JulAug01/bobja01.pdf). Usacac.army.mil. 11 October 2011. . Retrieved 17 October 2011.

[66] Captain Adam Geibel Ambush at Serzhen Yurt: Command-Detonated Mines in the Second Chechen War (http://findarticles.com/p/articles/mi_m0FDF/is_1_31/ai_78974282) Engineer: The Professional Bulletin for Army Engineers, Feb, 2001

[67] "Land of the warlords" (http://www.guardian.co.uk/elsewhere/journalist/story/0,,1796576,00.html). *The Guardian* (London). 13 June 2006. . Retrieved 23 May 2010.

[68] Williams, Stuart (16 April 2009). "Russia ends 10-year Chechnya operation" (http://news.smh.com.au/breaking-news-world/russia-ends-10year-chechnya-operation-20090416-a8mi.html). *The Sydney Morning Herald*. . Retrieved 2009-04-17.

[69] Beslan's unanswered questions (http://www.iht.com/articles/2006/05/30/opinion/edaslan.php) International Herald Tribune, 30 May 2006

[70] Russia censured over Chechen man (http://news.bbc.co.uk/2/hi/europe/5219254.stm) BBC
[71] U.S. Response to Human Rights Commission Resolution on Chechnya (http://geneva.usmission.gov/press2000/0427chechnya.html) U.S. Mission Geneva
[72] Russian Federation 2001 Report (http://web.amnesty.org/web/ar2001.nsf/webeurcountries/RUSSIAN+Federation?OpenDocument) Amnesty International
[73] Chechnya Overview (http://www.ushmm.org/conscience/alert/chechnya/) Holocaust Memorial Museum
[74] European Court Rules Against Moscow (http://iwpr.net/?p=crs&s=f&o=239843&apc_state=henicrs2005) Institute for War and Peace Reporting, 2 March, 2005M
[75] Russia: Chechen Mass Grave Found (http://www.nytimes.com/2008/06/21/world/europe/21briefs-CHECHENMASSG_BRF.html?partner=rssnyt&emc=rss), Agence France-Presse, 21 June 2008
[76] Amnesty International Issues Reports on Disappearances (http://www.jamestown.org/chechnya_weekly/article.php?articleid=2373419), The Jamestown Foundation, 24 May 2007
[77] A vexing reminder of war in Chechnya's booming capital (http://www.iht.com/articles/2008/04/29/europe/journal.php), *International Herald Tribune*, 29 April 2008
[78] Georgia says gorge 'under control' (http://news.bbc.co.uk/2/hi/europe/2231955.stm) BBC News, 2 September 2002
[79] UN helicopter shot down in Georgia (http://news.bbc.co.uk/2/hi/europe/1586098.stm) BBC News, 8 October 2001
[80] Указы Президента ЧРИ А-Х. Садулаева (http://chechenpress.net/events/2006/05/27/06.shtml), Chechenpress, 27.05.06
[81] "Убивал – не убивал, попал – не попал" (http://www.kommersant.ru/k-vlast/get_page.asp?DocID=695544), Kommersant, 07.08.2006
[82] Law enforcers killed 72 militants in Chechnya in 2007 (http://en.rian.ru/russia/20080116/97117813.html), RIA Novosti, 16/ 01/ 2008
[83] http://www.ihf-hr.org/documents/doc_summary.php?sec_id=&d_id=4402
[84] Smokescreen Around Chechnya (http://www.worldpress.org/Europe/2048.cfm) The Moscow Times, 18 March 2005
[85] Russian TV accuses military of censorship (http://news.bbc.co.uk/2/hi/world/monitoring/media_reports/615937.stm), BBC News, 23 January 2000
[86] "Kremlin Stifles Critical Coverage Of Chechnya" (http://www.ifex.org/en/content/view/full/68793/). Ifex.org. . Retrieved 17 October 2011.
[87] Silencing Chechnya (http://www.themoscowtimes.com/stories/2005/01/27/005.html) Moscow Times, 27 January 2005
[88] Russia Bars ABC News for Interview With Separatist (http://www.nytimes.com/2005/08/02/international/europe/02cnd-russia.html?pagewanted=all), The New York Times, 2 August 2005
[89] POLL FINDS A PLURALITY OF RUSSIANS DISTRUST RAMZAN (http://www.jamestown.org/publications_details.php?volume_id=421&issue_id=4037&article_id=2372009) The Jamestown Foundation, 27 March 2007
[90] Chechen official puts death toll for 2 wars at up to 160,000 (http://www.iht.com/articles/2005/08/15/news/chech.php) International Herald Tribune, 16 August 2005
[91] Russia: Chechen Official Puts War Death Toll At 160,000 (http://www.rferl.org/featuresarticle/2005/08/b23f8d99-f15d-4b40-882c-975598c29ae3.html) RFE/RL, 16 August 2005
[92] Death Toll Put at 160,000 in Chechnya (http://www.themoscowtimes.com/stories/2005/08/16/011.html) The Moscow Times, 16 August 2005
[93] Chechnya war (http://www.alertnet.org/db/crisisprofiles/RU_WAR.htm?v=in_detail), Reuters AlertNet, 11 April 2007
[94] Amnesty International Issues Reports on Disappearances (http://www.jamestown.org/chechnya_weekly/article.php?articleid=2373419) Jamestown Foundation, 24 May 2007
[95] Civil and military casualties of the wars in Chechnya (http://www.hrvc.net/htmls/references.htm) Russian-Chechen Friendship Society
[96] "Chechnya Conflict and Environmental Implications" (http://www.american.edu/TED/ice/chechnya.htm). American.edu. . Retrieved 17 October 2011.
[97] Chechen Republic // GENERAL INFORMATION (http://www.kommersant.com/p-92/r_436/Chechen_Republic/), Kommersant, 10 Mar. 2004
[98] Chechnya habitat 'ravaged by war' (http://news.bbc.co.uk/2/hi/europe/5108416.stm), BBC News, 22 June 2006
[99] Military operations greatly alter Chechen mountain life (http://www.watchdog.cz/index.php?show=000000-000002-000001-000110-000048&lang=1), Prague Watchdog, 4 May 2003
[100] 'In the Caucasus, you can buy anything' (http://weekly.ahram.org.eg/2004/723/sc211.htm), Al-Ahram Weekly, 2004
[101] Chechnya: Land Mines Seen As Continuing Scourge (http://www.rferl.org/featuresarticle/2004/10/8f24150a-e534-42a8-80d9-198ae5453f89.html) RFE/RL, 19 October 2004
[102] Chechnya (http://www.icbl.org/lm/2004/chechnya), LM Report 2004, 8 Feb 2005
[103] http://www.watchdog.cz/index.php?show=000000-000005-000003-000001&lang=1
[104] "May 2001: Summary of main news related to the conflict in Chechnya" (http://www.watchdog.cz/index.php?show=000000-000005-000001-000182-000001-000005&lang=1). Watchdog.cz. . Retrieved 17 October 2011.
[105] The battle for the soul of Chechnya (http://www.guardian.co.uk/chechnya/Story/0,,2214769,00.html), The Guardian, 22 November 2007
[106] Chechnya Weekly from the Jamestown Foundation (http://www.jamestown.org/chechnya_weekly/article.php?articleid=2373840)
[107] [MSF Activity Reports on The Russian Federation: 2006 http://www.doctorswithoutborders.org/news/russianfederation.cfm], Doctors Without Borders

[108] Russian demographic statistics 2008 (http://www.gks.ru/wps/PA_1_0_S5/Documents/jsp/Detail_default.jsp?category=1112178611292&elementId=1140096846203) Rosstat Retrieved on Oct-05-2009

[109] A determined spirit guides Grozny (http://www.boston.com/bostonglobe/editorial_opinion/oped/articles/2007/11/14/a_determined_spirit_guides_grozny/?page=2), The Boston Globe, 14 November 2007

[110] Grozny's lost boys (http://www.smh.com.au/news/world/groznys-lost-boys/2008/03/21/1205602658064.html), *Sydney Morning Herald*, 22 March 2008

[111] A Mystery Malady in Chechnya (http://www.genocidewatch.org/Chechnyarussiaamysterymaladyinchechnyamar06.htm), Los Angeles Times, 10 March 2006

[112] Large numbers of street children discovered in Chechnya (http://www.watchdog.cz/?show=000000-000002-000001-000186&lang=1), Prague Watchdog, 23 March 2007

[113] (http://www.macaudailytimesnews.com/index.php?option=com_content&task=view&id=7314&Itemid=33)

[114] Employment and unemployment in Russia August 2009 (http://www.gks.ru/bgd/free/B04_03/IssWWW.exe/Stg/d03/193.htm) Rosstat, Retrieved on Oct-05-2009

[115] Чечня – лидер по уровню безработицы среди регионов России (http://www.rosbaltsouth.ru/2007/12/05/437738.html), 5.12.2007

[116] Amnesty International Urgent Action (http://www.smu.edu/humanrights/aiurgent.html), Amnesty International, 25 January 2008

[117] "The Consequences of War for Education and Culture in Chechnya" (http://www.idee.org/lreport2.html). Idee.org. 29 September 2000. . Retrieved 17 October 2011.

[118] "Spring rebuilding in Chechnya" (http://www.iht.com/articles/2006/05/03/news/chech.php). *International Herald Tribune*. 29 March 2009. . Retrieved 17 October 2011.

[119] The Crisis in Chechnya and the Northern Caucasus at a Glance (http://www.theirc.org/news/the_crisis_in_chechnya_and_the_northern_caucasus_at_a_glance.html), IRC, 31 Jan 2006

[120] The warlord and the spook (http://economist.com/world/displaystory.cfm?story_id=9254176) The Economist, 31 March 2007

[121] Chechnya's Walking Wounded (http://205.188.238.181/time/printout/0,8816,901031006-490663,00.html) Time (magazine)/CNN, 28 Sep. 2003

[122] Island lessons for Russian war vet (http://findarticles.com/p/articles/mi_qn4176/is_20030430/ai_n14548271), Oakland Tribune, 30 Apr 2003

[123] The Geography of OMON Deployments in the North Caucasus (http://jamestown.org/chechnya_weekly/article.php?articleid=2374082), The Jamestown Foundation, 3 April 2008

[124] For Russians, Police Rampage Fuels Fear (http://www.washingtonpost.com/wp-dyn/articles/A4009-2005Mar26.html) *Washington Post*, 27 March 2005

[125] Russia: Police Brutality Shows Traces Of Chechnya (http://www.rferl.org/featuresarticle/2005/06/da84eb4b-5f23-4876-8d61-bc4d6f4f6260.html) RFE/RL, 20 June 2005

[126] Political turmoil erupts again in deadly protests (http://www.iht.com/articles/2005/11/02/news/briefs.php) IHT, 2 November 2005

[127] Migrants flee town after racial violence (http://english.people.com.cn/200609/14/eng20060914_302534.html) People's Daily, 14 September 2006

[128] Teenager Admits to Over 30 Murders (http://www.themoscowtimes.com/stories/2007/05/29/011.html) The Moscow Times, 29 May 2007

[129] Nationalists rally in Russian town near Chechnya (http://www.reuters.com/article/homepageCrisis/idUSL05224442._CH_.2400) Reuters, 5 Jun 2007

[130] Racist Violence Plagues Russian Army (http://iwpr.net/?p=crs&s=f&o=159879&apc_state=henicrs2000) IWPR, 15-Sep-00

[131] Dokka Umarov speech (http://blip.tv/file/get/Kavkazcenter-873.wmv)

[132] Johnson, David (19 April 2002). "separatists kill 18 pro-Russians in Chechnya, Putin says war is over" (http://www.cdi.org/Russia/202-3.cfm). *Russia Weekly* (Washington, D.C.: Center for Defense Information). . Retrieved 2007-12-19.

[133] "Chechen peace amid gunfire" (http://edition.cnn.com/2002/WORLD/europe/12/21/chechnya.life.otsc/index.html). Cable News Network. 21 December 2002. . Retrieved 2007-12-19.

[134] Sakker, Stephen (10 July 2006). "Sergey Ivanov: "The war in Chechnya is over"" (http://www.inosmi.ru/translation/228674.html) (in Russian). London: British Broadcasting Corp.. . Retrieved 2007-12-19.

[135] Borisov, Tim (10 July 2007). "Ramzan Kadyrov: Since the war ended forever" (http://www.rg.ru/2007/07/10/reg-kavkaz/kadirov.html) (in Russian). Moscow: Rossiiskaya Gazeta. . Retrieved 2007-12-19.

[136] "The Situation in Chechnya" (http://web.archive.org/web/20080216043846/http://www.soma.on.ca/XXXV/Background+Guides/Security+Council+--+Topic+2+--+Situation+in+Chechnya.pdf) (PDF). Ontario: Southern Ontario Model United Nations Assembly. 2007. p. 5. Archived from the original (http://www.soma.on.ca/XXXV/Background Guides/Security Council -- Topic 2 -- Situation in Chechnya.pdf) on 2008-02-16. . Retrieved 2007-12-19.

[137] Blomfield, Adrian (6 July 2006). "Chechnya's new leader: a boxer with his own army" (http://www.telegraph.co.uk/news/main.jhtml?xml=/news/2006/03/06/wchech06.xml). *The Daily Telegraph* (London: Telegraph Media Group). . Retrieved 2007-12-19.

[138] Romanov, Pyotr (11 July 2006). "Outside View: End of Caucasian war" (http://wpherald.com/articles/243/1/Outside-View-End-of-Causasian-war/Demise-of-Shamil-Basayev.html). *World Peace Herald* (Washington, D.C.: News World Communications). . Retrieved 2007-12-19.

[139] Blomfield, Adrian (27 March 2007). "In the front line of Putin's secret war" (http://www.telegraph.co.uk/news/main.jhtml?xml=/news/2007/03/27/wchech27.xml). *The Daily Telegraph* (London). . Retrieved 23 May 2010.

[140] Russia Factbook (https://www.cia.gov/library/publications/the-world-factbook/geos/rs.html) Central Intelligence Agency

[141] John Pike. "Second Chechnya War" (http://www.globalsecurity.org/military/world/war/chechnya2.htm). Globalsecurity.org. . Retrieved 17 October 2011.

[142] Russian Federation What justice for Chechnya's disappeared? (http://asiapacific.amnesty.org/library/Index/ENGEUR460152007)

[143] The Alkhazurovo Operation: Are Chechnya's separatists on the Rebound? (http://www.jamestown.org/chechnya_weekly/article.php?articleid=2374081)

[144] "Operation Enduring Freedom" (http://www.icasualties.org/oef/). iCasualties. . Retrieved 17 October 2011.

[145] Ингушетия: хроника терактов, обстрелов, похищений (http://kavkaz-uzel.ru/newstext/chronics/id/1196026.html)

[146] Дагестан: хроника террора (1996–2007 гг.) (http://kavkaz-uzel.ru/newstext/chronics/id/790621.html)

[147] Articles – Containing Russia (http://www.realclearpolitics.com/articles/2007/04/containing_russia.html). RealClearPolitics (2007-04-30). Retrieved on 2010-11-25.

[148] Commissioner Hammarberg meets Putin and Medvedev (http://www.coe.int/t/commissioner/Activities/news2008/080425Putin_en.asp) Retrieved: 8-26-08

[149] Russian Caucasus 'stabilising': EU Commissioner (http://russiatoday.ru/news/news/23950) Retrieved: 8-26-08

[150] Thousands still missing in Chechnya (http://russiatoday.ru/news/news/23832) Retrieved: 8-26-08

[151] Грани.Ру // Политика / Россия / Десять лет без права (http://www.grani.ru/Politics/Russia/m.149075.html). Grani.ru (2009-03-26). Retrieved on 2010-11-25.

[152] Shchedrov, Oleg; Buribayev, Aydar; Pearce, Tim (27 March 2009). "Russia mulls lifting tight Chechnya security regime" (http://www.reuters.com/article/latestCrisis/idUSLR961502). Moscow: Reuters. . Retrieved 2009-03-28.

[153] Грани.Ру // Война / Медведев: ФСБ должна сохранить контроль над Чечней (http://www.grani.ru/War/Chechnya/m.149153.html). Grani.ru (2009-03-27). Retrieved on 2010-11-25.

Bibliography

- (http://www.amazon.com/dp/1592281001) "Three Worlds Gone Mad" Author: Robert Young Pelton
- *A Dirty War: A Russian Reporter in Chechnya* (http://books.google.com/books?id=8T31JQAACAAJ&dq) Author: Anna Politkovskaya
- *A Military History of Russia: From Ivan the Terrible to the War in Chechnya* (http://books.google.com/books?id=DbR62llvLh0C&printsec=frontcover) Author: David R. Stone (preview available)
- *A Small Corner of Hell: Dispatches from Chechnya* (http://books.google.com/books?id=M0NgDHDnpqgC&printsec=frontcover) Author: Anna Politkovskaya (preview available)
- *Allah's Mountains: The Battle for Chechnya* (http://books.google.com/books?id=NPkH-7BCB6AC&printsec=frontcover) Author: Sebastian Smith (preview available)
- *Chechnya: From Nationalism to Jihad* (http://books.google.com/books?id=VhtNIDj6evUC&printsec=frontcover) Author: James Hughes (preview available)
- *Chechnya: From Past To Future* (http://books.google.com/books?id=mPZeN5Wh1e4C&printsec=frontcover) Author: Richard Sakwa and others (preview available)
- *Chechnya: Life in a War-Torn Society* (http://books.google.com/books?id=BbYP8pOVv-AC&printsec=frontcover) Author: Valery Tishkov (preview available)
- *Chechnya: The Case for Independence* (http://books.google.com/books?id=5z4hAAAACAAJ) Author: Tony Wood
- *Chechnya: To the Heart of a Conflict* (http://books.google.com/books?id=MvQyHQAACAAJ) Author: Andrew Meier
- *Chienne de Guerre: A Woman Reporter Behind the Lines of the War in Chechnya* (http://books.google.com/books?id=90Q2GdifewwC) Author: Anne Nivat
- *Crying Wolf: The Return of War to Chechnya* (http://books.google.com/books?id=FDb-GwAACAAJ) Author: Vanora Bennett
- *My Jihad* (http://books.google.com/books?id=NukGAAAACAAJ) Author: Aukai Collins
- *One Soldier's War* (http://books.google.com/books?id=QDvJGAAACAAJ) Author: Arkady Babchenko

- *Open Wound: Chechnya 1994–2003* (http://books.google.com/books?id=taoIAAAACAAJ) Author: Stanley Greene
- *Putin's Russia* (http://books.google.com/books?id=gQMOAAAACAAJ) Author: Anna Politkovskaya
- *Russia's Chechen Wars 1994–2000: Lessons from Urban Combat* (http://books.google.com/books?id=coTg0jV7rLIC&printsec=frontcover) Author: Olga Oliker (preview available)
- *Russia's Islamic Threat* (http://books.google.com/books?id=cSGFhTEP49IC&printsec=frontcover) Author: Gordon M. Hahn
- *Russia's Restless Frontier: The Chechnya Factor in Post-Soviet Russia* (http://books.google.com/books?id=Tcab0VXTqnQC&printsec=frontcover) Author: Dmitri Trenin, Anatol Lieven (preview available)
- *Russia's Wars with Chechnya 1994–2003* (http://books.google.com/books?id=zPgeAQAACAAJ) Author: Michael Orr
- *Russian Military Reform, 1992–2002* (http://books.google.com/books?id=7JLYiPmzD5oC&pg=PA160&dq) Author: Anne Aldis, Roger N. McDermott
- *Russo-Chechen Conflict, 1800–2000: A Deadly Embrace* (http://books.google.com/books?id=qSZa6_wnSiIC&printsec=frontcover) Author: Robert Seely (preview available)
- *The Angel of Grozny: Orphans of a Forgotten War* (http://books.google.com/books?id=iljEKQAACAAJ) Author: Asne Seierstad
- *The Chechen Wars: Will Russia Go the Way of the Soviet Union?* (http://books.google.com/books?id=inc4KfEHymYC&printsec=frontcover) Author: Matthew Evangelista (preview available)
- *The Lone Wolf and the Bear: Three Centuries of Chechen Defiance of Russian Rule* (http://books.google.com/books?id=OuzqrrzVspEC&printsec=frontcover) Author: Moshe Gammer (preview available)
- *The Oath: A Surgeon Under Fire* (http://books.google.com/books?id=vcMMAAAACAAJ) Author: Khassan Baiev
- *The Wolves of Islam: Russia and the Faces of Chechen Terror* (http://books.google.com/books?id=_LXfR7wNWTUC&printsec=frontcover) Author: Paul J. Murphy (preview available)
- *"Welcome to Hell": Arbitrary Detention, Torture, and Extortion in Chechnya* (http://books.google.com/books?id=uNHy6VQXGhYC&printsec=frontcover) Author: Human Rights Watch (preview available)

External links

Timelines and chronologies

- BBC Timeline: Chechnya (http://news.bbc.co.uk/1/hi/world/asia-pacific/country_profiles/2357267.stm)

Summaries

- CHECHNYA: TWO FEDERAL INTERVENTIONS (http://www.da.mod.uk/colleges/csrc/document-listings/caucasus/P29) Conflict Studies Research Centre
- Second Chechnya War – 1999–??? (http://www.globalsecurity.org/military/world/war/chechnya2.htm) GlobalSecurity.Org

Human rights issues

- Video: Is it safe in Chechnya? A European human rights body has described the situation in Russia's Chechen republic as critical (21 April 2008) (http://russiatoday.ru/news/news/23746/video)
- Council of Europe resolutions on 'The human rights situation in the Chechen Republic':
  - Resolution 1323 (2003) (http://assembly.coe.int/Mainf.asp?link=http://assembly.coe.int/Documents/AdoptedText/TA03/ERES1323.htm)
  - Resolution 1403 (2004) (http://assembly.coe.int/Mainf.asp?link=http://assembly.coe.int/Documents/AdoptedText/ta04/ERES1403.htm)
- Human Rights Violations in Chechnya (http://www.hrvc.net/main.htm) Society for the Russian-Chechen Friendship

- The Trauma of ongoing War in Chechnya (http://www.doctorswithoutborders.org/publications/reports/2004/chechnya_report_9-9-04.pdf) Doctors Without Borders

Articles

- "The North Caucasus," Russian Analytical Digest No. 22 (5 June 2007) (http://www.isn.ethz.ch/pubs/ph/details.cfm?lng=en&id=31618)
- Critical media coverage of Chechnya stifled (http://www.ifex.org/en/content/view/full/68793/)
- Shifting Battlefields of the Chechen War (April 2006) (http://www.jamestown.org/publications_details.php?volume_id=416&issue_id=3697&article_id=2371008)
- The Chechen resistance movement: 2006 in review (http://www.jamestown.org/publications_details.php?volume_id=421&issue_id=3971&article_id=2371800) Jamestown Foundation
- ISN Case Study: The North Caucasus on the Brink (August 2006) (http://www.isn.ch/pubs/ph/details.cfm?id=22365)

Memorial (society)

Type	Non-profit NGO
Founded	1987
Location	Russia
Services	History of totalitarianism, protecting human rights
Website	memo.ru [1] (down) Irkutsk section [2] Krasnoyarsk section [3] Ryazan section [4]

Memorial (Russian: Мемориал) is an international historical and civil rights society that operates in a number of post-Soviet states. It focuses on recording and publicising the Soviet Union's totalitarian past, but also monitors human rights in post-Soviet states.

Mission and activities

Memorial's full official name is *International Volunteer Public Organization "MEMORIAL Historical, Educational, Human Rights And Charitable Society.* According to its charter, Memorial aims:

- "To promote mature civil society and democracy based on the rule of law and thus to prevent a return to totalitarianism"
- "To assist formation of public consciousness based on the values of democracy and law, to get rid of totalitarian patterns, and to establish firmly human rights in practical politics and in public life"
- "To promote the revelation of the truth about the historical past and perpetuate the memory of the victims of political repression exercised by totalitarian regimes." This is done, in particular, by keeping an electronic database of the victims of political terror in the USSR.[5]

Memorial organizes assistance, both legal and financial, for the victims of the Gulag. It also conducts research into the history of political repression and publicizes the findings in books, articles, exhibitions, museums, and websites of its member organisations.

History

Andrei Sakharov wrote that Lev Ponomaryov, Yuri Samodurov, Vyacheslav Igrunov, Dmitri Leonov, Arseny Roginsky and others put forth an initiative to create a memorial complex to victims of Joseph Stalin's repression in the late 1980s. The idea suggested creating a monument, a museum, an archive, a library. This led to an all-Union informal movement which expanded the original goals. It organized a petition to the 19th Conference of the CPSU. The petition resulted in the conference decreeing the creation of the monument to victims of repressions. A decision of the 22nd Congress of the CPSU was earlier ignored.[6] [7]

The *Memorial* as the historical and educational society was founded at the conference held in the Moscow Aviation Institute January 26–28, 1989.

In 1991 a Civil Rights Defense Center "MEMORIAL" was founded.[8]

A poll was carried out in Moscow streets of the names of the candidates to the Public Council of the society. Among others, Alexander Solzhenitsyn was named, but he refused to join and in his talk with Andrei Sakharov he motivated this decision by his opinion that it was not right to restrict the scope of the project to the Stalin era only, since the repressive era in Russia started as early as 1917.[6]

The *Memorial* as the International Volunteer Public Organization "MEMORIAL Historical, Educational, Human Rights And Charitable Society" was officially founded by the founding conference held on April 19, 1992.[9]

After the dissolution of the Soviet Union the society became international, with organizations in post-Soviet states: Russia, Ukraine, Kazakhstan, Latvia, and Georgia, as well as in Italy (since April 20, 2004).[10]

Political work

Through the efforts of the society, on October 30, 1990, the *Memorial to the Victims of the Gulag* (a simple stone from Solovki) was erected at the Lubyanka Square in Moscow, near the KGB headquarters beside the Iron Felix (the latter was removed in August 1991).

The efforts of Memorial were behind the *Law on Rehabilitation of Victims of Political Repression*, which was passed in 1991. In 1991 Memorial also contributed to the Supreme Soviet of the RSFSR officially making October 30 a Day of Remembrance for the Victims of Political Repression.

Archives

Memorial also helps individuals to find documents, graves, etc., of politically persecuted relatives. As of 2005, Memorial had a database of over 1,300,000 names of such people.[11] The archives were used by British historian Orlando Figes when he was researching his 2008 book *The Whisperers: Private Lives in Stalin's Russia.*[12]

Virtual Gulag

One of Memorial's main projects at the moment is the creation of the Virtual Gulag Museum, which will bring together research and archives from all over the ex-Soviet Union to commemorate and record the existence of the Gulag and the suffering of its victims.[13]

Kovalevsky Forest

Memorial are trying to build a National Memorial Museum Complex in Kovalevsky Forest to commemorate 4,500 victims of the Red Terror.[14] Memorial discovered the bodies in 2002.[15]

Media

Memorial funds or helps to produce various publications and films.

- *The Crying Sun*, 2007, a documentary focusing on the life of people from the mountainous village of Zumsoy in Chechnya, and their struggle to preserve their cultural identity in the face of military raids and enforced disappearances by the Russian army and guerilla fighters. (Produced in collaboration with WITNESS, 25 minutes long.)[16]

Awards

In 2004, Memorial was among the four recipients of the Right Livelihood Award, sometimes called the alternative Nobel Prize, for its work in documenting violations of human rights in Russia and other former states in the USSR.[17] Quoting the RLA jury: "... for showing, under very difficult conditions, and with great personal courage, that history must be recorded and understood, and human rights respected everywhere, if sustainable solutions to the legacy of the past are to be achieved." In the same year, The UN refugee agency (UNHCR) named Memorial the winner of the annual Nansen Refugee Award for its wide range of services on behalf of forced migrants and internally displaced people in the Russian Federation, as well as refugees from Africa, Asia and the Middle East.[18]

In 2009, Memorial won the Sakharov Prize, in memory of the murdered Memorial activist Natalya Estemirova.[19] Announcing the award, President of the European Parliament Jerzy Buzek said that the assembly hoped "to contribute to ending the circle of fear and violence surrounding human rights defenders in the Russian Federation".[19] Oleg Orlov, the chairman of Memorial, commented that the prize represents "much-needed moral support at a difficult time for rights activists in Russia",[20] and that he considers the prize "a mark of the high value placed on the work of Memorial and that of all of our colleagues - Russian rights activists who are working in a very difficult situation".[21] A cash reward, which comes with the prize, of €50,000 is to be awarded to Memorial in December 2009.[19]

Confiscation of digital archive

On 4 November 2008, Memorial's St Petersburg office which houses archives on the Gulag was raided by the authorities and 12 computer hard disks containing the entire digital archive of the atrocities committed under Stalin, representing 20 years of work, were confiscated. The information was being used to develop "a universally accessible database with hundreds of thousands of names." Office director Irina Flinge believes that they were targeted because their organization is on the wrong side of Putinism, specifically the idea "that Stalin and the Soviet regime were successful in creating a great country".[22] [23]

Officially, the raid was in relation to an article published in the *Novy Peterburg* newspaper in June 2007.[24] Memorial denies any link to the article. Some human rights lawyers in Russia have speculated that the raid is retaliation for Memorial screening a banned film *Rebellion: the Litvinenko Case*, about the murder of Russian ex-spy Alexander Litvinenko.[13] [25] According to writer Orlando Figes, the raid "was clearly intended to intimidate Memorial".[26] Allison Gill, director of Human Rights Watch in Moscow, has said "This outrageous police raid shows the poisonous climate for non-governmental organisations in Russia [...] This is an overt attempt by the Russian government [...] to silence critical voices."[26] The raid also prompted an open letter to Dmitry Medvedev from academics from all over the world, condemning the seizure.[13] The United States has declared that it is "deeply concerned" about the raid: State Department spokesman Sean McCormack said: "Unfortunately, this action against Memorial is not an isolated instance of pressure against freedom of association and expression in Russia."[13]

On March 20, 2009, the court of Dzerzhinsky District decided that the search on December 4, 2008, in Memorial with confiscation of 12 HDDs with information about victims of political repressions was carried out with procedural violations, and actions of law enforcement bodies were illegal,[27] [28] [29] and eventually the 12 hard drives, as well as optical discs and some papers, were returned to Memorial[30] [31].

Activities in Chechnya

Memorial also had an office in Chechnya, to monitor human rights issues there. It was frequently raided by the authorities.

A Memorial activist Natalia Estemirova, who investigated murders and abductions in Chechnya, was herself abducted in Grozny and shot to death in Ingushetia on 15 July 2009[32] . It is suggested her death is connected to her investigations of government-backed militias in the country.[33] . Memorial's chairman Oleg Orlov accused Ramzan Kadyrov of being behind the murder,[34] and claimed that Kadyrov had openly threatened her[35] . Kadyrov denied his involvement[36] and sued Memorial for defamation, targeting Orlov personally with his complaint.[36] [37]

On 18 July 2009, Memorial suspended its activities in the republic, stating "We cannot risk the lives of our colleagues even if they are ready to carry on their work".[38]

Activists

- Natalia Estemirova
- Svetlana Gannushkina
- Sergei Kovalev
- Nikita Petrov
- Viktor Popkov
- Arseny Roginsky, president
- Lidia Yusupova

References

[1] http://www.memo.ru
[2] http://www.memorial.ru
[3] http://www.krasnoyarsk.memorial.ru
[4] http://www.ryazan.memorial.ru
[5] Жертвы политического террора в СССР (in Russian) (http://lists.memo.ru/)
[6] Andrei Sakharov, *Gorky, Moscow, Later Everywhere*, 1990, Chekhov Publishing Corp. (Russian edition), pp. 101–102 (http://www.iseu.by/rus/memoria/sakharov/sakharov/memoirs/sacharov4_3.htm)
[7] Sakharov, Andrei; translated by Antonina Bouis (1991). *Moscow and Beyond, 1986 to 1989*. Knopf. pp. 168. ISBN 9780394587974.
[8] "Civil Rights Defense Center "MEMORIAL" (http://www.memo.ru/hr/index.htm)
[9] Memorial Charter (http://www.memo.ru/eng/about/charter.htm)
[10] Memorial-Italia (http://www.memorial-italia.it/frontend/?rr=chi_siamo)
[11] FAQ about Memorial (http://www.rightlivelihood.org/memorial_faq.html)
[12] BBC (http://news.bbc.co.uk/2/hi/europe/7798497.stm)
[13] Timesonline – *Gulag files seized during police raid on rights group* (http://www.timesonline.co.uk/tol/news/world/europe/article5333440.ece)
[14] *A national museum to the victims of Stalinist repression: words not deeds?* (http://www.opendemocracy.net/od-russia/catriona-bass/national-museum-to-victims-of-stalinist-repression-words-not-deeds?utm_source=feedblitz&utm_medium=FeedBlitzEmail&utm_content=201210&utm_campaign=0), opendemocracy.net
[15] На Ржевском полигоне почтили память жертв «красного террора» (http://predanie.org/content/view/230/16/)
[16] http://www.16beavergroup.org/monday/archives/002222.php
[17] 2004 Right Livelihood Award: Memorial (Russia) (http://www.rightlivelihood.org/memorial.htm)
[18] http://www.unhcr.org/news/NEWS/40920a244.html
[19] "Russia rights group wins EU prize" (http://news.bbc.co.uk/2/hi/europe/8320851.stm). BBC. 22 October 2009. .
[20] "Political Sakharov Prize Goes To Russian Rights Activists" (http://www.forextv.com/Forex/News/ShowStory.jsp?seq=1101965&category=&displaycategory=Political). Forex TV. 22 October 2009. .
[21] "Russia's Memorial group wins EU's Sakharov Prize" (http://en.rian.ru/russia/20091022/156556061.html). RIA Novosti. 22 October 2009. .
[22] Galpin, Richard. Stalin's new status in Russia (http://news.bbc.co.uk/2/hi/europe/7798497.stm). *BBC*. December 27, 2008.
[23] Report on the December 2008 raid on Memorial's St Petersburg office (http://www.opendemocracy.net/russia/article/Eleven-hard-disks)
[24] Memorial will have the property back but not the reputation (http://www.fontanka.ru/2009/01/20/140/), Fontanka.Ru, January 20, 2009 (in Russian)
[25] www.opendemocracy.net (http://www.opendemocracy.net/russia/article/russia-raid-on-Memorial-HQ)
[26] Guardian (http://www.guardian.co.uk/world/2008/dec/07/russian-police-seize-archive-repression)
[27] 'Memorial' reverted the searches (http://www.kommersant.ru/doc.aspx?DocsID=1142280), Kommersant, March 21, 2008 (in Russian)
[28] HDDs will be returned to "Memorial" in presence of the Ombudsman (http://www.fontanka.ru/2009/03/27/116/), Fontanka.Ru, March 27, 2009 (in Russian)
[29] Memorial Vindicated Again (http://seansrussiablog.org/2009/03/31/memorial-vindicated-again/), by Sean Guillory, March 31, 2009
[30] Memorial got back its confiscated HDDs (http://www.lenizdat.ru/a0/ru/pm1/c-1074447-0.html), Lenizdat.Ru, May 6, 2009 (in Russian)
[31] http://www.novayagazeta.spb.ru/2009/32/6
[32] "Vow to catch Chechnya assassins" (http://news.bbc.co.uk/2/hi/europe/8153613.stm). *BBC News*. 16 July 2009. . Retrieved 22 May 2010.
[33] timesonline.com (http://news.bbc.co.uk/2/hi/europe/8152351.stm)
[34] According to Orlov, "Я знаю, я уверен в том, кто виновен в убийстве Наташи Эстемировой. Мы все этого человека знаем. Зовут его Рамзан Кадыров, это президент Чеченской республики.

[35] (http://www.grani.ru/Politics/Russia/President/m.154035.html) "Она рассказывала, что Кадыров ей угрожал, говорил буквально: "Да, у меня руки по локоть в крови. И я не стыжусь этого. Я убивал и буду убивать плохих людей."
[36] Chechen leader sues rights group after activist murder (http://www.google.com/hostednews/afp/article/ALeqM5jHhf17Jf1bDaZ7jT9MYFvB_V_LQA), AFP, 18 July 2009. Retrieved on 19 July 2009.
[37] Schwirtz, Michael. Chechen Leader Sues Over Accusations of Ordering Activist's Death (http://www.nytimes.com/2009/07/18/world/europe/18chechnya.html), *The New York Times*, 18 July 2009. Retrieved on 20 July 2009.
[38] BBC (http://news.bbc.co.uk/2/hi/europe/8157454.stm)

Nobel Peace Prize

The Nobel Prize in Peace	
Awarded for	Outstanding contributions in Peace
Presented by	Norwegian Nobel Committee
Country	Norway
First awarded	1901
Official website	Nobelprize.org [1]

The ***Nobel Peace Prize*** (Norwegian, Swedish and Danish: *Nobels fredspris*) is one of the five Nobel Prizes bequeathed by the Swedish industrialist and inventor Alfred Nobel.

Background

According to Nobel's will, the Peace Prize shall be awarded to the person who

Alfred Nobel

> "...shall have done the most or the best work for fraternity between nations, for the abolition or reduction of standing armies and for the holding and promotion of peace congresses.[2]"

Alfred Nobel's will further specified that the prize be awarded by a committee of five people chosen by the Norwegian Parliament.

Nobel died in 1896 and he did not leave an explanation for choosing peace as a prize category. As he was a trained chemical engineer, the categories for chemistry and physics were obvious choices. The reasoning behind the peace prize is less clear. According to the Norwegian Nobel Committee, his friendship with Bertha von Suttner, a peace activist and later winner of the prize, profoundly influenced his decision to include peace as a category.[3] Some Nobel scholars suggest it was Nobel's way to compensate for developing destructive forces. His inventions included dynamite and ballistite, both of which were used violently during his lifetime. Ballistite was used in war [4] and the Irish Republican Brotherhood, an Irish nationalist organization, carried out dynamite attacks in the 1880s.[5] Nobel was also instrumental in turning Bofors from an iron and steel company to an armaments company.

It is unclear why Nobel wished the Peace Prize to be administered in Norway, which was ruled in union with Sweden at the time of Nobel's death. The Norwegian Nobel Committee speculates that Nobel may have considered Norway better suited to awarding the prize, as it did not have the same militaristic traditions as Sweden. It also notes that at the end of the nineteenth century, the Norwegian parliament had become closely involved in the Inter-Parliamentary Union's efforts to resolve conflicts through mediation and arbitration.[3]

Nomination and selection

The Norwegian Parliament appoints the Norwegian Nobel Committee, which selects the Nobel Peace Prize laureate.

The Norwegian Nobel Institute in Oslo, Norway.

Nomination

Each year, the Norwegian Nobel Committee specifically invites qualified people to submit nominations for the Nobel Peace Prize.[6] The statutes of the Nobel Foundation specify categories of individuals who are eligible to make nominations for the Nobel Peace Prize.[7] These nominators are;

- Members of national assemblies and governments and members of the Inter-Parliamentary Union,
- Members of the Permanent Court of Arbitration and the International Court of Justice at the Hague,
- Members of Institut de Droit International,
- University professors of history, social sciences, philosophy, law and theology, university presidents and directors of peace research and international affairs institutes,
- Former recipients, including board members of organizations that have previously won the prize,
- Present and past members of the Norwegian Nobel Committee, and
- Former permanent advisers to the Norwegian Nobel Institute.

The 14th Dalai Lama and Archbishop Desmond Tutu, Nobel Peace Prize laureates.

Nominations must usually be submitted to the Committee by February 1 of the year in question. Nominations by committee members can be submitted up to the date of the first Committee meeting after this deadline.[7]

In 2009, a record 205 nominations were received,[8] but the record was broken again in 2010 with 237 nominations; in 2011, the record was broken once again with 241 nominations.[9] The statutes of the Nobel Foundation do not allow information about nominations, considerations or investigations relating to awarding the prize to be made public for at least 50 years after a prize has been awarded.[10] Over time many individuals have become known as "Nobel Peace Prize Nominees", but this designation has no official standing.[11] Nominations from 1901 to 1956, however, have been released in a database.[12]

Selection

Nominations are considered by the Nobel Committee at a meeting where a short list of candidates for further review is created. This short list is then considered by permanent advisers to the Nobel institute, which consists of the Institute's Director and the Research Director and a small number of Norwegian academics with expertise in subject areas relating to the prize. Advisers usually have some months to complete reports, which are then considered by the Committee to select the laureate. The Committee seeks to achieve a unanimous decision, but this is not always possible. The Nobel Committee typically comes to a conclusion in mid-September, but occasionally the final decision has not been made until the last meeting before the official announcement at the beginning of October.[13]

Awarding the prize

The Chairman of the Norwegian Nobel Committee presents the Nobel Peace Prize in the presence of the King of Norway on 10 December each year (the anniversary of Nobel's death). The Peace Prize is the only Nobel Prize not presented in Stockholm. The Nobel laureate receives a diploma, a medal and a document confirming the prize amount.[14] As of 2009, the prize was worth 10 million SEK (about US$1.4 million). The Nobel Peace Prize Ceremony is held at the Oslo City Hall.

Obverse of the Nobel Peace Prize Medal presented to Sir Ralph Norman Angell in 1933; the Imperial War Museum, London.

Criticism

General criticism

Unlike the scientific and literary Nobel Prizes, usually issued in retrospect often two or three decades after the awarded achievement, the Peace Prize has been awarded for more recent or immediate achievements, or with the intention of encouraging future achievements. Some commentators[15] have suggested that to award a peace prize on the basis of unquantifiable contemporary opinion is unjust or possibly erroneous, especially as many of the judges cannot themselves be said to be impartial observers.

A feature story in Aftenposten claimed that the main general criticism (in 2011) were: "*The Nobel Committee* ought to recruit members with [more of a] professional and international background... that can do just as good a job as retired MPs of Norway", "There is too little openness about the criteria that the committee uses when they choose a recipient of the prize", and "the adherence to Nobel's will should be more strict".[16]

Norway's national and political goals regarding the prize have been described (in 2006) as "never before has the prize been a better instrument for nation building and a more valuable support of Norway's foreign policy and economical interests", according to "Øivind Stenersen [historian] and his co-authors".[17]

Criticism of individual conferments

The awards given to Lê Đức Thọ and Henry Kissinger, prompted two dissenting Committee members to resign.[18] The awards given to Yitzhak Rabin, Shimon Peres and Yasser Arafat,[19] [20] Lê Đức Thọ,[21] Henry Kissinger,[21] Jimmy Carter,[22] Al Gore, and Barack Obama[23] [24] [25] have been much-debated.

Alleged omissions

Foreign Policy magazine has listed Mohandas Gandhi, Eleanor Roosevelt, Václav Havel, Ken Saro-Wiwa, Sari Nusseibeh and Corazon Aquino as people who "never won the prize, but should have".[26] Other notable omissions that have drawn criticism include Pope John Paul II[27] and Dorothy Day.[28] It was widely reported that Irena Sendler had been nominated for the 2007 prize, which was jointly won by the Intergovernmental Panel on Climate Change and Al Gore.[29] [30] [31]

The omission of Mohandas Gandhi has been particularly widely discussed, including in public statements by various members of the Nobel Committee.[32] [33] The Committee has confirmed that Gandhi was nominated in 1937, 1938, 1939, 1947 and, finally, a few days before his death in January 1948.[34] The omission has been publicly regretted by later members of the Nobel Committee.[32] Geir Lundestad, Secretary of Norwegian Nobel Committee in 2006 said, "The greatest omission in our 106 year history is undoubtedly that Mahatma Gandhi never received the Nobel Peace prize. Gandhi could do without the Nobel Peace prize, whether Nobel committee can do without Gandhi is the question".[35] In 1948, following Gandhi's death, the Nobel Committee declined to award a prize on the ground that "there was no suitable living candidate" that year. Later, when the Dalai Lama was awarded the Peace Prize in 1989, the chairman of the committee said that this was "in part a tribute to the memory of Mahatma Gandhi".[36]

Notes

[1] http://nobelprize.org

[2] "Excerpt from the Will of Alfred Nobel" (http://nobelprize.org/alfred_nobel/will/short_testamente.html). Nobel Foundation. . Retrieved 2008-03-31.

[3] "Why Norway?" (http://nobelpeaceprize.org/en_GB/about_peaceprize/why-norway/). The Norwegian Nobel Committee. . Retrieved 2009-10-11.

[4] Altman, L. (2006). Alfred Nobel and the prize that almost didn't happen (http://www.nytimes.com/2006/09/26/health/26docs.html?pagewanted=1&ei=5070&en=919b88628e82140e&ex=1160884800). *New York Times*. Retrieved 14 October 2006.

[5] BBC History - 1916 Easter Rising - Profiles - The Irish Republican Brotherhood (http://www.bbc.co.uk/history/british/easterrising/profiles/po17.shtml) *BBC*

[6] "Nomination for the Nobel Peace Prize" (http://nobelprize.org/nomination/peace/index.html). Nobel Foundation. . Retrieved 2009-09-10.

[7] "Who may submit nominations?" (http://nobelpeaceprize.org/en_GB/nomination_committee/who-can-nominate/). The Norwegian Nobel Committee. . Retrieved 2009-09-10.

[8] ""President Barack Obama wins Nobel Peace Prize"" (http://news.yahoo.com/s/ap/eu_nobel_peace). Associated Press on yahoo.com. . Retrieved 2009-10-09.

[9] "Nominations for the 2011 Nobel Peace Prize" (http://nobelpeaceprize.org/en_GB/nomination_committee/nomination-2011/). Nobel Foundation. . Retrieved 2011-10-07.

[10] "Nominations for the 2009 Nobel Peace Prize" (http://nobelpeaceprize.org/en_GB/nomination_committee/nomination-2009/). The Norwegian Nobel Committee. . Retrieved 2009-10-11.

[11] Who may submit nominations - Nobels fredspris (http://www.nobelprize.org/nobel_prizes/peace/nomination/nominators.html)

[12] "Nomination Database — The Nobel Peace Prize, 1901-1956" (http://www.nobelprize.org/nobel_prizes/peace/nomination/database.html). Nobelprize.org. . Retrieved 2011-09-11.

[13] "How are Laureates selected?" (http://nobelpeaceprize.org/en_GB/nomination_committee/selection-process/). The Norwegian Nobel Committee. . Retrieved 2009-09-10.

[14] What the Nobel Laureates Receive (http://nobelprize.org/award_ceremonies/prize.html). nobelprize.org.

[15] Murphy, Clare (10 August 2004). "The Nobel: Dynamite or damp squib?" (http://news.bbc.co.uk/2/hi/middle_east/3724734.stm). *BBC online* (BBC News). . Retrieved 2009-10-11.

[16] Aspøy, Arild (2011-10-04). "Fredsprisens gråsoner". *Aftenposten*: p. 4. "Nobelkomiteen bør ta inn medlemmer med faglig og internasjonal bakgrunn... som gjøre en like god jobb som pensjonerte stortingsrepresentanter."

[17] Aspøy, Arild (2011-10-04). "Fredsprisens gråsoner". *Aftenposten*: p. 4. "Aldri tidligere hadde fredsprisen vært et bedre instrument for nasjonsbygging og en mer verdifull støtte for norsk utenrikspolitikk og økonomiske interesser"

[18] Tønnesson, Øyvind (29 June 2000). "Controversies and Criticisms" (http://nobelprize.org/peace/articles/controversies/index.html). Nobelprize.org. . Retrieved 27 February 2010.

[19] Said, Edward (1996). *Peace and Its Discontents: Essays on Palestine in the Middle East Peace Process*. Vintage. ISBN 0679767258.

[20] Gotlieb, Michael (24 October 1994). "Arafat tarnishes the Nobel trophy". *The San Diego Union — Tribune*: p. B7.

[21] "Worldwide criticism of Nobel peace awards" (http://archive.timesonline.co.uk/tol/viewArticle.arc?articleId=ARCHIVE-The_Times-1973-10-18-06-006&pageId=ARCHIVE-The_Times-1973-10-18-06). *The Times* (London). 18 October 1973. . Retrieved 2009-10-11.

[22] Douglas G. Brinkley. *The Unfinished Presidency: Jimmy Carter's Journey to the Nobel Peace Prize* (1999)

[23] "Surprised, humbled Obama awarded Nobel Peace Prize" (http://news.yahoo.com/s/ap/20091009/ap_on_re_eu/eu_nobel_peace). Associated Press. . Retrieved 2009-10-09.

[24] Otterman, Sharon (2009-10-09), "World Reaction to a Nobel Surprise" (http://thelede.blogs.nytimes.com/2009/10/09/world-reaction-to-a-nobel-surprise/?hp#bozoanchor), *The New York Times*, , retrieved 2009-10-09

[25] "Obama Peace Prize win has Americans asking why?" (http://www.reuters.com/article/GCA-BarackObama/idUKTRE5983AM20091009?virtualBrandChannel=11621&sp=true). reuters.com. 2009-10-09. . Retrieved 2009-10-09.

[26] Kenner, David. (7 October 2009). "Nobel Peace Prize Also-Rans" (http://www.foreignpolicy.com/articles/2009/10/07/nobel_peace_prize_also_rans). *Foreign Policy*. Retrieved 10 October 2009

[27] "Pope John Paul II deserves the Nobel Peace Prize" (http://www.the-kingdom.ie/news/story/?trs=kfidmhidsn). *The Kingdom*. 6 June 2005. . Retrieved 2009-10-10.

[28] Roberts, Nancy L. (1984). "Dorothy Day and the Catholic Worker" (http://books.google.com.au/books?id=Wx5A4UE05QYC&source=gbs_navlinks_s). ISBN 9780873959384. .

[29] Hevesi, Dennis (13 May 2008). "Irena Sendler, Lifeline to Young Jews, Is Dead at 98" (http://www.nytimes.com/2008/05/13/world/europe/13sendler.html?ref=world). The New York Times. . Retrieved 2010-05-05.

[30] Woo, Elaine (13 May 2008). "Irena Sendler, 98; saved 2,500 children in the Holocaust" (http://www.boston.com/bostonglobe/obituaries/articles/2008/05/13/irena_sendler_98_saved_2500_children_in_the_holocaust/). The Boston Globe. . Retrieved 2010-05-05.

[31] de Quetteville, Harry (15 March 2007). "Poland honours heroine who saved children" (http://www.telegraph.co.uk/news/uknews/1545602/Poland-honours-heroine-who-saved-children.html). Telegraph. . Retrieved 2010-05-05.
[32] Tønnesson, Øyvind (1 December 1999). "Mahatma Gandhi, the Missing Laureate" (http://nobelprize.org/nobel_prizes/peace/articles/gandhi/index.html). The Nobel Foundation. . Retrieved 2007-10-17.
[33] http://nobelprize.org/prize_announcements/peace/ask_questions.html
[34] "The Nomination Database for the Nobel Peace Prize, 1901-1956: Gandhi" (http://nobelprize.org/nomination/peace/nomination.php?key1=candname&log1=LIKE&string1=gandhi&action=advsearch&log10=OR&key2=candname&log2=LIKE&string2=&log11=OR&key3=candname&log3=LIKE&string3=&startyear=&endyear=&order1=year&order2=nomname&order3=cand1name&submit2.x=0&submit2.y=0&submit2=Go). Nobelprize.org. . Retrieved 2008-10-13.
[35] (http://www.icrs.ugm.ac.id/wednesday-forum-schedule/111-relevance-of-gandhian-philosophy-in-the-21st-century) Relevance of Gandhian Philosophy in the 21st Century
[36] Presentation Speech by Egil Aarvik, Chairman of the Norwegian Nobel Committee (http://nobelprize.org/nobel_prizes/peace/laureates/1989/presentation-speech.html)

See also

- Nobel Foundation
- Nobel Museum
- Nobel Peace Center
- Nobel Peace Prize Concert

External links

- "The Nobel Peace Prize" (http://nobelprize.org/nobel_prizes/peace/) – Official site of the Nobel Foundation.
- "The Nobel Peace Prize" (http://nobelpeaceprize.org) – Official webpage of the Norwegian Nobel Institute for the Norwegian Nobel Committee.
- "All Nobel Laureates in Peace" (http://www.nobel.se/peace/laureates/index.html) – Index webpage on the official site of the Nobel Foundation.
- "The Nobel Prize Award Ceremonies" (http://nobelprize.org/award_ceremonies/) – Official hyperlinked webpage of the Nobel Foundation.
- "The Nobel Prize Medals and the Medal for the Prize in Economics" (http://nobelprize.org/nobel_prizes/medals/) – By Birgitta Lemmel; an article on the history of the design of the medals featured on the official site.
- "National Peace Nobel Prize shares 1901-2009 by citizenship (or home of organization) at the time of the award." (http://www.idsia.ch/~juergen/pea.html) – From J. Schmidhuber (2010): Evolution of National Nobel Prize Shares in the 20th Century (http://www.idsia.ch/~juergen/nobelshare.html) at arXiv:1009.2634v1 (http://arxiv.org/abs/1009.2634)
- "The Nomination Database for the Nobel Prize in Peace, 1901-1956" (http://nobelprize.org/peace/nomination/database.html) – Database featured on the official site of the Nobel Foundation.
- "What the Nobel Laureates Receive" (http://nobelprize.org/award_ceremonies/prize.html) – Featured link in "The Nobel Prize Award Ceremonies".

Chechen people

Chechens (Noxçiy)

S. Mansur • K. Kishiev • P. Zakharov
T. Tchermoeff • K. Nuradilov • M. Terloeva

Total population
1,500,000 worldwide (2009)
Regions with significant populations

Russia	(including Chechnya) 1,360,253[1]
Chechnya	1,031,647[1]
Ingushetia	95,403[1]
Dagestan	87,867[1]
Rostov Oblast	15,469[1]
Moscow	14,465[1]
Stavropol Krai	13,208[1]
Volgograd Oblast	12,256[1]
Tyumen Oblast	10,623[1]
Astrakhan Oblast	10,019[1]
Europe	100,000 (not including Russian Federation)[2]
Turkey	70,000[3]
Kazakhstan	35,000[1]
Jordan	10,000[1]
Azerbaijan	5,000[2]
Egypt	5,000[2]
Syria	4,000[2]
Georgia	10,000 (including 9,000 Kist people)
Iraq	2,500[4]
Iran	N/A (estimates from 2,000-10,000)
United States	500
Canada	100
	All data from 2009

Languages
Chechen
Religion
Predominantly Sunni Islam (of Shafi`i school)
Related ethnic groups
Ingush, Batsbi, Kists.

Chechens (Chechen: Нохчи *Noxçi*; old-Chechen: Nakhchu, Nakhchij, Nakhch Qam) constitute the largest native ethnic group originating in the North Caucasus region. They refer to themselves as **Noxçi** (singular Noxçi or Noxço). Also known as Sadiks (Isod people), Gargareans, Malkhs (Malkhoi). The isolated mountain terrain of the Caucasus and the strategic value outsiders have placed on the areas settled by Chechens has contributed much to the Chechen community ethos and helped shape national character. Chechen and Ingush peoples are collectively known as the Vainakh.[5]

Origins of the word Chechen

The term "Chechen" is ultimately believed to derive from the Iranian name for the Noxçi and it first occurs in Arabic sources from the 8th century. According to popular tradition, the Russian term "Chechen" comes from the name of the village of Chechen-Aul, where the Chechens defeated Russian soldiers in 1732. The word "Chechen", however, occurs in Russian sources as early as 1692 and the Russians probably derived it from the Kabardian "Shashan".[6]

Geography and diaspora

The Chechen people are mainly inhabitants of Chechnya, Russian Federation. There are also significant Chechen populations in other subdivisions of Russia (especially in Dagestan, Ingushetia and Moscow). A smaller numbers of Chechens are widely scattered in Siberia and the Russian Far East.

Outside Russia, countries with significant Chechen diaspora populations are Turkey, Kazakhstan, Azerbaijan, and the Middle East (especially Jordan, Egypt, Syria and Iraq). These are mainly descendants of people who had to leave Chechnya during the Caucasian War (which led to the annexation of Chechnya by the Russian Empire around 1850) and the 1944 Stalinist deportation in the case of Kazakhstan.

More recently, tens of thousands of Chechen refugees settled in the European Union and elsewhere as the result of the First and Second Chechen Wars, especially in the wave of emigration to the West after 2002.[7]

History

The Chechens are one of the Vainakh peoples, who have lived in the highlands of the North Caucasus region since prehistory (there is archeological evidence of historical continuity dating back since 3,000 B.C.[8]). In the Middle Ages, the lowland of Chechenya was dominated by the Khazars and then the Alans. Local culture was also subject to Byzantine influence and some Chechens converted to Eastern Orthodox Christianity. Gradually, Islam prevailed, although the Chechens' own pagan religion was still strong until at least the 19th century. Society was organised along feudal lines. The North Caucasus was devastated by the Mongol invasions of the 13th century and those of Tamerlane in the 14th.[9] [10]

In the late Middle Ages, the Little Ice Age forced the Chechens down from the hills into the lowlands where they came into conflict with the Terek and Greben Cossacks who had also begun to move into the region. The Caucasus was also the focus for three competing empires: Ottoman Turkey, Persia and Russia. As Russia expanded southwards from the 16th century, clashes between Chechens and the Russians became more frequent. In the late 18th century Sheikh Mansur led a major Chechen resistance movement. In the early 19th century, Russia embarked on full-scale conquest of the North Caucasus in order to protect the route to its new territories in Transcaucasia. The campaign was led by General Yermolov who particularly disliked the Chechens, describing them as "a bold and dangerous people".[11] Angered by Chechen raids, Yermolov resorted to a policy of "scorched earth" and deportations; he also founded the fort of Grozny (now the capital of Chechnya) in 1818. Chechen resistance to Russian rule reached its peak under the leadership of the Dagestani Shamil in the mid-19th century. The Chechens were finally defeated after a long and bloody war.[12] In the aftermath large numbers of *muhajir* refugees emigrated or were forcibly deported to the Ottoman Empire.[13] [14] [15] Since then there have been various Chechen rebellions against Russian power, as well as nonviolent resistance to Russification and the Soviet Union's collectivization and antireligious campaigns.

In 1944 Moscow's oppression reached its apogee as all Chechens, together with several other peoples of the Caucasus, were ordered by Joseph Stalin to be deported *en masse* to Kazakhstan and Siberia and at least one-quarter and perhaps half of the entire Chechen nation perished in the process.[13] [16] [17] Though "rehabilitated" in 1956 and allowed to return the next year, the survivors lost economic resources and civil rights and, under both Soviet and post-Soviet governments, they have been the objects of (official and unofficial) discrimination and discriminatory public discourse.[13] [18] Chechen attempts to regain independence in the 1990s after the fall of the Soviet Union have led to two devastating wars with the new Russian state since 1994.

Language

The main language of the Chechen people is Chechen. Chechen belongs to the family of Nakh languages (North-Central Caucasian languages). Literary Chechen is based on the central lowland dialect. Other related languages include Ingush, which has speakers in the nearby Ingushetia, and Batsi, which is the language of the people in the adjoining part of Georgia. At various times in their history, Chechens used Georgian, Arabic and Latin alphabets; as of 2008, the official one is now the Cyrillic alphabet.

In 1989, 73.4% spoke Russian,[19] though this figure has declined due to the wars for a large number of reasons (including the lack of proper education, the refusal to learn the language, and the mass dispersal of the Chechen diaspora due to the war).

Many Chechens also speak, or learn to speak, Turkish. This is due to historical and cultural reasons (Turkish was once the lingua franca of the region), as well as the presence of a large Chechen diaspora in Turkey (and now, within the Turkish sections of German cities).

Most Chechens living in their homeland can understand Ingush with ease. The two languages are not truly mutually intelligible, but it is easy for Chechens to learn how to understand the Ingush language and vice versa over time after hearing it for a while. This situation is often compared to Spanish and Italian (or, by some, Spanish and Portuguese or Catalan), Serbo - Croatian and Slovenian, etc.

A large number of Chechens also are now able to speak English (and, for some, French) due to its status as a global *lingua franca* and as the language of international interaction.

Chechens in the diaspora often speak the language of the country they live in (Polish, Japanese, Georgian, etc.).

Physical appearance

Chechens belong to the Caucasoid type, exhibiting traits typical of European and Caucasian peoples. The majority of Chechens are dark-haired (medium to dark brown or black), but there are Chechens with blonde or even red hair, while eye color ranges from blue to brown and skin tone is typically rather pale and light (though there are some Chechens with darker complexions). Like other Caucasian peoples, Chechens are typically slender and tall, though there are many exceptions to this rule.

Origins and Genetics

Origins

Chechens are a Nakh people, and discussion of their origins is intertwined with the discussion of the mysterious origins of Nakh peoples as a whole.

Linguistically, Nakh peoples are distantly related to Dagestani peoples (such as Avars, Dargins, Lezghins, Laks, etc.), as they all speak languages in the Nakho-Dagestani, or Northeast Caucasian language family. However, this relationship is not a close one: the Nakho-Dagestani family is of comparable or greater time-depth than Indo-European, meaning Chechens are only as linguistically related to Avars or Dargins as the French are to the Russians or Iranians.

Nakh peoples such as Chechens are thought to either be descended from original settlers of the Caucasus (North and/or South)[20] [8] or supposedly Nakh-speaking ethnic minorities in the Northeastern regions of the ancient state of Urartu (whose people also spoke a language that was possibly related to the Nakh languages).[21] The two theories are not mutually incompatible, and there has been much evidence that seems to link both of the two together (either by dual origins or the "return" theory, in which the Nakh peoples originally lived in the Caucasus and then returned).

It should be noted that Chechen genetics show a high level of genetic diversity (see section below).

Proposed Nakh placenames have been found in numerous areas of the South Caucasus, most prominently in Eastern Georgia, North-Central Georgia/South Ossetia, Nakhichivan, and Eastern Armenia (i.e. the modern Republic of Armenia). There are also a span of Nakh placenames in the North Caucasus outside modern Nakh territory, particularly in North Ossetia and Balkaria (the Balkars are suspected by some to be partial Nakh descendants, later Alanized and then Turkified).

In particular, the Chechens are descended from the *Dzurdzuks*, a group well known in the Georgian chronicles (*Dourts* in the Armenian version). Other groups linked Amjad Jaimoukha traces the name Dzurdzuk to an ancient city north of Lake Urmia, near Nakhichevan (Nakhichevan is thought to be a Nakh placename by some). Other groups attributed to being the ancestors of the Chechens and Ingush include the *Kists* (in the Georgian chronicles), *Gargareans* (from the Nakh root **gergara**; reported by Strabo to have "returned" from the South Caucasus to the North Caucasus, fleeing the wars in the South) and the *Nakhchmateans* (Armenian chronicles).

Genetics

Genetic tests on Chechens, though sparse and not sufficiently thorough so far, have shown roots in the Caucasus as well as strong connections to and influences from the Middle East as well as Europe. As is the case with many other Caucasian peoples, Chechens are more connected with the Middle East on the Y-dna side, but more "European" on the mitochondrial X-chromosome DNA.[22] However, it was found that Chechens (as well as Caucasians as a whole) placed closer to Kurds and Persians than other European peoples (on the mtDNA), despite being far closer to Europe than the Middle East on the X-chromosome as a whole.

Y-DNA

The most recent and most reliable study on Chechens, by Balanovsky *et al.* in 2011[23] sampled a total of 330 Chechens from three sample locations (one in Malgobek, one in Achkoi-Martan, and one from two sites in Dagestan) and found the following frequencies:

N	J2	J1	L	G2	R1a	Q	R1b	N	I
330	56.7%	20.9%	7%	5.5%	3.9%	3%	1.8%	0.6%	0.5%

- J2- (*56.7%*[23]) Associated with Mediterranean, South Caucasian and Fertile Crescent populations, with its peaks at 87.4% in Ingushetia and 72% in Georgia's Kazbegi region (near Mount Kazbek). In the North Caucasus, the largest frequencies are those of Nakh peoples (Chechens (56.7%) and Ingush (88.8%)[23] . Other notable values were found among North Caucasian Turkic peoples (Kumyks (25%)[24] and Balkars(24%)[25]). It is notable that according to both Nasidze's study in 2004 and then a later study on Dagestani peoples by Yunusbaev in 2006, J2 suddenly collapses as one enters the territory of non-Nakh Northeast Caucasian peoples, dropping suddenly to very low values among Dagestani peoples.[26] [22] [27] [23] The overwhelming bulk of Chechen J2 is of the subclade **J2a4b***(J2-M67), of which the highest frequencies by far are found among Nakh peoples- Chechens were 55.2% according to the Balanovsky study, while Ingush were 87.4%.
- J1- (*20.9%*[23]). In Balanovsky, it was found at 25% in Chechnya, 21% in Malgobek Chechens and 16% in Dagestani Chechens. It was found at much higher levels in Dagestan. As is the case with the whole of the Caucasus, Chechen J1 is almost universally J1*.
- L- Associated with South Asia, and the Caucasus. In Balanovsky's study, Chechens were found to be 7.0% L, and this was all L3.[23]
- Other haplogroups that appeared consistently appeared at lower frequencies included G2 (5.5%), R1a (3.9%), Q (3%) and R1b-M269 (1.8%). However, R2, which was not detected in Balanovsky (possibly because it was not tested for), accounted for as much as 16% of Chechen males in a previous study by Ivan Nasidze.[28]

Overall, tests have shown consistently that Chechens are most closely related to Ingush, Circassians, Georgians, and Iranians (especially Northwestern Iranians), occasionally showing a kinship to other peoples in some tests. Balanovsky's study showed the Ingush to be the Chechens' closest relatives by far.[27] [28] []

mtDNA

A 2004 study showed Chechens to be extremely diverse on the X-chromosome, with 18 different haplogroups out of only 23 samples.[22] Chechens clustered closest to Azeris, Georgians and Kabardins. They clustered closer to European populations than Middle Eastern populations this time, but were significantly closer to Western European populations (British and Basque) than to Eastern European populations (Russians and other Slavs, as well as Estonians), despite living in the East. They actually clustered about as close to Basques as they did to Ingush (Chechens also cluster closer to many other populations than Ingush, such as Armenians and Abazins), but the Chechens were the closer to the Ingush than any other population, the disbalance probably largely being due to the uniqueness of the Ingush on the X-chromosome among those tested.[22]

Culture

Prior to the adoption of Islam, the Chechens practiced a unique blend of religious traditions and beliefs. They partook in numerous rites and rituals, many of them pertaining to farming; these included rain rites, a celebration that occurred on the first day of plowing, as well as the Day of the Thunderer Sela and the Day of the Goddess Tusholi.

Chechen society is structured around *tukhum* (unions of clans) and about 130 *teip*, or clans. The teips are based more on land and one-side lineage than on blood (as exogamy is prevalent and encouraged), and are bonded together to form the Chechen nation. Teips are further subdivided into *gar* (branches), and gars into *nekye* (patronymic families). The Chechen social code is called *nokhchallah* (where *Nokhchuo* stands for "Chechen") and may be loosely translated as "Chechen character". The Chechen code of honour implies moral and ethical behaviour, generosity and the will to safeguard the honor of women.

In addition to sparse written record from the Middle Ages, Chechens traditionally remember history through the illesh, a collection of epic poems and stories.

Chechens today have a strong sense of nation, which is enforced by the old clan network and nokhchalla- the obligation to clan, tukhum, etc. This is often combined with old values transmuted into a modern sense. They are mythically descended from the epic hero, Turpalo-Nokhchuo (the Chechen Hero). There is a strong theme of representing the nation with its national animal, the wolf.

Due to their strong dependence on the land, its farms and its forests (and indeed, the national equation with the wolf), Chechens have a strong sense of affection for nature. According to Chechen philosopher Apty Bisultanov, ruining an ant-hill or hunting Caucasian goats during their mating season were considered extremely sinful.[29] It is notable that the glasnost era Chechen independence movement, *Bart* (unity) in fact originated as a simple environmentalist organization in the republic's capital of Grozny.[30]

Chechen culture puts a strong value on the concept of freedom. This asserts itself in a number of ways. Much like Scots and Albanians, a large majority of the nation's national heroes fought for independence (or otherwise, like the legendary Zelimkhan, robbed from the nation deemed the oppressor in order to feed Chechen children in a Robin Hood-like fashion). A common greeting in the Chechen language, *marsha oylla*, is literally translated as "enter in freedom". The word for freedom also encompasses notions of peace and prosperity.

Chechens are often referred to as the "French of the Caucasus", for a number of reasons (it is notable that the Circassians are the "English of the Caucasus", and the Georgians are the "Italians of the Caucasus"). This comparison may refer to etiher political/historical traits, or to personality characteristics. Compared to their natives, Chechens have, like the French, historically been a comparably liberal people, though this is often obscured in the modern day. Like the French, who overthrew their age-old monarchy in the French revolution, the Chechens had a similar revolution a century or two earlier[31] , and like the French, they bore the distinction (for a period) of being the only egalitarian society in an area full of monarchic states. Like the French, the Chechens preferred swift, revolutionary (and often violent) methods to realize the change they wished to see- unlike the Circassians (called the "English of the Caucasus" both for their political and personality characteristics) who preferred more gradualist methods.[32] In the more personality/national character sense (generally the more common use), like the French, they have a reputation for being witty and clever.[33]

Religion

Chechnya is predominantly Muslim. Most of the Chechens belong to the Shafi'i school of thought of Sunni Islam, while a minority belong to the Hanafi.[13] Some adhere to the mystical Sufi tradition of Muridism, while about half of Chechens belong to Sufi brotherhoods, or tariqah. The two Sufi tariqas that spread in the North Caucasus were the Naqshbandiya and the Qadiriya (the Naqshbandiya is particularly strong in Dagestan and eastern Chechnya, whereas the Qadiriya has most of its adherents in the rest of Chechnya and Ingushetia). Some of the modern Chechen rebels are Salafis, but these form a small minority of the group and are often viewed suspiciously by non-Salafis who protectively guard their national customs against encroachment (hence, the phrase "Muhammad may have been an Arab, but Allah is surely Chechen"). According to some, the view of the Chechens as being an obsessively pious, intolerant, fundamentalist Muslim group is highly incorrect (and largely encouraged by the Russian media for political purposes).[34] [35] [36]

A Chechen man prays during the battle for Grozny. The flame in the background is coming from a gas pipeline which was hit by shrapnel. (January 1995)

See also

- Vainakh peoples
- Bats people, a related ethnic group in Georgia
- Ingush people, a related ethnic group in Ingushetia
- Kist people, a related ethnic group in Georgia
- Peoples of the Caucasus
- Nakh peoples
- Northeast Caucasian peoples

References

[1] Russian Census of 2002 (http://www.perepis2002.ru/index.html?id=17)(**Russian**)
[2] Chechens in the Middle East: Between Original and Host Cultures (http://belfercenter.ksg.harvard.edu/publication/12785/chechens_in_the_middle_east.html), Event Report, Caspian Studies Program
[3] Kristiina Markkanen: Chechen refugee came to Finland via Baku and Istanbul (http://www.hs.fi/english/article/Chechen+refugee+came+to+Finland+via+Baku+and+Istanbul/1135246619648) (Englisch)
[4] Chechens in the Middle East (http://belfercenter.ksg.harvard.edu/publication/12785/chechens_in_the_middle_east.html)
[5] Arutiunov, Sergei. (1996). "Ethnicity and Conflict in the Caucasus" (http://src-h.slav.hokudai.ac.jp/sympo/Proceed97/Arutiunov5.html). Slavic Research Center
[6] Jaimoukha p.12
[7] Chechnya's Exodus to Europe, North Caucasus Weekly Volume: 9 Issue: 3, The Jamestown Foundation, January 24, 2008
[8] Bernice Wuethrich (19 May 2000). "Peering Into the Past, With Words" (http://www.sciencemag.org/cgi/content/full/288/5469/1158). *Science* **288** (5469): 1158. doi:10.1126/science.288.5469.1158. .
[9] Jaimoukha pp.33-34
[10] Dunlop p.3

[11] Dunlop p.14
[12] Jaimoukha (p.50): "The Chechens suffered horrific losses in human life during the long war. From an estimated population of over a million in the 1840s, there were only 140,000 Chechens left in the Caucasus in 1861..."
[13] "Who are the Chechens?" (http://web.archive.org/web/20060915080123/http://socrates.berkeley.edu/~bsp/caucasus/articles/nichols_1995-chechen.pdf). Archived from the original (http://socrates.berkeley.edu/~bsp/caucasus/articles/nichols_1995-chechen.pdf) on 2006-09-15. . by Johanna Nichols, University of California, Berkeley.
[14] Dunlop p.29ff. Dunlop writes (p.30): "In 1860, according to Soviet-era figures, 81,360 Chechens left for Turkey; a second emigration took place in 1865, when an additional 22,500 Chechens left. More than 100,000 Chechens were thus ethnically 'cleansed' during this process. This was perhaps a majority of their total population..."
[15] Jaimoukha p.50
[16] Jaimoukha p.58
[17] Dunlop, Chapter 2 "Soviet Genocide", particularly pp.70-71 ("How many died?")
[18] Jaimoukha p.60
[19] Mikhailov, Valentin. *Chechnya and Tatarstan*
[20] Johanna Nichols (February 1997). "The Ingush (with notes on the Chechen): Background information" (http://ingush.berkeley.edu:7012/ingush_people.html). *University of California, Berkeley*. . Retrieved 2007-02-10.
[21] Jaimoukha. **Chechens**. Page 29
[22] I. Nasidze, E. Y. S. Ling, D. Quinque *et al.*, "Mitochondrial DNA and Y-Chromosome Variation in the Caucasus," *Annals of Human Genetics* (2004) 68,205–221. http://www.eva.mpg.de/genetics/pdf/Caucasus_big_paper.pdf
[23] Oleg Balanovsky *et al.*, "Parallel Evolution of Genes and Languages in the Caucasus Region," *Molecular Biology and Evolution* 2011
[24] Yunusbaev 2006
[25] Battaglia, Vincenza; Fornarino, Simona; Al-Zahery, Nadia; Olivieri, Anna; Pala, Maria; Myres, Natalie M; King, Roy J; Rootsi, Siiri et al. (24 December 2008). "Y-chromosomal evidence of the cultural diffusion of agriculture in southeast Europe" (http://www.draganprimorac.com/wp-content/uploads/2010/05/Battaglia.pdf). *European Journal of Human Genetics* **17** (6): 820–830. doi:10.1038/ejhg.2008.249. PMC 2947100. PMID 19107149. .
[26] Yunusbaev 2006.
[27] Caciagli et al, 2009. *The key role of patrilineal inheritance in the genetic variation of Dagestani highlanders.*
[28] Nasidze et al."Mitochondrial DNA and Y-Chromosome Variation in the Caucasus",' 'Annals of Human Genetics **(2004)**
[29] http://chechen.8m.com/history/bisult_brnfree.html
[30] Wood, Tony. *Chechnya: The Case for Independence*. Page 46
[31] Jaimoukha, Amjad. "The Chechens: A Handbook". Page 14
[32] Manning, Paul. "Just Like England: On the Liberal Institutions of the Circassians". Available online in pdf format here: http://www.circassianworld.com/pdf/Paul_Manning.pdf
[33] http://gatchina3000.ru/brockhaus-and-efron-encyclopedic-dictionary/113/113665.htm (in Russian)
[34] "Shattering the Al Qaeda-Chechen Myth: Part 1" (http://web.archive.org/web/20040129132549/http://www.jamestown.org/publications_details.php?volume_id=13&&issue_id=590). Archived from the original (http://www.jamestown.org/publications_details.php?volume_id=13&&issue_id=590) on 2004-01-29. ., by Brian Glyn Williams, The Jamestown Foundation, October 2, 2003
[35] Wood, Tony. *Chechnya: the Case for Independence*. p127-145
[36] Jaimoukha, Amjad. *The Chechens: A Handbook*. Throughout book.

Sources

- Amjad Jaimoukha *The Chechens: A Handbook* (London, New York: Routledge, 2005)
- Lechi Ilyasov *The Diversity of the Chechen Culture: From Historical Roots to the Present* (Moscow, 2009), (http://www.zhaina.com/history/205-the-diversity-of-the-chechen-culture.html)
- John B. Dunlop *Russia Confronts Chechnya: Roots of a Separatist Conflict* (Cambridge University Press, 1998)

gag:Çeçenner

Amnesty International

Type	Non-profit NGO
Founded	July 1961 by Peter Benenson in Britain
Location	Global General secretariat in London
Key people	Salil Shetty (Secretary-General)
Services	Protecting human rights
Method	Media attention, direct-appeal campaigns, research, lobbying
Members	More than 3 million members and supporters[1]
Motto	It is better to light a candle than to curse the darkness.[2]
Website	www.amnesty.org [3]

Amnesty International (commonly known as **Amnesty** and **AI**) is an international non-governmental organisation whose stated mission is "to conduct research and generate action to prevent and end grave abuses of human rights, and to demand justice for those whose rights have been violated."[4]

Following a publication of Peter Benenson's article "The Forgotten Prisoners" in *The Observer* 28 May 1961,[5] Amnesty was founded in London the same year. Amnesty draws attention to human rights abuses and campaigns for compliance with international laws and standards. It works to mobilise public opinion to put pressure on governments that let abuse take place.[4] The organisation was awarded the 1977 Nobel Peace Prize for its "campaign against torture",[6] and the United Nations Prize in the Field of Human Rights in 1978.[7]

In the field of international human rights organisations (of which there were 300 in 1996),[8] Amnesty has the longest history and broadest name recognition, and "is believed by many to set standards for the movement as a whole."[8]

History

1960s

Amnesty International was founded in London in July 1961 by English labour lawyer Peter Benenson.[9] According to his own account, he was travelling in the London Underground on 19 November 1960, when he read of two Portuguese students from Coimbra who had been sentenced to seven years of imprisonment in Portugal for allegedly "having drunk a toast to liberty".[a][10] Researchers have never traced the alleged newspaper article in question.[a] In 1960, Portugal was ruled by the authoritarian Estado Novo regime.[11] Anti-regime conspiracies were vigorously repressed by the Portuguese state police and deemed anti-Portuguese. In his significant newspaper article "The Forgotten Prisoners", Benenson later described his reaction as follows: "Open your newspaper any day of the week and you will find a story from somewhere of someone being imprisoned, tortured or executed because his opinions or religion are unacceptable to his government [...] The newspaper reader feels a sickening sense of impotence. Yet if these feelings of disgust could be united into common action, something effective could be done."[12]

Benenson worked with friend Eric Baker. Baker was a member of the Religious Society of Friends who had been involved in funding the British Campaign for Nuclear Disarmament as well as becoming head of Quaker Peace and Social Witness, and in his memoirs Benenson described him as "a partner in the launching of the project".[13] In consultation with other writers, academics and lawyers and, in particular, Alec Digges, they wrote via Louis Blom-Cooper to David Astor, editor of *The Observer* newspaper, who, on 28 May 1961, published Benenson's article "The Forgotten Prisoners". The article brought the reader's attention to those "imprisoned, tortured or executed because his opinions or religion are unacceptable to his government"[12] or, put another way, to violations, by governments, of articles 18 and 19 of the Universal Declaration of Human Rights (UDHR). The article described these violations occurring, on a global scale, in the context of restrictions to press freedom, to political oppositions, to timely public trial before impartial courts, and to asylum. It marked the launch of "Appeal for Amnesty, 1961", the aim of which was to mobilise public opinion, quickly and widely, in defence of these individuals, whom Benenson named "Prisoners of Conscience". The "Appeal for Amnesty" was reprinted by a large number of international newspapers. In the same year Benenson had a book published, *Persecution 1961*, which detailed the cases of nine prisoners of conscience investigated and compiled by Benenson and Baker (Maurice Adin, Ashton Jones, Agostinho Neto, Patrick Duncan, Olga Ivinskaya, Luis Taruc, Constantin Noica, Antonio Amat and Hu Feng).[14] In July 1961 the leadership had decided that the appeal would form the basis of a permanent organisation, which on 30 September 1962 was officially named 'Amnesty International' (Between the 'Appeal for Amnesty, 1961' and September 1962 the organisation had been known simply as 'Amnesty'.)[15]

What started as a short appeal soon became a permanent international movement working to protect those imprisoned for non-violent expression of their views and to secure worldwide recognition of Articles 18 and 19 of the UDHR. From the very beginning, research and campaigning were present in Amnesty International's work. A library was established for information about prisoners of conscience and a network of local groups, called 'THREES' groups, was started. Each group worked on behalf of three prisoners, one from each of the then three main ideological regions of the world: communist, capitalist and developing.

By the mid-1960s Amnesty International's global presence was growing and an International Secretariat and International Executive Committee was established to manage Amnesty International's national organisations, called 'Sections', which had appeared in several countries. The international movement was starting to agree on its core principles and techniques. For example, the issue of whether or not to adopt prisoners who had advocated violence, like Nelson Mandela, brought unanimous agreement that it could not give the name of 'Prisoner of Conscience' to such prisoners. Aside from the work of the library and groups, Amnesty International's activities were expanding to helping prisoner's families, sending observers to trials, making representations to governments, and finding asylum or overseas employment for prisoners. Its activity and influence was also increasing within intergovernmental organisations; it would be awarded consultative status by the United Nations, the Council of Europe and UNESCO before the decade ended.

1970s

Leading Amnesty International in the 1970s were key figureheads Seán MacBride and Martin Ennals. While continuing to work for prisoners of conscience, Amnesty International's purview widened to include "fair trial" and opposition to long detention without trial (UDHR Article 9), and especially to the torture of prisoners (UDHR Article 5). Amnesty International believed that the reasons underlying torture of prisoners, by governments, were either to obtain information or to quell opposition by the use of terror, or both. Also of concern was the export of more sophisticated torture methods, equipment and teaching by the superpowers to "client states", for example by the United States through some activities of the CIA.

Amnesty International drew together reports from countries where torture allegations seemed most persistent and organized an international conference on torture. It sought to influence public opinion in order to put pressure on national governments by organising a campaign for the 'Abolition of Torture' which ran for several years.

Amnesty International's membership increased from 15,000 in 1969[16] to 200,000 by 1979.[17] This growth in resources enabled an expansion of its program, 'outside of the prison walls', to include work on "disappearances", the death penalty and the rights of refugees. A new technique, the 'Urgent Action', aimed at mobilising the membership into action rapidly was pioneered. The first was issued on 19 March 1973, on behalf of Luiz Basilio Rossi, a Brazilian academic, arrested for political reasons.

At the intergovernmental level Amnesty International pressed for application of the UN's Standard Minimum Rules for the Treatment of Prisoners and of existing humanitarian conventions; to secure ratifications of the two UN Covenants on Human Rights in 1976); and was instrumental in obtaining additional instruments and provisions forbidding its practice. Consultative status was granted at the Inter-American Commission on Human Rights in 1972.

In 1976 Amnesty's British Section started a series of fund-raising events that came to be known as The Secret Policeman's Balls series. They were staged in London initially as comedy galas featuring what the Daily Telegraph called "the crème de la crème of the British comedy world"[18] including members of comedy troupe Monty Python, and later expanded to also include performances by leading rock musicians. The series was created and developed by Monty Python alumnus John Cleese and entertainment industry executive Martin Lewis working closely with Amnesty staff members Peter Luff (Assistant Director of Amnesty 1974–1978) and subsequently with Peter Walker (Amnesty Fund-Raising Officer 1978-1982). Cleese, Lewis and Luff worked together on the first two shows (1976 and 1977). Cleese, Lewis and Walker worked together on the 1979 and 1981 shows, the first to carry what the Daily Telegraph described as the "rather brilliantly re-christened" *Secret Policeman's Ball* title.[18]

The organisation was awarded the 1977 Nobel Peace Prize for its "campaign against torture"[6] and the United Nations Prize in the Field of Human Rights in 1978.[7]

1980s

By 1980 Amnesty International was drawing more criticism from governments. The USSR alleged that Amnesty International conducted espionage, the Moroccan government denounced it as a defender of lawbreakers, and the Argentine government banned Amnesty International's 1983 annual report.[19]

1986 Faroe postage stamp celebrating Amnesty's 25th anniversary – Painting by 11 year old Rannvá Kunoy

Throughout the 1980s, Amnesty International continued to campaign against torture, and on behalf of prisoners of conscience. New issues emerged, including extrajudicial killings, military, security and police transfers, political killings; and disappearances.

Towards the end of the decade, the growing numbers worldwide of refugees was a very visible area of Amnesty International's concern. While many of the world's refugees of the time had been displaced by war and famine, in adherence to its mandate, Amnesty International concentrated on those forced to flee because of the human rights violations it was seeking to prevent. It argued that rather than focusing on new restrictions on entry for asylum-seekers, governments were to address the human rights violations which were forcing people into exile.

Apart from a second campaign on torture during the first half of the decade, two major musical events occurred, designed to increase awareness of Amnesty and of human rights (particularly among younger generations) during the mid- to late-1980s. The 1986 Conspiracy of Hope tour, which played five concerts in the U.S., and culminated in a daylong show, featuring some thirty-odd acts at Giants Stadium, and the 1988 Human Rights Now! world tour.

Human Rights Now!, which was timed to coincide with the 40th anniversary of the United Nations' Universal Declaration of Human Rights (UDHR), played a series of concerts on five continents over six weeks. Both tours featured some of the most famous musicians and bands of the day.

1990s

Throughout the 1990s, Amnesty International continued to grow, to a membership of over 3 million in over 150 countries and territories,[1] led by Senegalese Secretary General Pierre Sané. Amnesty continued to work on a wide range of issues and world events. For example, South African groups joined in 1992 and hosted a visit by Pierre Sané to meet with the apartheid government to press for an investigation into allegations of police abuse, an end to arms sales to the African Great Lakes region and the abolition of the death penalty. In particular, Amnesty International brought attention to violations committed on specific groups, including refugees, racial/ethnic/religious minorities, women and those executed or on Death Row. The death penalty report *When the state kills* (ISBN 978-0-691-10261-0) and the 'Human Rights are Women's Rights' campaign were key actions for the latter two issues. During the 1990s, Amnesty International was forced to react to human rights violations occurring in the context of a proliferation of armed conflict in Angola, East Timor, the Persian Gulf, Rwanda, and the former Yugoslavia. Amnesty International took no position on whether to support or oppose external military interventions in these armed conflicts. It did not (and does not) reject the use of force, even lethal force, or ask those engaged to lay down their arms. Instead, it questioned the motives behind external intervention and selectivity of international action in relation to the strategic interests of those sending troops. It argued that action should be taken to prevent human rights problems becoming human rights catastrophes, and that both intervention and inaction represented a failure of the international community.

Amnesty International was proactive in pushing for recognition of the universality of human rights. The campaign 'Get Up, Sign Up' marked 50 years of the UDHR. Thirteen million pledges were collected in support, and the Decl music concert was held in Paris on 10 December 1998 (Human Rights Day). At the intergovernmental level, Amnesty International argued in favour of creating an United Nations High Commissioner for Human Rights (established 1993) and an International Criminal Court (established 2002).

After his arrest in London in 1998 by the Metropolitan Police, Amnesty International became involved in the legal battle of Senator Pinochet, a former Chilean President, who sought to avoid extradition to Spain to face charges. Lord Hoffman had an indirect connection with Amnesty International, and this led to an important test for the appearance of bias in legal proceedings in UK law. There was a suit[20] against the decision to release Senator Pinochet, taken by the then British Home Secretary Mr Jack Straw, before that decision had actually been taken, in an attempt to prevent the release of Senator Pinochet. The English High Court refused[21] the application and Senator Pinochet was released and returned to Chile. This legal challenge was a novel attempt to use legal process to challenge a decision before it was taken and could be seen as hard to reconcile with the rule of law, as it was predicated on a presumption that the Home Secretary had erred in law whatever the reasons were for the decision.

2000s

After 2000, Amnesty International's agenda turned to the challenges arising from globalisation and the reaction to the 11 September 2001 attacks in the United States. The issue of globalisation provoked a major shift in Amnesty International policy, as the scope of its work was widened to include economic, social and cultural rights, an area that it had declined to work on in the past. Amnesty International felt this shift was important, not just to give credence to its principle of the indivisibility of rights, but because of what it saw as the growing power of companies and the undermining of many nation states as a result of globalisation.[22]

In the aftermath of the 11 September attacks, the new Amnesty International Secretary General, Irene Khan, reported that a senior government official had said to Amnesty International delegates: "Your role collapsed with the collapse of the Twin Towers in New York".[23] In the years following the attacks, some believe that the gains made by human rights organisations over previous decades had possibly been eroded. Amnesty International argued that human rights were the basis for the security of all, not a barrier to it. Criticism came directly from the Bush administration and *The Washington Post*, when Khan, in 2005, likened the US government's detention facility at Guantanamo Bay, Cuba, to a Soviet Gulag.[24] [25]

During the first half of the new decade, Amnesty International turned its attention to violence against women, controls on the world arms trade and concerns surrounding the effectiveness of the UN. With its membership close to two million by 2005,[26] Amnesty continued to work for prisoners of conscience.

In 2007, the organisation appeared to endorse pro-choice for abortion.[27] However, the organisation responded by saying that it had only done this for limited situations.[28]

Amnesty International reported, concerning the Iraq war, on 17 March 2008, that despite claims the security situation in Iraq has improved in recent months, the human rights situation is disastrous, after the start of the war five years ago in 2003.[29]

In 2008 Amnesty International launched a mobile donating campaign in the United States, which allows supporters to make $5 micro-donations by sending a text message to the short code 90999 with the keyword RIGHTS. Amnesty International's mobile fund raising campaign was created in partnership with Mgive and the Mobile Giving Foundation.[30]

In 2009 Amnesty International accused Israel and the Palestinian Hamas movement of committing war crimes during Israel's January offensive in Gaza, called Operation Cast Lead, that resulted in the deaths of more than 1400 Palestinians and 13 Israelis.[31] The 117-page Amnesty report charged Israeli forces with killing hundreds of civilians and wanton destruction of thousands of homes. Amnesty found no evidence of Palestinian militants using human shields to stop Israeli attacks, but accused Hamas of launching attacks from buildings in which Palestinian civilians were sheltering. A subsequent United Nations Fact Finding Mission on the Gaza Conflict was carried out; Amnesty stated that its findings were consistent with those of Amnesty's own field investigation, and called on the UN to act promptly to implement the mission's recommendations.[32]

2010s

In February 2010, Amnesty suspended Gita Sahgal, its gender unit head, after she criticized Amnesty for its links with Moazzam Begg, Director of a campaign group called Cageprisoners. She had called the links "a gross error of judgment" that risked Amnesty's reputation on human rights, and said it was wrong to ally with "Britain's most famous supporter of the Taliban".[33] [34] [35] [36] Amnesty responded that Sahgal was not suspended "for raising these issues internally... [Begg] speaks about his own views ..., not Amnesty International's."[37] Among those who spoke up for Saghal were Salman Rushdie ("Amnesty ... has done its reputation incalculable damage.... It looks very much as if Amnesty's leadership is suffering from a kind of moral bankruptcy, and has lost the ability to distinguish right from wrong"), Member of Parliament Denis MacShane, Joan Smith, Christopher Hitchens, Martin Bright, Melanie Phillips, and Nick Cohen.[38] [39] [40] [41] [42] [43] [44] [45]

In February 2011, Amnesty requested that Swiss authorities start a criminal investigation of former U. S. President George W. Bush and arrest him.[46]

In July 2011, Amnesty International celebrated its 50 years with an animated short film directed by Carlos Lascano, produced by Eallin Motion Art and Dreamlife Studio, with music by Academy Award winner Hans Zimmer and nominee Lorne Balfe. The film shows that the fight for humanity is not yet over.[47]

Principles

A vital part of AI's mandate is the so-called "violence clause". It sets prisoners of conscience apart from the other categories of prisoners on whose behalf the movement works. If a prisoner is serving a sentence imposed, after a fair trial, for activities involving violence, AI will not ask the government to release the prisoner.

AI does not judge whether recourse to violence is justified or not. However, AI does not oppose the political use of violence in itself since The Universal Declaration of Human Rights, in its preamble, foresees situations in which people could "be compelled to have recourse, as a last resort, to rebellion against tyranny and oppression".

AI neither supports nor condemns the resort to violence by political opposition groups in itself, just as AI neither supports nor condemns a government policy of using military force in fighting against armed opposition movements. However, AI supports minimum humane standards that should be respected by governments and armed opposition groups alike. When an opposition group tortures or kills its captives, takes hostages, or commits deliberate and arbitrary killings, AI condemns these abuses.[48]

Work

> “Amnesty International's vision is of a world in which every person enjoys all of the human rights enshrined in the Universal Declaration of Human Rights and other international human rights standards.
>
> In pursuit of this vision, Amnesty International's mission is to undertake research and action focused on preventing and ending grave abuses of the rights to physical and mental integrity, freedom of conscience and expression, and freedom from discrimination, within the context of its work to promote all human rights.”
>
> —Statute of Amnesty International, 27th International Council meeting, 2005

Amnesty International primarily targets governments, but also reports on non-governmental bodies and private individuals ("non-state actors").

There are six key areas which Amnesty deals with:

- Women's, children's, minorities' and indigenous rights
- Ending torture
- Abolition of the death penalty
- Rights of refugees
- Rights of prisoners of conscience
- Protection of human dignity.

Some specific aims are to: abolish the death penalty, end extra judicial executions and "disappearances," ensure prison conditions meet international human rights standards, ensure prompt and fair trial for all political prisoners, ensure free education to all children worldwide, decriminalise abortion,[49] fight impunity from systems of justice, end the recruitment and use of child soldiers, free all prisoners of conscience, promote economic, social and cultural rights for marginalized communities, protect human rights defenders, promote religious tolerance, protect LGBT rights,[50] stop torture and ill-treatment, stop unlawful killings in armed conflict, uphold the rights of refugees, migrants, and asylum seekers, and protect human dignity.

To further these aims, Amnesty International has developed several techniques to publicise information and mobilise public opinion. The organisation considers as one of its strengths the publication of impartial and accurate reports. Reports are researched by: interviewing victims and officials, observing trials, working with local human rights activists, and monitoring the media. It aims to issue timely press releases and publishes information in newsletters and on web sites. It also sends official missions to countries to make courteous but insistent inquiries.

Campaigns to mobilise public opinion can take the form of individual, country, or thematic campaigns. Many techniques are deployed, such as direct appeals (for example, letter writing), media and publicity work, and public demonstrations. Often, fund-raising is integrated with campaigning.

In situations which require immediate attention, Amnesty International calls on existing urgent action networks or crisis response networks; for all other matters, it calls on its membership. It considers the large size of its human resources to be another of its key strengths.

The role of Amnesty International has an immense impact on getting citizens onboard with focusing on human rights issues. These groups influence countries and governments to give their people justice with pressure and in man power. An example of Amnesty International's work, which began in the 1960s by writing letters to free imprisoned people that were put there for non-violent expressions. The group now has power, attends sessions, and became a source of information for the U.N. The increase in participation of non-governmental organizations changes how we live today. Felix Dodds states in a recent document that, "In the 1972 there were 39 democratic countries in the world; by 2002, there were 139." This shows that non-governmental organizations make enormous leaps within a short period of time for human rights.

Country focus

Amnesty reports disproportionately on relatively more democratic and open countries,[51] arguing that its intention is not to produce a range of reports which statistically represents the world's human rights abuses, but rather to apply the pressure of public opinion to encourage improvements. The demonstration effect of the behaviour of both key Western governments and major non-Western states is an important factor: as one former Amnesty Secretary-General pointed out, "for many countries and a large number of people, the United States is a model," and according to one Amnesty manager, "large countries influence small countries."[8] In addition, with the end of the Cold War, Amnesty felt that a greater emphasis on human rights in the North was needed to improve its credibility with its Southern critics by demonstrating its willingness to report on human rights issues in a truly global manner.[8]

According to one academic study, as a result of these considerations the frequency of Amnesty's reports is influenced by a number of factors, besides the frequency and severity of human rights abuses. For example, Amnesty reports significantly more (than predicted by human rights abuses) on more economically powerful states; and on countries which receive US military aid, on the basis that this Western complicity in abuses increases the likelihood of public pressure being able to make a difference.[8] In addition, around 1993–94, Amnesty consciously developed its media relations, producing fewer background reports and more press releases, to increase the impact of its reports. Press releases are partly driven by news coverage, to use existing news coverage as leverage to discuss Amnesty's human rights concerns. This increases Amnesty's focus on the countries the media is more interested in.[8]

Amnesty's country focus is similar to that of some other comparable NGOs, notably Human Rights Watch: between 1991 and 2000, Amnesty and HRW shared eight of ten countries in their "top ten" (by Amnesty press releases; 7 for Amnesty reports).[8] In addition, six of the 10 countries most reported on by Human Rights Watch in the 1990s also made *The Economist's* and *Newsweek's* "most covered" lists during that time.[8]

Rank	Country	#Press Releases	% Total
1	United States	136	4.24
2	Israel (inc. West Bank and Gaza Strip)	128	3.99
3	Indonesia and East Timor	119	3.71
	Turkey	119	3.71
4	People's Republic of China	115	3.58
5	Serbia and Montenegro	104	3.24
6	United Kingdom	103	3.21
7	India	85	2.65
8	USSR and Russian Federation	80	2.49
9	Rwanda	64	2.00

10	Sri Lanka	59	1.84
Source: Ronand et al. (2005:568)[8] Data for 1986–2000			

Rank	Country	#Reports	% Total
1	Turkey	394	3.91
2	USSR and Russian Federation	374	3.71
3	People's Republic of China	357	3.54
4	United States	349	3.46
5	Israel (inc. West Bank and Gaza Strip)	323	3.21
6	South Korea	305	3.03
7	Indonesia and East Timor	253	2.51
8	Colombia	197	1.96
9	Peru	192	1.91
10	India	178	1.77
Source: Ronand et al. (2005:568)[8] Data for 1986–2000			

Artists For Amnesty

Amnesty International, through its "Artists For Amnesty" program has also endorsed various cultural media works for what its leadership often consider accurate or educational treatments of real-world topics which fall within the range of Amnesty's concern:

- *A is for Auschwitz*
- *At the Death House Door*
- *Blood Diamond*[52]
- *Bordertown*
- *Catch a Fire*
- *In Prison My Whole Life*
- *Invictus*
- *Lord of War*
- *Rendition*
- *The Constant Gardener*
- *Tibet: Beyond Fear*
- *Trouble the Water*

Organisation

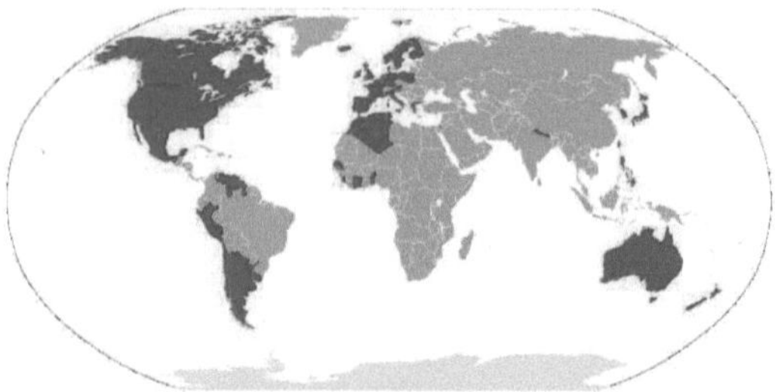

Amnesty International Sections, 2005

The Amnesty Canadian headquarters in Ottawa.

Amnesty International is largely made up of voluntary members, but retains a small number of paid professionals. In countries in which Amnesty International has a strong presence, members are organised as 'sections'. Sections coordinate basic Amnesty International activities normally with a significant number of members, some of whom will form into 'groups', and a professional staff. Each have a board of directors. In 2005 there were 52 sections worldwide. 'Structures' are aspiring sections. They also coordinate basic activities but have a smaller membership and a limited staff. In countries where no section or structure exists, people can become 'international members'. Two other organisational models exist: 'international networks', which promote specific themes or have a specific identity, and 'affiliated groups', which do the same work as section groups, but in isolation.

The organisations outlined above are represented by the International Council (IC) which is led by the IC Chairperson. Members of sections and structures have the right to appoint one or more representatives to the Council according to the size of their membership. The IC may invite representatives from International Networks and other individuals to meetings, but only representatives from sections and structures have voting rights. The function of the IC is to appoint and hold accountable internal governing bodies and to determine the direction of the movement. The IC convenes every two years.

The International Executive Committee (IEC), led by the IEC Chairperson, consists of eight members and the IEC Treasurer. It is elected by, and represents, the IC and meets biannually. The role of the IEC is to take decisions on behalf of Amnesty International, implement the strategy laid out by the IC, and ensure compliance with the organisation's statutes.

The International Secretariat (IS) is responsible for the conduct and daily affairs of Amnesty International under direction from the IEC and IC. It is run by approximately 500 professional staff members and is headed by a Secretary General. The IS operates several work programmes; International Law and Organisations; Research; Campaigns; Mobilisation; and Communications. Its offices have been located in London since its establishment in the mid-1960s.

Amnesty International is financed largely by fees and donations from its worldwide membership. It does not accept donations from governments or governmental organisations.

- *Amnesty International Sections, 2005*
  Algeria; Argentina; Australia; Austria; Belgium (Dutch speaking); Belgium (French speaking); Benin; Bermuda; Canada (English speaking); Canada (French speaking); Chile; Côte d'Ivoire; Denmark; Faroe Islands; Finland;

France; Germany; Greece; Guyana; Hong Kong; Iceland; Ireland; Israel; Italy; Japan; Korea (Republic of); Luxembourg; Mauritius; Mexico; Morocco; Nepal; Netherlands; New Zealand; Norway; Peru; Philippines; Poland; Portugal; Puerto Rico; Senegal; Sierra Leone; Slovenia; Spain; Sweden; Switzerland; Taiwan; Togo; Tunisia; United Kingdom; United States of America; Uruguay; Venezuela

- *Amnesty International Structures, 2005*
  Belarus; Bolivia; Burkina Faso; Croatia; Curaçao; Czech Republic; Gambia; Hungary; Malaysia; Mali; Moldova; Mongolia; Pakistan; Paraguay; Slovakia; South Africa; Thailand; Turkey; Ukraine; Zambia; Zimbabwe
- *IEC Chairpersons*
  Seán MacBride, 1965–1974; Dirk Börner, 1974–1977; Thomas Hammarberg, 1977–1979; José Zalaquett, 1979–1982; Suriya Wickremasinghe, 1982–1985; Wolfgang Heinz, 1985–1996; Franca Sciuto, 1986–1989; Peter Duffy, 1989–1991; Annette Fischer, 1991–1992; Ross Daniels, 1993–1997; Susan Waltz, 1996–1998; Mahmoud Ben Romdhane, 1999–2000; Colm O Cuanachain, 2001–2002; Paul Hoffman, 2003–2004; Jaap Jacobson, 2005; Hanna Roberts, 2005–2006; Lilian Gonçalves-Ho Kang You, 2006–2007; Peter Pack, 2007–present
- *Secretaries General"*

Secretary General	Office	Origin
Peter Benenson	1961–1966	Britain
Eric Baker	1966–1968	Britain
Martin Ennals	1968–1980	Britain
Thomas Hammarberg	1980–1986	Sweden
Ian Martin	1986–1992	Britain
Pierre Sané	1992–2001	Senegal
Irene Khan	2001–2010	Bangladesh
Salil Shetty	2010 –	India

Criticism

Criticism of Amnesty International includes claims of excessive pay for management, underprotection of overseas staff, associating with organizations with a dubious record on human rights protection, selection bias, ideological/foreign policy bias against either non-Western countries[53] or Western-supported countries, criticism of Amnesty's policies relating to abortion,[54] assertion that "defensive jihad" is not antithetical to human rights,[55] and organisational continuity.[53] [56] Governments who have criticised Amnesty include those of Israel, Iran, Saudi Arabia, the Democratic Republic of the Congo,[57] the People's Republic of China,[58] Vietnam,[59] Russia[60] and the United States,[61] for what they assert is one-sided reporting or a failure to treat threats to security as a mitigating factor. The actions of these governments—and of other governments critical of Amnesty International—have been the subject of human rights concerns voiced by Amnesty. As of February 2011, Amnesty is engaged in a dispute with the British union Unite over Amnesty allegedly attempting to de-recognize some of its foreign-based workers' rights.[62]

Pay Controversy

In February 2011, newspaper stories in the UK revealed that Khan had received a payment of UK £533,103 from Amnesty International following her resignation from the organisation on 31 December 2009,[63] a fact pointed to from Amnesty's records for the 2009–2010 financial year. The sum paid to her was in excess of four times her annual salary of £132,490.[63] The deputy secretary general, Kate Gilmore – who also resigned in December 2009 – received an ex-gratia payment of £320,000.[63] [64] Peter Pack, the chairman of Amnesty's international executive committee, initially stated on 19 February 2011, "The payments to outgoing secretary general Irene Khan shown in the accounts of AI (Amnesty International) Ltd for the year ending March 31st 2010 include payments made as part of a confidential agreement between AI Ltd and Irene Khan."[64] and that "It is a term of this agreement that no further comment on it will be made by either party."[63]

The payment and AI's initial response to its leakage to the press led to considerable outcry. Philip Davies, the Conservative MP for Shipley, decried the payment, telling the *Daily Express*, "I am sure people making donations to Amnesty, in the belief they are alleviating poverty, never dreamed they were subsidizing a fat cat payout. This will disillusion many benefactors."[64] On 21 February Peter Pack issued a further statement, in which he said that the payment was a "unique situation" that was "in the best interest of Amnesty's work" and that there would be no repetition of it.[63] He stated that "the new secretary general, with the full support of the IEC, has initiated a process to review our employment policies and procedures to ensure that such a situation does not happen again."[63] Pack also stated that Ammesty was "fully committed to applying all the resources that we receive from our millions of supporters to the fight for human rights".[63] On February 25, Pack issued a more complete statement intended for internal circulation among Amnesty members and staff. This in turn had been made public by Amnesty International Netherlands.[65] In summary, it states that Amnesty's International Executive Committee (IEC) in 2008 had decided not to prolong Khan's contract for a third term. In the following months, IEC discovered that due to British employment law, it had to choose between the three options of either offering Khan a third term, discontinuing her post and potentially risking legal consequences, or signing a confidential agreement and issuing a pay compensation.

See also

- 100 Days Campaign
- The Secret Policeman's Balls

Notes

a. Anthropologist Linda Rabben refers to the origin of Amnesty as a "creation myth" with a "kernel of truth": "The immediate impetus to form Amnesty did come from Peter Benenson's righteous indignation while reading a newspaper in the London tube on 19 November 1960."[66] Historian Tom Buchanan traced the origins story to a radio broadcast by Peter Benenson in 1962. The 4 March 1962 BBC news story did not refer to a "toast to liberty", but Benenson said his tube ride was on 19 December 1960. Buchanan was unable to find the newspaper article about the Portuguese students in *The Daily Telegraph* for either month. Buchanan found many news stories reporting on the repressive Portuguese political arrests in *The Times* for November 1960.[67]

References

[1] "Who we are" (http://www.amnesty.org/en/who-we-are). Amnesty International. . Retrieved 2 June 2011.

[2] "History – The Meaning of the Amnesty Candle" (http://www.amnesty.ca/about/history/history_of_amnesty_international/meaning_of_the_Amnesty_candle.php). Amnesty International. . Retrieved 4 June 2008.

[3] http://www.amnesty.org/

[4] "About Amnesty International" (http://www.amnesty.org/en/who-we-are/about-amnesty-international). Amnesty International. . Retrieved 20 July 2008.

[5] Peter Benenson. " The Forgotten Prisoners (http://www.guardian.co.uk/uk/1961/may/28/fromthearchive.theguardian)", *The Observer*, 28 May 1961. Retrieved 28 May 2011.

[6] The Nobel Prize in Peace 1977 (http://nobelprize.org/nobel_prizes/peace/laureates/1977/press.html)

[7] United Nations Prize in the field of Human Rights (http://www.ohchr.org/Documents/Press/previous_recipients.pdf)

[8] James Ronand, Howard Ramos, Kathleen Rodgers (2005), "Transnational Information Politics: NGO Human Rights Reporting, 1986–2000" (http://www.mcgill.ca/files/rgchr/ISQsubmission.pdf), International Studies Quarterly (2005) 49, 557–587

[9] Childs, Peter; Storry, Mike, eds (2002). "Amnesty International". *Encyclopedia of Contemporary British Culture*. London: Routledge. pp. 22–23.

[10] Elizabeth Keane (2006). *An Irish Statesman and Revolutionary: The Nationalist and Internationalist Politics of Sean MacBride*. I.B.Tauris. ISBN 978-1-84511-125-0.

[11] Douglas L. Wheeler, Walter C. Opello (2010). Historical Dictionary of Portugal. p.xxvi. Scarecrow Press, 2010

[12] Benenson, Peter (28 May 1961). "The forgotten prisoners" (http://web.archive.org/web/20090116041137/http://www.amnestyusa.org/about-us/the-forgotten-prisoners-by-peter-benenson/page.do?id=1101201). The Observer. Archived from the original (http://www.amnestyusa.org/about-us/the-forgotten-prisoners-by-peter-benenson/page.do?id=1101201) on 16 January 2009. . Retrieved 19 September 2006.

[13] Benenson, P. (1983). Memoir

[14] Buchanan, T. (2002). "The Truth Will Set You Free': The Making of Amnesty International". *Journal of Contemporary History* **37** (4): 575–97. doi:10.1177/00220094020370040501. JSTOR 3180761.

[15] *Amnesty International Report 1962*. Amnesty International. 1963.

[16] *Amnesty International Report 1968-69*. Amnesty International. 1969.

[17] *Amnesty International Report 1979*. Amnesty International. 1980.

[18] Monahan, Mark (4 October 2008). "Hot ticket: The Secret Policeman's Ball at the Royal Albert Hall, London" (http://www.telegraph.co.uk/culture/theatre/3561631/Hot-ticket-The-Secret-Policemans-Ball-at-the-Royal-Albert-Hall-London.html). *The Daily Telegraph.* .

[19] Amnesty International is accused of espionage (http://www.amnesty.org/russia/pdfs/justice-report-eng.pdf) Archived (http://web.archive.org/20110612050116/http://www.amnesty.org/russia/pdfs/justice-report-eng.pdf) June 12, 2011 at the Wayback Machine

[20] "Legal lessons of Pinochet case" (http://news.bbc.co.uk/1/hi/uk/617425.stm). *BBC News*. 2 March 2000. . Retrieved 23 April 2010.

[21] uncredited (31 February 2000). "Pinochet appeal fails" (http://news.bbc.co.uk/1/hi/uk/625198.stm). BBC News. . Retrieved 9 February 2009.

[22] Amnesty International News Service "Amnesty International 26th International Council Meeting Media briefing" (http://www.amnesty.org/en/library/asset/ORG10/005/2003/en/497640ed-d6a4-11dd-ab95-a13b602c0642/org100052003en.html), 15 August 2003. Retrieved 9 January 2011.

[23] *Amnesty International Report 2002*. Amnesty International. 2003.

[24] "'American Gulag'" (http://www.washingtonpost.com/wp-dyn/content/article/2005/05/25/AR2005052501838.html). The Washington Post. 26 May 2005. . Retrieved 2 October 2006.

[25] "Bush says Amnesty report 'absurd'" (http://news.bbc.co.uk/1/hi/world/americas/4598109.stm). BBC. 31 May 2005. . Retrieved 2 October 2006.

[26] *Amnesty International Report 2005: the state of the world's human rights*. Amnesty International. 2004. ISBN 978-1-887204-42-2.

[27] "Amnesty International Becomes a Pro-Choice Organization" (http://archive.newsmax.com/archives/ic/2007/8/21/153220.shtml). Archive.newsmax.com. 21 August 2007. . Retrieved 18 March 2010.

[28] Women's Rights | Amnesty International USA (http://www.amnestyusa.org/women/pdf/SRR_Resource_Toolkit.pdf)

[29] "Reports: 'Disastrous' Iraqi humanitarian crisis" (http://edition.cnn.com/2008/WORLD/meast/03/17/iraq.humanitarian/index.html). CNN. 17 March 2008. . Retrieved 17 March 2008.

[30] "Mobile Giving Foundation- Charities" (http://www.mobilegiving.org/Charities.aspx). Mobilegiving.org. . Retrieved 18 March 2010.

[31] Koutsoukis, Jason (3 July 2009). "Israel used human shields: Amnesty" (http://www.theage.com.au/world/israel-used-human-shields-amnesty-20090702-d6j2.html). Melbourne: Fairfax Digital. . Retrieved 3 July 2009.

[32] "UN must ensure Goldstone inquiry recommendations are implemented" (http://www.amnesty.org/en/news-and-updates/news/israel-gaza-implementation-un-fact-finding-mission-recommendations-crucial-justi). 15 September 2009. .

[33] Aaronovitch, David, "How Amnesty chose the wrong poster-boy; Collaboration with Moazzam Begg, an extremist who has supported jihadi movements, looks like a serious mistake," The Times, 9 February 2010, accessed 10 February 2010 (http://www.timesonline.co.uk/tol/comment/columnists/david_aaronovitch/article7019817.ece)

[34] ""Amnesty chief suspended after attacking group's links to 'Britain's most famous Taliban supporter'", Daily Mail, 9 February 2010, accessed 10 February 2010" (http://www.dailymail.co.uk/news/article-1249649/Amnesty-turmoil-suspending-chief-attacked-groups-links-Muslim-jihadists.html). London: Dailymail.co.uk. 9 February 2010. . Retrieved 18 March 2010.

[35] "Bright, Martin, "Gita Sahgal: A Statement", "Spectator", 7 February 2010, accessed 10 February 2010" (http://www.spectator.co.uk/martinbright/5759197/gita-sahgal-a-statement.thtml). Spectator.co.uk. 7 February 2010. . Retrieved 18 March 2010.

[36] "Joan Smith: Amnesty shouldn't support men like Moazzam Begg; A prisoner of conscience can turn into an apologist for extremism," *[[The Independent* (http://www.independent.co.uk/opinion/commentators/joan-smith/joan-smith-amnesty-shouldnt-support-men-like-moazzam-begg-1895848.html)], *11 February 2010, accessed 11 February 2010]*

[37] ""Amnesty International on its work with Moazzam Begg and Cageprisoners," 11 February 2010, accessed 11 February 2010" (http://www.amnestyusa.org/document.php?id=ENGNAU20100211115380&lang=e). Amnestyusa.org. 11 February 2010. . Retrieved 18 March 2010.

[38] "Salman Rushdie's statement on Amnesty International" (http://www.timesonline.co.uk/tol/news/uk/article7034773.ece), *The Sunday Times*, 21 February 2010

[39] MacShane, Member of British Parliament, Denis (10 February 2010). "Letter To Amnesty International from" (http://www.human-rights-for-all.org/spip.php?article11). . Retrieved 17 February 2010.

[40] Phillips, Melanie (14 February 2010). "The human wrongs industry spits out one of its own" (http://www.spectator.co.uk/melaniephillips/5774326/the-human-wrongs-industry-spits-out-one-of-its-own.thtml). *The Spectator*. . Retrieved 23 February 2010.

[41] Smith, Joan, "Joan Smith: Amnesty shouldn't support men like Moazzam Begg; A prisoner of conscience can turn into an apologist for extremism", *[[The Independent* (http://www.independent.co.uk/opinion/commentators/joan-smith/

joan-smith-amnesty-shouldnt-support-men-like-moazzam-begg-1895848.html)], *11 February 2010, accessed 17 February 2010]*

[42] Hitchens, Christopher, "Christopher Hitchens: Amnesty International's suspension of conscience", The *[[National Post* (http://network.nationalpost.com/np/blogs/fullcomment/archive/2010/02/17/christopher-hitchens-amnesty-international-s-suspension-of-conscience.aspx)], *17 February 2010, accessed 17 February 2010]*

[43] Bright, Martin, "Amnesty International, Moazzam Begg and the Bravery of Gita Sahgal", *[[The Spectator* (http://www.spectator.co.uk/martinbright/5757557/amnesty-international-moazzam-begg-and-the-bravery-of-gita-sahgal.thtml)], *7 February 2010]*

[44] "Misalliance; Amnesty has lent spurious legitimacy to extremists who spurn its values," *[[The Times* (http://www.timesonline.co.uk/tol/comment/leading_article/article7024113.ece)], *12 February 2010, accessed 17 February 2010]*

[45] Cohen, Nick, "We abhor torture – but that requires paying a price; Spineless judges, third-rate politicians and Amnesty prefer an easy life to fighting for liberty," *[[The Observer* (http://www.guardian.co.uk/commentisfree/2010/feb/14/nick-cohen-human-rights-binyam-mohamed)], *14 February 2010, 17 February 2010]*

[46] "USA: TORTURE, WAR CRIMES, ACCOUNTABILITY: VISIT TO SWITZERLAND OF FORMER US PRESIDENT GEORGE W. BUSH AND SWISS OBLIGATIONS UNDER INTERNATIONAL LAW: AMNESTY INTERNATIONAL'S MEMORANDUM TO THE SWISS AUTHORITIES" (http://amnesty.org/en/library/asset/AMR51/009/2011/en/e82562ec-75c9-4092-9a3a-d2d51484e67d/amr510092011en.html). Amnesty International. 6 February 2011. . Retrieved 8 February 2011.

[47] AMNESTY INTERNATIONAL - 50 years on Vimeo (http://vimeo.com/24146622)

[48] AI's FOCUS (http://www.amnesty-volunteer.org/aihandbook/ch3.html#violence)

[49] "Amnesty International defends access to abortion for women at risk" (http://web.archive.org/web/20110725004934/http://news.amnesty.org/index/ENGPOL300122007). 14 June 2007. Archived from the original (http://news.amnesty.org/index/ENGPOL300122007) on July 25, 2011. .

[50] Sexual Orientation and Gender Identity | Amnesty International (http://www.amnesty.org/en/sexual-orientation-and-gender-identity)

[51] Amnesty International "Amnesty International response to Andrés Ballesteros et al." (http://www.amnesty.org/en/library/asset/AMR23/006/2007/en/dom-AMR230062007en.pdf), *AMR 23/006/2007*, 21 February 2007. Retrieved on 4 February 2009.

[52] *About this film* - Blood Diamond (http://www.amnestyusa.org/business-and-human-rights/conflict-diamonds/about-this-film/page.do?id=1101509)

[53] Bernstein, Dennis (2002). "Interview: Amnesty on Jenin – Dennis Bernstein and Dr. Francis Boyle Discuss the Politics of Human Rights" (http://cosmos.ucc.ie/cs1064/jabowen/IPSC/articles/article0004573.html). Covert Action Quarterly. Archived (http://www.webcitation.org/5infq6M8l) from the original on 5 August 2009. . Retrieved 5 August 2009.

[54] Crary, David (2007-07-27). "Furor Over Amnesty's Abortion Stance" (http://www.usatoday.com/news/topstories/2007-07-26-1742525477_x.htm). *USA Today*. . Retrieved 2010-05-25.

[55] Hasan Suroor (2 April 2010). "The Hindu : News / International : Row over support for "defensive jihad"" (http://beta.thehindu.com/news/international/article364915.ece). Chennai, India: Beta.thehindu.com. . Retrieved 8 April 2010.

[56] CNSNews.com – Top Human Rights Group Blasted for 'Defensive Jihad' Comments (http://www.cnsnews.com/news/article/63765)

[57] DR Congo blasts Amnesty International report on repression (http://web.archive.org/web/20060103214347/http://www.namibian.com.na/Netstories/2000/January/Africa/aggression.html), *The Namibian*, 14 January 2000. Retrieved 15 May 2006.

[58] The U.S. and China This Week (http://www.uscpf.org/news/2001/02/021601.htm), U.S.-China Policy Foundation, 16 February 2001. Retrieved 15 May 2006.

[59] " The Cream of The Diplomatic Crop from Ha Noi. (http://www.thienlybuutoa.org/Misc/cream_of_the_diplomatic_crop.htm)", THIÊN LÝ BỬU TÒA. Retrieved 15 May 2006.

[60] " Russian official blasts Amnesty International over Chechnya refugees (http://www.hrvc.net/news8-03/23b-8-03.html)", Human Rights Violations in Chechnya, 22 August 2003. Retrieved 15 May 2006.

[61] Press Briefing By Scott McClellan (http://georgewbush-whitehouse.archives.gov/news/releases/2005/05/20050525-3.html#l), The White House, 25 May 2005. Retrieved 30 May 2006.

[62] Amnesty International threatens workers' rights (http://www.unitetheunion.org/news__events/latest_news/amnesty_international_threaten.aspx)

[63] Tania Mason, Charity Commission has 'no jurisdiction' over board member's payment from Amnesty (http://www.civilsociety.co.uk/finance/news/content/8390/charity_commission_has_no_jurisdiction_over_board_members_payment_from_amnesty), civilsociety.co.uk, 21 February 2011. Retrieved 21 February 2011.

[64] John Chapman, Amnesty boss gets secret £500,000 payout (http://www.express.co.uk/posts/view/229903/Amnesty-boss-gets-secret-500-000-payout), express.co.uk, 19 February 2011. Retrieved 21 February 2011.

[65] Peter Pack, A letter to all AI members and staff from the International Executive Committee. (http://www.amnesty.nl/documenten/IEC letter PP 25 February 2011.pdf), amnesty.nl, 25 February 2011. Retrieved 01 March 2011.

[66] Rabben, Linda (2001). "Amnesty International: Myth and Reality" (http://www.bu.edu/agni/essays/print/2001/54-rabben.html). *AGNI* (Boston, Massachusetts: Boston University) (54). . Retrieved 25 September 2008.

[67] Buchanan, Tom (October 2002). "'The Truth Will Set You Free': The Making of Amnesty International". *Journal of Contemporary History* **37** (4): 575–597. doi:10.1177/00220094020370040501. JSTOR 3180761.

Further reading

- Amnesty International (2005). *Amnesty International Report 2006: The State of the World's Human Rights.* Amnesty International. ISBN 978-0-86210-369-9.
- Clarke, Anne Marie (2001). *Diplomacy of Conscience: Amnesty International and Changing Human Rights Norms*. Princeton University Press. ISBN 978-0-691-05743-9.
- Hopgood, Stephen (2006). *Keepers of the Flame: Understanding Amnesty International.* Cornell University Press. ISBN 978-0-8014-4402-9.
- Power, Jonathan (1981). *Amnesty International: The Human Rights Story*. McGraw-Hill. ISBN 978-0-08-028902-1.
- Sellars, Kirsten (April 2002). *The Rise and Rise of Human Rights*. Sutton Publishing Ltd. ISBN 978-0-7509-2755-0.

External links

- Amnesty International official site (http://www.amnesty.org/)
- Is Amnesty International Biased? (http://www.globalpolicy.org/ngos/credib/2003/1306interview.htm), 2002 discussion by Dennis Bernstein and Dr. Francis Boyle
- Amnesty International Head Irene Khan on The Unheard Truth: Poverty and Human Rights (http://www.democracynow.org/2009/10/16/amnesty_international_head_irene_khan_on) – video by *Democracy Now!*
- Amnesty International Promotion to Eliminate the Death Penalty (http://shorts.nthword.com/2010/06/ad-of-week-amnesty-international-death.html) – video by TBWA/Paris and Pleix for Amnesty International France

Martin Ennals Award for Human Rights Defenders

The **Martin Ennals Award for Human Rights Defenders**, called also "the Nobel Prize for human rights", was created in 1993 to honour and protect individuals around the world who demonstrate exceptional courage in defending and promoting human rights. Its principal aim is to provide special protection ("protective publicity") to human rights defenders who are at risk by focusing international media attention on their plight, mainly through television, radio, internet and the press, particularly in their country of origin.

The award carries a cash prize of 20,000 Swiss francs to be used by the award winners to support their work in the field of human rights.

The annual ceremony takes place in Geneva in October.

The award is named after Martin Ennals, past secretary general of Amnesty International.

An international jury, composed of representatives of ten leading human rights organizations, selects the award winner each year. Members of the Jury include Amnesty International, Human Rights Watch, International Federation of Human Rights, World Organisation Against Torture, Front Line Defenders, International Commission of Jurists, Human Rights First, International Service for Human Rights, Diakonie Germany, and Huridocs.

Recipients

- 1994: Harry Wu (China)
- 1995: Asma Jahangir (Pakistan)
- 1996: Clement Nwankwo (Nigeria)
- 1997: Bishop Samuel Ruiz García (Mexico)
- 1998: Dr. Eyad El Sarraj (Palestina)
- 1999: Natasha Kandic (Yugoslavia)
- 2000: Immaculée Birhaheka (DR Congo)
- 2001: Peace Brigades International (Colombia)
- 2002: Jacqueline Moudeina (Chad)
- 2003: Alirio Uribe Muñoz (Colombia)
- 2004: Lidia Yusupova (Russia)
- 2005: Aktham Naisse (Syria)
- 2006: Akbar Ganji (Iran) and Arnold Tsunga (Zimbabwe)
- 2007: Rajan Hoole (Sri Lanka), Kopalasingham Sritharan (Sri Lanka) and Pierre Claver Mbonimpa (Burundi)
- 2008: Mutabar Tadjibaeva (Uzbekistan)
- 2009: Emad Baghi (Iran)
- 2010: Muhannad Al-Hassani (Syria)
- 2011: Kasha Jacqueline Nabagesera (Uganda)

External links

The International Secretariat of the Martin Ennals Award is based in Geneva, for images and documentation see:

- Martin Ennals Award website [1]

References

[1] http://www.martinennalsaward.org/index.html

Thorolf Rafto Memorial Prize

The Professor Thorolf Rafto Memorial Prize (*Raftostiftelsen*) is a human rights award established in the memory of the Norwegian human right activist, Thorolf Rafto.

Organization

The prize is awarded annually by the Rafto Foundation for Human Rights, which was founded in the humanistic tradition of the Helsinki Accords in order to promote the fundamental human rights of intellectual and political freedom. Today, the foundation is based at the Human Rights House in Bergen, Norway. The major work of the foundation, including the organization of the award ceremony is done by a small team of professional staff and volunteers. The award ceremony takes place at Den Nationale Scene in Bergen annually in November.

The initial idea of the Rafto Prize was to provide a basic informative platform for the laureates that would help to receive further attention from the international media and support from political and non-political organisations. By awarding the Rafto Prize, the Rafto Foundation for Human Rights seeks to bring attention to independent voices that due to oppressive and corruptive regimes are not always heard. For example, four Rafto Laureates have subsequently received further international assistance and were awarded the Nobel Peace Prize. Aung San Suu Kyi, Jose Ramos-Horta, Kim Dae-jung and Shirin Ebadi were awarded the Rafto Prize prior to the Nobel Peace Prize.[1]

History

Thorolf Rafto was a professor of Economic History at the Norwegian School of Economics and Business Administration (NHH). He was also well known for his political activism in Eastern Europe, especially in Hungary, Czechoslovakia and Poland. During a visit to Prague in 1979 to hold a lecture for students excluded from universities for political reasons, Rafto was arrested and brutally beaten up by the communist security police. Inflicted injuries dramatically weakened his health. On 4 November 1986 Thorolf Rafto died. [2]

However, his friends and colleagues agreed to establish a foundation that would continue Rafto's work such as promotion of freedom of speech and political expression in Eastern Europe. It was also decided to introduce a prize for human right activists. Nevertheless, the fall of the Iron Curtain and consequential democratization of Eastern European states led to a reconsideration the status of the foundation. Meanwhile it had opened new possibilities to work with other geographical regions in a promotion of human rights. Already in 1990, the Rafto Prize was awarded to a Burmese democratic leader, Aung San Suu Kyi who, in the following year 1991, received the Nobel Peace Prize for her non-violent struggle for democracy and human rights. For the first years, the foundation was based at the Norwegian School of Economics and Business Administration. From 1997, the Rafto Foundation was relocated to the Human Rights House of Bergen, Norway. [3]

Ceremony

The Rafto Prize is awarded annually on the first Sunday in November and since 1990, the official ceremony takes place at the National Theatre of Bergen. Among the invited guests are representatives from Bergen municipality and the Norwegian government, academics, supporters and partners of the Rafto Foundation and family members of the Rafto family.

Criteria and Nomination Process

The annual deadline for nominations is 1 April. Voluntary organisations, institutions and individuals worldwide, with knowledge or interest in human rights are allowed to nominate candidates for the Rafto Prize. Former recipients of the prize can also nominate candidates, although candidates who are nominated by themselves or by their staff or by honorary officers will not be taken into consideration. After the deadline, all applications are carefully considered by the prize committee and the final decision is usually released at the press conference at Rafto House in September.[4]

List of Laureates

Year	Laureate(s)	Country
2010	Bishop José Raúl Vera López	Mexico
2009	Malahat Nasibova	Azerbaijan
2008	Pastor Bulambo Lembelembe Josué[5] [6]	Democratic Republic of the Congo
2007	National Campaign on Dalit Human Rights	India
2006	Thich Quang Do	Vietnam
2005	Lidia Yusupova	Russia
2004	Rebiya Kadeer	China
2003	Paulos Tesfagiorgis	Eritrea
2002	Sidi Mohammed Daddach	Western Sahara
2001	Shirin Ebadi	Iran
2000	Kim Dae-jung	South Korea
1999	Gennady Grushevoy	Belarus
1998	ECPAT	Thailand
1997	The Romani people, represented by Ian Hancock	Romani people
1996	Palermo Anno Uno	Italy
1995	Union of the Committees of Soldiers' Mothers of Russia	Russia
1994	Leyla Zana	Turkey
1993	The people of East Timor, represented by José Ramos-Horta	East Timor
1992	Preah Maha Ghosananda	Cambodia
1991	Jelena Bonner	Russia
1990	Aung San Suu Kyi	Burma
1989	Doina Cornea FIDESZ (Dr Peter Molnar)	Romania Hungary
1988	Trivimi Velliste	Estonian SSR

1987	Jiří Hájek	Czechoslovakia

References

[1] *Raftostiftelsen* (Store norske leksikon) (http://www.snl.no/Raftostiftelsen)
[2] *Thorolf Rafto* (Store norske leksikon) (http://www.snl.no/Thorolf_Rafto)
[3] *Thorolf Rafto/utdypning* (Store norske leksikon) (http://www.snl.no/.nbl_biografi/Thorolf_Rafto/utdypning)
[4] *About the Rafto Foundation* (Rafto Foundation for Human Rights) (http://www.rafto.org/?page=38)
[5] "Prestigious human rights prize to Eastern Congo" (http://www.norway.org/policy/news/rafto_08_en.htm). *Norwegian Ministry of Foreign Affairs* (Norway.org). 3 October 2008. . Retrieved 2008-10-06.
[6] Berglund, Nina (25 September 2008). "Congo church leader wins Rafto Prize" (http://www.aftenposten.no/english/local/article2674921.ece). Aftenposten. . Retrieved 2008-09-25.

External links

- Rafto Laureates (http://www.rafto.org/)

International Federation for Human Rights

fidh Fédération internationale des ligues des droits de l'Homme	
Type	Federation of Human Rights Organisations Non-profit NGO
Founded	1922
Location	Global International secretariat in Paris, France.
Key people	Souhayr Belhassen (President since 2007) Ales Bialatski (Vice President)[1] René Cassin Joseph Paul-Boncour Victor Basch
Services	Protect human rights defenders, ensure effective human rights, and justice for all, globalisation with due respect for human rights.
Method	Fact-finding missions, judicial observations, training, exchange programs, research, permanent lobbying of intergovernmental organisations, mobilizing public opinion.
Members	164 human rights organisations in more than 100 countries
Motto	Human Rights for All.[2]
Website	www.fidh.org [3]

The **International Federation for Human Rights** (**FIDH**) is a non-governmental federation for human rights organizations. Founded in 1922, FIDH is the oldest international human rights organisation worldwide and today brings together 164 member organisations in over 100 countries.

FIDH is nonpartisan, nonsectarian, and independent of any government. Its core mandate is to promote respect for all the rights set out in the Universal Declaration of Human Rights, the International Covenant on Civil and Political Rights, and the International Covenant on Economic, Social and Cultural Rights.[4] [5]

FIDH co-ordinates and supports the actions of its members and is their contact with intergovernmental organisations. The FIDH has a consultative status with the United Nations, UNESCO and the Council of Europe, and the status of observer with the African Commission on Human and Peoples' Rights.

Overview

FIDH was established in 1922, when it united ten national organizations. It is a federation of 164 human rights organizations[6] in nearly 100 countries. Among which are the French *Ligue des droits de l'homme* (LDH) and the Palestinian Society for the Protection of Human Rights. FIDH coordinates and supports the activities of its member organizations, at the local, regional and international levels. Like its members, FIDH is not linked to any party or religion, and is independent. FIDH has a consultative status before the United Nations, UNESCO and the Council of Europe, and observer status before the African Commission on Human and Peoples' Rights, the Organisation internationale de la Francophonie and the International Labour Organization.[7]

FIDH also has "regular contact" with the European Union, Organization for Security and Cooperation in Europe, Organization of American States, United Nations Development Programme, World Trade Organization, International Monetary Fund, World Bank, and Organisation for Economic Co-operation and Development.[7]

FIDH's mandate "is to contribute to the respect of all the rights defined in the Universal Declaration of Human Rights." It aims to make "effective improvements in the protection of victims, the prevention of Human Rights violations and the sanction of their perpetrators." Its priorities are established by its World Congress and International Board (22 members) with the support of its International Secretariat (30 staff members).[7]

Funding

FIDH's total income in 2005 was €3,503,106 (nearly US$4.5m), of which €2,803,294 (over US$3.5m) came from "grants and donations," comprising approximately 80% of its income. FIDH's finances lack transparency, as funding sources are not itemized on its website or in financial statements, and no response was received to letters requesting this information. Instead, FIDH lists general figures and provides a financial summary: "FIDH relies heavily on donations from the public and from private businesses, contributions from its member organizations and on the commitment of its voluntary workers. It also receives grants from international and national bodies, and from foundations..."[7]

Priorities

Protecting human rights defenders: The Observatory for the Protection of Human Rights Defenders, FIDH's joint program with the World Organization Against Torture (OMCT), works for the implementation of the UN Declaration on Human Rights Defenders, and supports the mandates of the UN Special Rapporteur on Human Rights Defenders and the Special Rapporteur of the African Commission. The Observatory advocates for the establishment of new mechanisms for the protection of human rights defenders, for example, within the Council of Europe and the OSCE. In 2004, the FIDH/OMCT Observatory for the Protection of Human Rights Defenders addressed 1,154 cases, in over 90 countries, with the collaboration of approximately 200 Human Rights organisations.[8] In 2005, the Observatory dealt with almost 850 cases, in approximately 60 countries, with the collaboration of about 400 human rights organizations, and sent 11 fact-finding and trial observation missions.

Justice for victims: fighting impunity: FIDH provides support and assistance to victims throughout their search for justice actions FIDH made a significant contribution to the establishment of the International Criminal Court (ICC), and in 2004 opened a permanent office at the ICC in The Hague. Currently, FIDH is involved in approximately 20 cases before domestic courts and the ICC, as well as in transitional justice processes in several countries. In 2005, FIDH transmitted the first applications by victims to participate in proceedings before the ICC, in relation to the investigation in the Democratic Republic of Congo. This led to the first decision of the ICC in January 2006 focusing on the regime for the participation of victims before the Court, in which all the applications transmitted by FIDH were accepted.

Advocating respect for human rights in the context of globalization: FIDH seeks to ensure the protection of economic, social and cultural rights, the primacy of human rights over trade law and the participation of civil society in international economic organizations. FIDH aims to strengthen the social responsibilities of corporations through dialogue with transnational corporations as well as through litigation. In 2005, FIDH obtained public commitments from Carrefour (the second largest retailer worldwide) to comply with and promote international human rights law.

Defending women's rights: FIDH campaigns against discrimination against women through its newly created Action Group for Women's Rights, headed by Shirin Ebadi, Nobel Peace Prize winner. The core aim of the movement is to work towards the effective implementation of the United Nations Convention for the Elimination of All Forms of Discrimination Against Women (CEDAW).[8] In this context, in 2005, FIDH organized fact-finding missions, submitted alternative reports to the CEDAW Committee, and launched a regional campaign in the broader

Middle East and North Africa.

Promoting respect for human rights in the context of counter-terrorism: Since 2002, FIDH has initiated and supported key proceedings before domestic courts, regional and international mechanisms, in cases concerning arbitrary measures and practices in the 'fight against terrorism'. FIDH campaigns within IGOs for the implementation of procedures to prevent human rights abuses. In 2005, FIDH reinforced its cooperation with the Center for Constitutional Rights (CCR) through supporting actions initiated by CCR, in particular in relation to Guantánamo and Abu Ghraib. FIDH also contributed significantly to the finalization of the draft UN Convention against Enforced Disappearances.

Activities

Monitoring and promoting human rights, assisting victims: These activities, including fact-finding and trial observation missions, research, advocacy and litigation, are implemented by independent human rights experts from all regions. Between 2004 and 2005, FIDH published over 550 press statements and organized approximately 90 international fact-finding and trial observation missions in over 60 countries.

Mobilizing the international community: FIDH provides guidance and support to its member organizations and other local partners in their interactions with international and regional inter-governmental organizations (IGOs). To ensure the effective implementation of these activities, FIDH has established delegations at the UN in Geneva and New York, at the European Union in Brussels and, since 2006, at the League of Arab States in Cairo. From 2004 to 2005, FIDH filed and supported over 500 cases before international IGOs. FIDH participates in standard-setting processes and promotes the establishment of monitoring mechanisms.

Supporting national NGOs and increasing their capacity: FIDH, together with its members and partners, implements cooperation programs at the national level, aimed at strengthening the capacity of human rights organizations. FIDH provides training and assists in creating opportunities for dialogue with authorities. From 2004 to 2005, FIDH undertook such programs in 32 countries in Africa, 16 in Latin America, 3 in Asia and 10 in the North Africa/Middle Eastern region.

Raising awareness: informing, alerting, bearing witness: FIDH draws public attention to the outcomes of its missions, its research findings and eyewitness accounts of human rights violations, by means of press releases, press conferences, open letters, mission reports, urgent appeals, petitions, and the FIDH website. In 2005, internet traffic on www.fidh.org amounted to approximately 2 million pages visited, and 400 references to FIDH per day were calculated on websites based in over 100 countries.

Structure

FIDH has its headquarters in Paris. It relies primarily on a pool of dedicated volunteers. The organizational structure consists of elected boards and a small body of permanent staff who support the activities of the board members and the mission delegates.

Every three years, the FIDH Congress gathers together member organizations to elect the International Board, fix the priorities of the organization and decide whether to grant membership to new partners or to exclude member organizations which no longer satisfy the requirements laid down in the organization's statutes.

The FIDH International Board reflects the diversity if its constituent organizations. It is composed of a President, Treasurer, 15 Vice-presidents and 5 Secretaries General, all of whom work on a voluntary basis and represent all regions of the world. Honorary Presidents have consultative status on the International Board. The International Board meets 3 times per year to define FIDH's political and strategic orientations and to draw up and approve the budget.

The Executive Board is composed of the President, the Treasurer and the 5 Secretaries General, and is responsible for the management of FIDH on a daily basis. It also draws on the particular expertise of mission delegates. The

Deputy Secretaries General, elected by the International Board, sit on the Executive Board with consultative status. This body meets once per month to take decisions on current concerns and requests submitted by member organizations.

The two Boards call on the expertise of other collaborators in FIDH's activities, including the permanent delegates to intergovernmental organizations and the mission delegates. The team of mission delegates gathers together several hundred individuals from all regions.

The International Secretariat is based in Paris. It implements decisions taken by the International and Executive Boards and ensures regular support to member organizations. The Secretariat employs 30 permanent staff, assisted by interns and volunteers.

References

[1] "Warning against Mr. Ales Bialatski" (http://www.fidh.org/Warning-against-Mr-Ales-Bialatski-President-of). International Federation for Human Rights. 16 February 2011. . Retrieved 3 June 2011.

[2] "FIDH's motto: Human Rights for All!" (http://www.fidh.org). FIDH. . Retrieved 1 September 2010.

[3] http://www.fidh.org/

[4] Contribution to the EU Multi-stakeholder Forum on CSR (Corporate Social Responsibility) (http://ec.europa.eu/enterprise/policies/sustainable-business/files/csr/documents/stakeholder_forum/fidh_en.pdf), 10 February 2009; accessed on 9 November 2009

[5] Information Partners (http://www.unhcr.org/refworld/partners.html), web site of the UNHCR, last updated 25 February 2010, 16:08 GMT (web retrieval 25 February 2010, 18:11 GMT)

[6] List of the FIDH's 164 organisations (http://www.fidh.org/164-organisations-de-defense-des-droits-de-l) (web retrieval 22 February 2010)

[7] NGO Monitor on FIDH (http://www.ngo-monitor.org/article/fidh_prioritizing_politics_over_protection) September 28, 2006; accessed 9 November 2009

[8] Acting FIDH (http://www.fidh.org/-Acting-FIDH-), on the website of the organization, accessed on 9 November 2009

External links

- FIDH (http://www.fidh.org)

Death threat

A **death threat** is a threat, often made anonymously, by one person or a group of people to kill another person or groups of people. These threats are usually designed to intimidate victims in order to manipulate their behavior, thus a death threat is a form of coercion. For example, a death threat could be used to dissuade a public figure from pursuing a criminal investigation or an advocacy campaign.

In many jurisdictions, death threats are a criminal offense. Death threats are often covered by coercion statutes. For instance, the coercion statute in Alaska says:

> A person commits the crime of coercion if the person compels another to engage in conduct from which there is a legal right to abstain or abstain from conduct in which there is a legal right to engage, by means of instilling in the person who is compelled a fear that, if the demand is not complied with, the person who makes the demand or another may inflict physical injury on anyone....[1]

Methods

A death threat can be communicated via a wide range of mediums, among these letters, newspaper publications, telephone calls, internet blogs,[2] and e-mail. If the threat is made against a political figure, it can also be considered treason. If a threat is against a non-living location that frequently contains living individuals (e.g. a building) it could be a terrorist threat. Sometimes death threats are part of a wider campaign of abuse targeting a person or a group of people (see terrorism, mass murder).

Here is an example of an actual death threat, from the book *Wordcrime* by John Olsson. This is a genuine example from a criminal case, provided by the Forensic Linguistics Institute, which analyzes all kinds of text, including traditional letters, ransom demands, hate mail, various texts via mobile phone; SMS device, etc., for authorship:

> Boris: I am one of the 4 employees still in the office. I have withheld my identity because I have realised that nothing is a secret any more, the author of the anonymous doc is now a public information. I write as a matter of genuine concern. We in the office are convinced that there is a real threat at your life, some mysterious people are looking for you (different people at different times). They are not genuine people. The cops are also looking for you, they say they want to return you to court, they look like there is more than meets the eye or more that we know of. regards

Death threats against a head of state

In some monarchies and republics, both democratic and authoritarian, threatening to kill the head of state and/or head of government (such as the sovereign, president, or prime minister) is considered a crime for which punishments vary. US law provides for up to 5 years in prison for threatening the President of the United States. In the United Kingdom, under the Treason Felony Act 1848, it is illegal to attempt to kill or deprive the monarch of her throne; this offense was originally punished with penal transportation and then was changed to the death penalty and currently the penalty is life imprisonment.

Osman warning, letter or notice

These are warnings of death threat or high risk of murder that are issued by British police or legal authorities to the expected victim.[3] They are used when there is intelligence of the threat, but there is not enough evidence to justify the police arresting the expected murderer.[4]

The warnings are named after a high-profile case, Osman v United Kingdom, of police failing to protect individuals despite some warning signs pointing at impending aggression. The murderer in this case said to the police: "Why didn't you stop me before I did it, I gave you all the warning signs?" The police had known that the murderer had posed a threat to several people, and had carried out criminal acts against some of them, but the police had not informed those at risk of the seriousness of the threat.[5] In September 1989 the family commenced a civil action in negligence against the police. This was dismissed by the High Court and then upheld on appeal in 1992. Further action was taken by the family in the European Commission of Human Rights beginning in November 1993 with a final report being issued in 1997.[6]

See also

- Assassination
- Bomb threat
- Coercion
- Extortion
- Assault
- Witness intimidation
- United States Federal Witness Protection Program
- United States Marshals Service
- Terrorism
- Hostage
- Interrogation
- Kidnapping
- Torture
- Secret Service
- Bulletproof vest
- Armour
- Undercover
- Contract killing
- Informant
- Stalking

References

[1] Alaska Statute 11.41.530(a)(1) (http://www.touchngo.com/lglcntr/akstats/Statutes/Title11/Chapter41/Section530.htm)
[2] *Blog death threats spark debate* (http://news.bbc.co.uk/1/hi/6499095.stm) BBC News retrieved September 30, 2007
[3] http://www.thescottishsun.co.uk/scotsol/homepage/news/2157509/Dads-death-threat-warning.html
[4] http://www.bedfordtoday.co.uk/bed-news/Beds-is-one-of-nations.4185282.jp
[5] http://www.timesonline.co.uk/tol/news/uk/crime/article4092890.ece
[6] http://a-level-law.com/tort/Negligence/osman.html

External links

- Judiciary Criminal Charges (http://72.14.207.104/search?q=cache:dkGiT5RMbqsJ:www.judiciary.state.nj.us/criminal/charges/terrthrt2.doc+death+threat+reasonable+believe+carried+out&hl=en&gl=us&ct=clnk&cd=1)
- (http://www.thetext.co.uk) The Forensic Linguistics Institute

Article Sources and Contributors

Lidia Yusupova *Source*: http://en.wikipedia.org/w/index.php?title=Lidia_Yusupova *Contributors*: Alex Bakharev, Altenmann, Asarelah, Buldri, Conscious, Espenrh, ForrestSjap, Grieg, HanzoHattori, Hippophaë, Hodja Nasreddin, Lomis, Marsal20, Moralist, Pechorin214, Rich Farmbrough, Samian, Sten, Tibetibet, 11 anonymous edits

Coordinator *Source*: http://en.wikipedia.org/w/index.php?title=Coordinator *Contributors*: Access Denied, Ace Class Shadow, Assassinslast, Astronautics, Cburnett, Croatnik, D6, DMG413, Darkhunger, DeadEyeArrow, Dispenser, Howrealisreal, Iceberg3k, IgorTrieste, John-1107, Lgusain, Loremaster, Lysy, Michael Hardy, Philip Trueman, Redxiv, Rjobidon, TFrenay, TheFarix, Tocapa, Wmahan, Yas, 43 anonymous edits

Human rights *Source*: http://en.wikipedia.org/w/index.php?title=Human_rights *Contributors*: 10metreh, 24.251.118.xxx, 3Juno3, 4lex, 9258fahsflkh917fas, A little insignificant, ARUNKUMAR P.R, Aao2107, Aar-bro, AaronSw, Aasgaard, Abelass, AbsolutDan, Abu Murtad, Adam McMaster, Adamsneyd, Adashiel, Addi-1690, Addihockey10, Addshore, AdiJapan, AdultSwim, Advisor5, Aeonx, Aetheling, Ahering@cogeco.ca, Ahoerstemeier, Aille, Airconswitch, Airplaneman, Aitias, Aj00200, Ajbpearce, Alan Liefting, Alananellie, Alansohn, Alarics, Alarm, Ale jrb, Alex756, AlexJP, Alexemanuel, AlexiusHoratius, Alexthe5th, Alienus, Aliyosufi, Allstarecho, Almafeta, Almagor35, AlphaEta, Alsandro, Altenmann, Altermike, AnakngAraw, Anarchia, Ancheta Wis, Andeggs, Andonic, Andre Engels, Andres, Andrew c, Andrwsc, Andy M. Wang, Andy Marchbanks, Andy pyro, AngelOfSadness, Ann Stouter, AnnaFrance, Antaeus Feldspar, Antandrus, Aogouguo, Apollon, Apollonia70, Aquillion, Arad, Arctic Night, ArglebargleIV, Aridd, Ark, Armaiti, Artaxiad, Arthena, Article29, Articnomad, Asarelah, Asifsaleh, Assyria 90, Athenean, Atlant, Auntof6, Avala, Awal, AxelBoldt, Az1568, Azeemahmed, BMF81, Babecorp, Baby gift idea, Bahahs, Balaji7, Bambuway, BankingBum, BanyanTree, Barcars, Bardslc01, Barek, Bcorr, Bdean1963, Becca9879, Beeblebrox, Behmod, Beland, Ben Ben, Bender235, Bensims2, Berkut, Besmirqe, Beyond My Ken, Beyond the classroom, Bhadani, Big Adamsky, Billcica, Billgunyon, Billysb1tch, Bjdehut, Bkell, Blanchardb, BlastOButter42, Blcfilm, Bll arch, Blogfidh, Bluaardvark, Bob f it, Bobbobbobbobson, Bobo The Ninja, Bobo192, Bogdangiusca, Bolivian Unicyclist, Bongwarrior, Bookandcoffee, Bookuser, Boothy443, BorgQueen, Boud, Bowlhover, Boyd Reimer, Bradz01214452701, BredoteauU2, Brenont, BrianGV, Brideshead, Brion VIBBER, Bristoltrolley, Brocach, Buffs, BusterD, Butros, Bwilkins, C mon, CENSORofWIKIPEDIA, CERminator, CIreland, Cactus.man, Cagliost, Calliopejen1, Calneva1977, Caltas, Cambodia123, Can't sleep, clown will eat me, CanadianLinuxUser, Cantiorix, Carlon, Carmichael95, Cassandra99, Catgut, Catquas, Cautious, Cedric31, Cenarium, Censor of Wikipedia, ChaosSorcerer91, CharlotteWebb, Charnell th, Chealer, Chelseawoman, Chesaguy, Chibi Goku, Chipmunker, Chmod007, Chowbok, ChrisJones, Christopher Connor, Christopher Kraus, Chwyatt, Ciaccona, Civil Engineer III, Ckincaid77, Clark89, Cloyle, Clubjuggle, Cnajmee, Cometstyles, Commissarusa, CommonsDelinker, Commsintern2, Connor2214, Contaldo80, Conversion script, Cordless Larry, Corpx, Courcelles, Cpl Syx, Craig Pemberton, CrazyChemGuy, CrazyRob926, Cuchullain, Cyferx, DARTH SIDIOUS 2, DBG2011, DCDuring, DJ Clayworth, DMacks, DVD R W, Dal2054, Dancter, DanielZ.thi, Danski14, Darigan, Dark Mage, Darkred, Darkspots, Darkwind, Darthgriz98, Davewild, David Biddulph, David Le Page, David.Monniaux, David91, DavidA, DavidBrooks, DavidLevinson, DavidSpencer.ca, Davidellerman, Davie4264, Davinhutchins, Davshul, Dawn Bard, Ddddoooo, Ddesignboy, Ddrd, DeadEyeArrow, DealPete, Debresser, Deeptrivia, Demonictouch, Deprifry, DerHexer, Derek Ross, Dergall, Descendall, Devinish, Dialecticexpert, Dicul, Diderot.alembert, Dirtybutclean, Disambigutron, Discospinster, Discover Toad, Djmckee1, Dmol, DocWatson42, Doctors of the world uk, Doffe, Doldrums, DominicBuch, Dominus, Doomedtx, Dougcweho, Dougweller, Download, Dpbsmith, Dpr, Dr.peter, Drawat123, Drtoddlandman, Dubkiller, Duffman, Durin, Dwarf Kirlston, Dycedarg, Earth, Easterbradford, Economic, Social and Cultural Rights, EdGl, Edi45, Editing19473, Edivorce, Edward321, Edwy, Ekki01, Ekotkie, El C, ElKevbo, Elassint, ElationAviation, Eldoffo, Elembis, Eléonore Dziurzynski, Eman2129, Emancipated, Emble64, Emily GABLE, Emmisa, Enkhbayar, Enviroboy, EoGuy, Epbr123, Es fecha, Esanchez7587, EscapingLife, Europeanhistorian, Evanhotep, Evenios, Everyking, Evin290, Ewebb49, Excirial, Fantastic4boy, Faradayplank, Favonian, Fay.farstad, Felixboy, Finalnight, Finnegans wake, FitzColinGerald, Fixer88, Flatterworld, Flipflopae, Flowerpotman, Fnlayson, Folantin, Foldo, Foxy12, Frazzydee, Fredrik, Freepalestine, Freiberg, FreplySpang, Fsotrain09, Funtimefreddie007, Fuseau, Fyyer, Fæ, GB fan, GRM7, Gabbe, Gabi S., Galoubet, Gdo01, Geeoharee, GeistOp, Gemma18, George100, Germaine01, Gerrit, Gfoley4, Gggh, Gianfranco, Giglett25, Gilliam, Ginginator, Giraffedata, Globalsolidarity, Gnevin, GoetheFromm, Gogo Dodo, Goon Noot, Goplat, Graham87, Greg kogan, Gregbard, Gromlakh, Grunners, Gsureshdurai, Gurch, Guthrie, Guy Peters, Guðsþegn, HJ Mitchell, HLindholt, HaeB, Hagerman, Hairy Dude, Hajor, Half price, Hallows AG, Hamamelis, HamburgerRadio, Harry 126, Harry128, Harryboyles, Haseo9999, Haymaker, Helenakwong, Hellogoodbye122, Hemlock Martinis, Hera1aphrodite, Here, Hermis, HexaChord, Himynameisbenny, HippiesRockWeed, Hirohisat, History2007, Hjr, Hma38, Hmains, Hodja Nasreddin, Hoffa2000, Hongooi, Hoping To Help, Howard Alexander, Hrhw, Hrolf123, Humanity2010, Humanrightsp3, Husond, I dream of horses, Iames, Ian Pitchford, Id447, Ifnord, Ifudofhumanrights, Ihrapune, Immunize, Imnotminkus, InMyHumbleOpinion, Indian Literati, Indon, InnerJustice, Inomyabcs, Insaninater, Insanity Incarnate, InsightADB, Into The Fray, Ireyes, Iridescence, Iridescent, Irmgard, IronGargoyle, Ishdarian, Ishootppl, Itsabouttime, Itsmejudith, Iwoz1, J. 'mach' wust, J. W. Love, J.delanoy, JCDenton2052, JCO312, JEN9841, JGHowes, JHanmer, JJGD, JW1805, Jackswiki, Jacob CARNEY, Jacob.jose, Jagged 85, Jagz, Jakew, Jam000qaz, Jared Preston, Jason Quinn, Jatkins, Jayjg, Jdavidb, Jeffreyn, Jegonzal, Jenarthur, Jevergreen, Jeyarajride, Jftw, Jfulgham, Jfwed, Jh51681, Jhessian Zombie, Jim, JimVC3, JimWae, Jimmyvanthach, Jmanigold, JoanneB, Jodiepoopoopoo, Johan1298, Johannes Rohr, Johannes.Ernst, John, Johnbrownsbody, Johnman239, Johnnie ong, Joie de Vivre, Jon72790, Joowwww, Jovianeye, Joy, Joyous!, Jpeob, Jrtayloriv, Jsc83, Jtankh, Judgesurreal777, Jujutacular, Jumbuck, JusticeforChildren, KHamsun, KJS77, KPH2293, Kaaveh Ahangar, Kahananite, Kaobear, Karam.Anthony.K, Kariteh, Karl-Henner, Karthikganapathy, Katana0182, Katieh5584, Katquack, Khazar, Khendon, Khoikhoi, Kimmelaar, King of kings121, Kipala, Kirachinmoku, Kit Berg, Kman665, Knezovjb, KnowledgeOfSelf, Konstock, Koyaanis Qatsi, Kreeve, Kubigula, Kukini, Kuru, Kurykh, Kylu, Kzollman, L Kensington, L'euphorie, LA2, LTJ, Lapicero, Lars Washington, Law, Lcalc, Ledenierhomme, Lemcke, Lerdsuwa, Leszek Jańczuk, Lethe, Letshearit, Letthecardsfall, Levineps, Lexda, Lightmouse, LilHelpa, LilyKitty, Lir, Littlealien182, Livedonzer, LizardJr8, Lmno, Logan, Lordmanwe, Lori Meyers100, Lot49a, LouisaDenier, Lowellian, Lucinor, Ludwigs2, Luna Santin, Lupin, Lupo, Lwray, Lynn Wilbur, M4gnum0n, M87, MCB, MDHupman, MER-C, Mac, Maclab, Madhero88, MagdalenaS, Majlesi5, MantisEars, Marekzp, Marielleh, Mark Renier, MarkSweep, Markaci, Marklar2007, Martinezmf2, Master Jay, Mateo SA, Materialscientist, Mattb112885, Matusz, Maunus, Max543, Maxcrc, Maximaximax, Maximum Nuts, Maziotis, Mboverload, McSly, Mchsmc, Mct475, Md84419, Megapixie, Mehrshad123, Meiskam, Mekri, Melsaran, Mendisd, Mentifisto, Merbenz, Meriddien, Meritus, Merlion444, Mermaid from the Baltic Sea, Merqurial, Mervyn Emrys, Meske, Metsavend, Mikko Paananen, Miltonzs, Mimithebrain, Mindmatrix, Mitch1981, Mitcheyyehctim, Mitoman1, Mitso Bel, Mjpieters, Mkaksone, Mlessard, Mon4ever, Monikahingorani, Moogwrench, Mootros, Moreschi, Morphh, Morwen, Mostlyharmless, Mr. Billion, Mr. Lefty, MrFish, MrOllie, Mrzaius, MuZemike, Munci, Mushroom, Mxn, NSD Student, NYScholar, Nableezy, Nahald, Nahlesu, Namorfilus, Nandesuka, Napzilla, Natalie West, NawlinWiki, Neilc, NellieBly, Nescio, Neutrality, Neverquick, Newsbreak, Ngethsamneang, Ngthsamneang, Nielsu, Nihiltres, Nikodemos, NimbusWeb, Nirvana2013, Nivix, Nk, Nnemo, Noctibus, Nomdewiki, Nopetro, Noraggingfoundation, Normann Z, Notinasnaid, Nposs, Nuview, NazismIsntCool, O^O, Odie5533, Olivier, Omphaloscope, Opelio, Orange Suede Sofa, Orangemike, Orpheus, Other Choices, Outerstyx, OwenX, Owerby, Oxymoron83, PCHS-NJROTC, PFrisbie, PIrish, PM800, PTSE, ParthianShot, Parveenkomal, Paul A, Pdcook, Pecher, Pedwe, Penbat, PennsylvaniaPatriot, Pepper, Peterdjones, Pexise, Pfhorrest, Pgan002, Pganas, Phil Bridger, Philip Baird Shearer, Philip Trueman, Phyesalis, Pi, Platewq, Pmanderson, Pogoman, Pol430, Pozasa001, Pretchan, Prisonerhealth, Proff Milenstine, Profg, Prolog, ProtectWomen, Prsephone1674, PseudoSudo, Pseudomonas, PurpleKiwi, Pwnage8, Qdcraw, Qe, Qqzzccdd, Quigley, Qxz, R'n'B, R022956, R27182818, RB972, RJII, RVJ, Radon210, Raggz, Randoley, Randy Schutt, Ranveig, RatedRestricted, Raul654, Raven in Orbit, Rdesaintloup, Rdsmith4, Reaper Eternal, Recognizance, Red King, Redthoreau, Redvers, Reedy, Reenem, Reinsbr, Rejectwater, RekishiEJ, Restrictedarea, RexNL, Rgsmith2b, RicciJoy, Rich Farmbrough, RichardF, Ridernyc, Rigel1, Rjensen, Rjwilmsi, Rknasc, Rob01225, RobDe68, Robert Blair, Robertisawesome7777, Romarin, Ronald11, Ronhjones, Roozbeh, Roscelese, Ryoutou, Ryulong, S, S Marshall, S. M. Sullivan, SMC, Sa.vakilian, Sanabituranima, Sander123, Santa Sangre, SarahRattray, Sardanaphalus, Sasanjan, SasiSasi, Sblovato, Scaife, Sceptre, SchuminWeb, Scientizzle, Scope creep, Seaphoto, SebastianHelm, Seegoon, Sentimmm33, SerenaT.Ishida, Shadowjams, Shahab, Shalom Yechiel, Shalom perutz, Shaolin129, Sheldon Novick, Shervin111, Shizhao, Shorne, Simoes, Simon00001, SimonP, Sintonak.X, SiobhanHansa, Sir Vicious, Skepticus, Skinnyweed, Skram, Sky Attacker, SkyWalker, Skysmith, Sligocki, SlimVirgin, Slp1, Smalljim, SmilesALot, Smt w, Smurdah, Smyth, Snowdog, Snowolf, Snowolfd4, Sod283, Solipsist, Sonicsuns, Soosim, Soumyasch, SpNeo, Spamicles, Speculoos, SpeedyGonsales, Split, Spotfixer, SpyMagician, Squirepants101, Ssidhu, Steinbock, Stenun, Steph-mals, Stephens101, Stephensonsix, Stephenw32768, Stepshep, Steven J. Anderson, Stevertigo, Stevietheman, Stirling Newberry, Stormie, StradivariusTV, Stratvic, StuffOfInterest, Su-Jada, Suffusion of Yellow, SuperMarioMan, Superstarnorway, Survivor, Suzshi, Svick, Swads, Swarm, TFCforever, Tail, Tajik, Targeman, TarigMubarak, Tarquin, Tasbian, Tassedethe, Tawker, Tayl1257, Taz Manchester, Tazmaniacs, Tchakra, TedE, Tedder, Teryx, Tetraedycal, The Ogre, The Thing That Should Not Be, TheKMan, TheLeopard, TheRealFennShysa, TheRedPenOfDoom, Thecheesykid, Thelaststand3, Theleftist, Themastertree, Themfromspace, Thesunkenroad, Thetan7, Thingg, ThirdwayNGO, Thompson.matthew, Thorsen, ThreeAnswers, Tibetibet, Tiddly Tom, Tide rolls, Tiesko, TigerShark, Til Eulenspiegel, Tim symonds, Timschocker, Timwi, Tkn20, Tlmglasgow, Tocino, Toddst1, Toitoine, Tomchiukc, Tomi, Tommo 87, Tommy2010, Tomtom001, Tomwsulcer, TonyClarke, Tonyfaull, Topbanana, Toussaint, Tpbradbury, Tra, TreasuryTag, Trent911, Tresiden, TreveX, Tripledot, Trivelt, Trudat2000, Trusilver, TruthIIPower, Twan4rm08, Tyla0x, USHRN, UW, UberCryxic, Ucanlookitup, Uirauna, Ultramarine, Uncle Dick, Uncle Milty, Unclefrankinson, Universalist55, User A1, Uwakina Steve Chuks, Valley2city, Vanished user 03, Vchapman, Verkhovensky, VeryVerily, Vgranucci, Viajero, Vijayykumar, Villedre, Vineet10, Vipinhari, Viriditas, Vohuman01, Voltaire77, Vranak, Vrenator, Vsmith, Vzbs34, WACourson, WBBM2020, WHeimbigner, WJBscribe, WLU, Waggers, Wakeyjamie, Warrior4321, Wavelength, Wayland, Wayne Slam, Weser, WheezingBill, Whiskey in the Jar, Whkoh, Why Not A Duck, Wickey-nl, Wiki alf, Wikidea, Wikignome0529, Wikignome0530, Wikinterpreter, Wildt, Wilfried Derksen, William Avery, William Bawl, Willking1979, Willscrlt, Wimt, WingateChristopher, Winsweek, Wknight94, Wmahan, Woland37, Woohookitty, Wrs1864, Wtmitchell, Wuzzy, X!, X911, XGeordieRiotZzX, XXcheesemuncherXx, Xaman, Xashaiar, Xezbeth, Xxshadow300, Yamara, YangYouRen, Yelloeyes, YellowMonkey, Yelyos, Yeoni, Yerpo, Ynhockey, Yo mumma smells, Yodakii, Yonghokim, Yorkshirian, Yuckfoo, Yun-Yuuzhan (lost password), Yvh11a, Z10x, Zahd, Zeeshanhasan, Zero Gravity, Zero g, Zfr, Zntrip, Zodon, Zoe12345, Zoeshearer, Zollerriia, Zootm, , , 2094 anonymous edits

First Chechen War *Source*: http://en.wikipedia.org/w/index.php?title=First_Chechen_War *Contributors*: 1297, 172, 8mmfilm!, Abune, Aivazovsky, Alaexis, Alansohn, Alex Bakharev, Animum, Arne Heise, ArrowmanCoder, Arthur Warrington Thomas, Articulatron, Ash sul, Askari Mark, Attilios, Auspx, AuthorAuthor, Aytta, Aytta2, BD2412, Barticus88, Belligero, Ben-Velvel, Björn-Isak Rosendahl, Black Falcon, Boris Barowski, Boud, Bryan Derksen, Buckshot06, Bunnyhop11, BurtAlert, CALR, CanisRufus, Charles Matthews, Chris the speller, Colchicum, Colemanm, Collins.mc, Crystallina, Cuaxdon, Curieux, Cyberodin, DabMachine, Dar-Ape, Darklilac, Dc76, De Administrando Imperio, Deepdish7, Descendall, Dimacq, Dl2000, Dpf90, Dreadstar, Ducksaye, EZ1234, Eastern6595, Eightofnine, Ejcunc, El C, Ericd, Everyking, Ezhiki, Farmount1989, FeelSunny, Following specific instructions whispered by a mysterious cat, Fratrep, Gab.popp, Gadfium, Gallaghb, Georg huegel, Geregen2, Ghfgdhnjgfd, Giraffedata, Gob Lofa, Grenavitar, Grey Fox-9589, Guinness man, Guldenat, Guyver85, Hadžija, HanzoHattori, Heavenlyblue, Hiron, Hodja Nasreddin, Ifroggie, Ihardlythinkso, Ilya1166, Ingsoc, Insufficient, Intgr, Ironman419, JForget, Jaro7788, Jdorney, Jean-Jacques Georges, John Vandenberg, Jokecrazy33, Jon Harald Søby, JoshNarins, Joy, Joyson Noel, JustAGal, Jxb311, Karkachev, King Critter, Kmaster, Koavf, Kocoum, Kolokol1, KrakatoaKatie, Kross, Kuban kazak, Kubigula, Kungfuadam, Kurlandlegionar, Kwertii, Kyng, Lapaz, Lareneg, Lightmouse, LilHelpa, LokiiT, Longhair, LtNOWIS, Ltx kurasan, Luna Santin, MER-C, MVNdude, Mad Max, Mahtava, Malachirality, Mav, MaxDel, McSly, Mega programmer, Mendels, Metalbootlegger, Meteor2017, Mike Rosoft, Mikko Paananen, Miyokan, Momoricks, Moonshiner, N-true, NEMT,

Nanobear, Nexcet, Nicke L, Nielswik, Nigel Ish, Noclador, Nug, Nymf, Olivier, Outlook, PFHLai, PasswordUsername, PatrickFisher, Pernambuco, PeterPredator, Petri Krohn, Peyre, Philip Trueman, Psysword, Publicus, RadioKirk, RashersTierney, Raymar2k, Reenem, Renata3, Richard a b, Rintrah, Rjwilmsi, Ruslanbek, Russavia, SFinside, Sanguinity, Schaper, Selfworm, Sentinel R, Seryo93, Sesel, ShakingSpirit, Sigma 7, SilentOne17, Sluzzelin, Spylab, Steven Zhang, Superzohar, Tabletop, Tassedethe, Terraflorin, The Rambling Man, Therexbanner, ThinkingTwice, Tim1357, TimBentley, Tnapoleao, Top Gun, Tycoon950, Tzartzam, VVPushkin, Vanished user 05, ViriiK, Vivin, Waorca, Who, Wikipediatastic, Wikipelli, Woohookitty, Wst, Yalens, Yamamoto Ichiro, Yitzhak1995, Zanturaeon, Zlatko, نجرت ماژ05, 421 anonymous edits

Second Chechen War *Source*: http://en.wikipedia.org/w/index.php?title=Second_Chechen_War *Contributors*: 172, 1984, 3man, ABF, AVIosad, Abune, Adamarthurryan, Aivazovsky, Akosiya, Akrabbim, Alaexis, Alansohn, Alcuin, Alex Bakharev, Alex9788, Alexander Iwaschkin, AlexiusHoratius, Alik Kirillovich, Alinor, Allstar86, Altenmann, Amakuru, Andres, Andris, Antandrus, Apoivre, Arbeit Sockenpuppe, Armyrifle9, Arne Heise, Arthena, Ash sul, Asperchu, Assassin3577, Asterion, Attilios, Auntof6, Auspx, Aytta, Az1568, BD2412, Bakeysaur99, Bdb484, Belligero, Belovedfreak, Ben Ben, Ben-Velvel, Bgpaulus, Björn-Isak Rosendahl, Black Falcon, Bofoc Tagar, Bogdan, BonesBrigade, Boowah59, BrokenSphere, Bryan Derksen, Buckshot06, CBM, Caesar Augustvs, Captain Obvious and his crime-fighting dog, Carbonite, Carlossuarez46, Carolmooredc, Cdamama, Choij, Closedmouth, Cmdrjameson, Cmoibenlepro, Cmp7, Coemgenus, Colchicum, Colemanm, ComaDivine, CryptoDerk, Cs, Cybercobra, Cyberodin, Cyrius, DMCer, Dakart, Darklilac, DarthJesus, Darz Mol, Dav2008, De Administrando Imperio, Deconstructhis, Deepdish7, Dekimasu, Demian12358, Descendall, Digitalme, DI2000, Dpktnyfzgjkjcf, Dtremenak, Eightofnine, EkoGraf, El C, Elmor rus, Ency, EndymiOn, Ericd, Esaborio, Eurosong, Everyking, Evstafiev, Exiledone, Extraordinary, Ezhiki, Fatih Kurt, Fedayee, FeelSunny, Fisenko, Fisherjs, Flyingcheese, Foodman, ForrestSjap, GCarty, Gab.popp, Gadfium, Gadig, Gaidash, Gaius Cornelius, Garret Beaumain, Gb-uk, Gene s, Giovanni33, GirasoleDE, Gnaboka, Good Olfactory, GreatWhiteNortherner, Greswik, Greyhood, Groober, Ground Zero, Guitar3000, Gurch, HanzoHattori, Hardscarf, Heqs, Hetar, Hirudo, HistoricWarrior007, Historymike, Hodja Nasreddin, Hourick, Hux, IJK Principle, ILovePlankton, Iamunknown, Ich, Illythr, Ilya1166, ImperialDragon, Iridescent, IvanAndreevich, J Milburn, J alladin, J04n, JackThursday, Jade Knight, Jagged, Jaro7788, Jdorney, Jersay, Jevansen, Joaquin008, John, JohnOwens, Jonathan P. Whelan, Joseph Solis in Australia, JoshNarins, Joyson Noel, JustAGal, Karkachev, KathrynLybarger, Kelly Martin, Kelvinc, Khoikhoi, Kingal86, Kingpin13, Kintetsubuffalo, Kmorozov, Koavf, Kocoum, Kolokol1, Kooo, KrakatoaKatie, Kuban kazak, Kungfuadam, Kurt Leyman, Kwertii, LWF, Lapsed Pacifist, Lareneg, Last Revanant, Leszek Jańczuk, LilHelpa, LiquidOcelot24, Lockeownzj00, LokiiT, Lorian, LtNOWIS, Lvivske, Machinarium, Mad Max, Magicmike, Man with one red shoe, Mansmokingacigar, Manxruler, Marcika, Marek69, MariusM, Martin451, Martpol, Materialscientist, Mattbr, MatthiasGutfeldt, Mattiabonasso, Mattisse, Mav, Mbiama Assogo Roger, Mboverload, MelR, Meredyth, Mestesso, Meteor2017, Mgiganteus1, Mikko Paananen, Mind my edits, Miyokan, Moonshiner, Moscvitch, Moshe Constantine Hassan Al-Silverburg, Mrevan, Mrtwig, MuffinxMonster420, Naddy, Nanobear, Nasredin, Nehwyn, Nejee16, Nescio, Nick-D, Nicke L, Nielswik, Nigel Ish, Nikola Smolenski, Niqollyab, Nivus, NoaResare, Nomad84, Nurg, Nv8200p, Nwe, Nymf, Ohconfucius, Ojan, PB54, PBP, PDH, PMPTNT, Parivindi, PasswordUsername, Paul Pieniezny, Paulburnett, Pearle, Perovic, PeterPredator, Peyre, Propugnatorfidei, Psysword, Pti, Publicus, Queenmomcat, R'n'B, RG2, RandomP, Reenem, Rettetast, RexNL, Reyk, Rich Farmbrough, Rjwilmsi, Robin Hood 1212, Ross555, Rune.welsh, Russavia, Rxnd, Ryulong, Salahx, Sam Hocevar, Samian, SamuelTheGhost, Sandstig, SawatariDaidoji, Scope creep, Seivad, Sentinel R, SergeiXXX, Shanoman, SilentOne17, Simon12, Simonides, Singhartha Ensueno, SkyWalker, Slightsmile, Slon02, Slowak, Sluzzelin, Smalljim, Smoothtofu, Sonicology, Spongesquid, Spylab, Squiddy, Squids and Chips, Staplovich, Stewacide, Stifle, Stonewhite, Storkk, StuRat, Supergodzilla2090, Supersix777777, Superzohar, Tabletop, Tassedethe, Tbhotch, TenOfAllTrades, Theocide, Therexbanner, ThomasHoughton, Tim1965, TimBentley, TimShell, Toi, Tokenizeman, Tom harrison, Tomeasy, Top Gun, Tpjv86b, Trandall1992, Transcendence, Trektosaturday, Trojan51, Twthmoses, Ufos8mycow00, VVPushkin, Valodzka, Vanished user 05, Vannin, Vary, Vmenkov, Vmrgrsergr, Volker89, Voyevoda, WRK, Wayward, WereSpielChequers, Wester, WhisperToMe, Who, Whosyourjudas, WilyD, Wisdom89, Woohookitty, YK Times, Yalens, Zoe, Zurishaddai, Δ, 689 anonymous edits

Memorial (society) *Source*: http://en.wikipedia.org/w/index.php?title=Memorial_%28society%29 *Contributors*: Abune, Al3xil, Altenmann, Art LaPella, Avoran, Bluemoose, BorgQueen, Brighterorange, Buldri, Dojarca, Esn, Espenrh, Fayenatic london, Fuseau, Gallus Gallicus, Gothbag, Graham87, GrizzledOldMan, Ground Zero, Hardscarf, Henry Flower, Hodja Nasreddin, Ilgiz, Inwind, JCO312, John of Reading, Kaihsu, Kuralyov, Lapsed Pacifist, Lom Konkreta, Lovok Sovok, Malick78, Marrante, Moralist, Moravice, Pauli133, Peltimikko, Raodorikku, Renata3, Rich Farmbrough, Rpyle731, Smallbones, Tabletop, Tataral, Ufinne, Vanished user 05, Wik, Xx236, 16 anonymous edits

Nobel Peace Prize *Source*: http://en.wikipedia.org/w/index.php?title=Nobel_Peace_Prize *Contributors*: .:Ajvol:., 0, 1000Faces, 130.94.122.xxx, 151.24.145.xxx, 17Drew, 198.209.100.xxx, 271828182, 9Nak, A More Perfect Onion, A-Nottingham, A-giau, ACSE, AMBerry, Abhijitsathe, Academic Challenger, Academic2007, Ace2209, Adam Bishop, Adam Keller, Adambro, Addihockey10, AdjustShift, Adlibber, Ahoerstemeier, Aiden Fisher, Aitias, Akamad, Alansohn, Aldaron, Allgood331, Alpha Quadrant (alt), Altenmann, AnakngAraw, Andjam, Andonic, Andre Engels, Andreworkney, Andrwsc, Andycjp, Anetode, AngryWriter, Anna Lincoln, Antandrus, Apeloverage, Apoc2400, Arcturus, Arielco, Arlekean, Arsenikk, ArséniureDeGallium, Artur1917, Asalon12, Asbestos, Asdfadsasdfsfasdafds, Ashleylynn99, Astuishin, Atif.t2, Atrix20, Avimonster, Axel-schwede, AxelBoldt, AxelHarvey, Azimuth1, BRG, BahHAHAHA, Bearcat, Beek100, Bellemichelle, Benevolent Spectator, Bennyhinn90210, Benphen, Bfigura, Bhv nobel, Bhvan, Biccat, Big Smooth, Binand, Bjdekker, Blix000, Blue Square Thing, BlueGuy213, BlytheG, Bobblewik, Bobo192, Bolivian Unicyclist, Bonadea, Bondkaka, BoojiBoy, BrOnXbOmBr21, Bradle, Brion VIBBER, British4peace, Brunton, Bruxism, Burgundavia, CDN99, Caiaffa, Calmypal, Calwatch, Camptown, Canadian Paul, Canderson7, Canjo, Cantus, Canuckian89, CapitalE, Cardibling, CardinalDan, Casey1817, Cburnett, Ccd1964, Cenarium, Chairmanriot, Cheeseyguy112, ChongDae, Chris S, Chris the speller, Chriselliswest, Chrishibbard7, Chrishmt0423, Chrism, Christian List, CieloEstrellado, Cinatyte, Clone1, Coffee, Colipon, CommonsDelinker, Conversion script, CoolMike, Cornischong, Corwin8, Cpt ricard, Crocodile Punter, Crumb, Cst17, Cubs197, Cybbe, Czhangrice, D, DARTH SIDIOUS 2, DB 103245, DIEXEL, DJ Clayworth, DM Andy, DMacks, DVdm, DabMachine, DanKorn, Dandelions, Dante Alighieri, Darkspots, Darth Panda, David Kernow, David Nemati, DavidSpanel, Davshul, Db099221, Dbfirs, DeLarge, DeadEyeArrow, Deadlock, Deagle AP, Deavenettel, Decato, Deco16-10, Delirium, Delldot, Dendlai, Deor, DerHexer, DerkMiller, Dersen, Deutschgirl, Dhcp, Diannaa, Digitalme, Dirtmerchant, Disavian, Discospinster, Disqualified Demon, Dlae, Dlohcierekim, Dmn, DoRullings, Doktorbuk, Dominic, Donama, Donreed, Dopey180, Douglas Burkinshaw, Dowew, Dpr, Dr bab, Dr4chess, Dragonnas, Duncharris, EVil-Aer, EamonnPKeane, Ebakunin, Ed g2s, Editoro, Edward321, EdwinHJ, Ekologkonsult, El barto9, Eliyak, Elizabeth A, Emerson7, Emhoo, Enfermero, Engleman, Entowynn, Eridani, ErrantX, Eshaparvathi, Esprit15d, Esrever, Esuzu, Etale, Etams, Etaoin, Everyking, Evil Monkey, Excirial, Fanatix, Fang Aili, Fennessy, Fılll, FisherQueen, Fiv5katz, Flibbertyjibbit, Flockmeal, Floul1, Flubeca, Formeruser-81, Franamax, Frankman, Fredpax, Friday, Fryede, G.e.e.kclub, GTBacchus, Gary King, Gauss, Gavia immer, Gbonline, Gdo01, Gegik, Gegorg, Genius101, Genobeeno, Gerbrant, Geschichte, Ggbroad, Ghostofnemo, Giants27, Giftlite, Gilliam, Glenn L, GnarlyLikeWhoa, GoShox, Goatchurch, Graculus, Graham87, Grblundell, Greenturtle09, GregorB, Gscshoyru, Gunnybunny1337, Gurch, Gurchzilla, Gustavf, Haha169, Hahah123, Hajor, Happyme22, Haza-w, Hdt83, Heine, Helixblue, Henryodell, Hephaestos, Hi237, HiDrNick, Highonlife, Hmains, Holmwood, Honshuzen, Hu12, Huangdi, Hvn0413, II MusLiM HyBRiD II, IRP, ISnortCrushedPolos, Icairns, Igoldste, Ikewu83, In flew Enza, Indon, Inge, Insomniacpuppy, Intelligentsium, Invincible Ninja, Iridescent, Isiod, Isyou, J.delanoy, JB82, JCO312, JW1805, JaGa, Jackfork, Jacob Poon, Jacob.jose, Jagged 85, Jakeslar, JaneGrey, Janmark, Jarry1250, Jaxl, Jay, JayJasper, Jazz77, Jeff G., Jeffreykegler, Jeppiz, Jerzy, Jfpierce, JialiangGao, Jiang, Jipzmate, Jnestorius, Joanjoc, JoanneB, Joao Xavier, Joey80, John, John Hill, John K, John Paul Parks, Jojit fb, JonTheMon, JonathanDP81, JonathanFreed, Jonkerz, Joost 99, Jorunn, Joseph Solis in Australia, Jpeob, Juansmith, Judyholiday, Junyi, KF, Kablammo, KansasCity, Katalaveno, Katemurton, Kawkaba, Kbdank71, Keesiewonder, Keith Lehwald, Kevin j, Khcf6971, Kimathi, Kimse, Kingturtle, Kkm010, KnowledgeOfSelf, Koavf, KoshVorlon, Koyaanis Qatsi, Kpjas, Kransky, Krich, Ktsquare, Kungfuadam, LA2, Lambanog, LarRan, LarryMac, Laurascudder, Lcawte, Ldud, LeaveSleaves, Leoadec, Leolaursen, Levineps, LiNERROR, Lightmouse, Lihaas, Limmerick007, Loadmaster, Lockesdonkey, LonelyBeacon, Lonelydarksky, Lord Emsworth, Luci Sandor, Lucideer, Lunchboxhero, Lunchscale, LuxFerum, Lysanzia, M.nelson, MAG1, MARKELLOS, MER-C, Mac, Mackan79, Macphisto, Macy, Makgraf, Manninp2, Marek69, Marginoferror, Marshall Williams2, MartinP1983, Matchups, MattWright, Mauro Bieg, Mav, Mawai, McGeddon, Mcorco2, Me mi mo, Med, Meegs, Mellifluous2008, Metageek, Metsavend, Mgimpel, Mic, Michael Ward, Michael riber jorgensen, Midway, Mike Rosoft, Mike333, Mikecraig, Miketedting, Miller17CU94, Mistico, Mjbt, Mmcculloch, Mmoehle, Moe Epsilon, Moggq, Mohammadahmad666, Mostafa Hussein, Mostlyharmless, Mothh, Movingboxes, Mpntod, Mr. Wheely Guy, MrWhipple, Mrego, Musicalmeg20, Mxn, NAHID, NSH001, NYScholar, Nabarry, Naddy, Nanobug, Naomib123, NapoliRoma, Nascar1996, NawlinWiki, Ndkl, Nergaal, NewEnglandYankee, Nick Cooper, NickW557, NickelShoe, Nielspeterqm, Nil Einne, Ninly, Nirvana2013, Nisselua, Nma wiki, NoahElhardt, Noahcs, Noctibus, Noeln94, NuclearWarfare, Nutmegger, Nwe, Nwt, OCNative, Obradovic Goran, Odengatan, Odgersfan83, Odie5533, Officiallyover, Ohconfucius, Ohnoitsjamie, Okapi, Olaf Davis, Omegastar, OneCoolKid, OneVoice, Onebravemonkey, Onebyone, OntarioQuizzer, Opelio, OpenToppedBus, Orncider, Ornithologician, Orzetto, Osomec, Ottestad, PGSable, Padawan3000, Paginate, Palnatoke, Panda, Paris75000, Pasky, Passw0rd, PatriceNeff, Patstuart, Pdboddy, Per aspera ad Astra, Peter Clarke, Pgarcia05, Pgk, Pharaoh Hound, Pharos, Phil Sandifer, Philip Trueman, PiMaster3, Pilotguy, Plasma east, Politic28, Ponyo, Praefectorian, Pre1mjr, Prof75, Professor Davies, Proffesorn, Proteus, PyroGamer, Pyroponce, Qertis, Quadell, Quelcrime, Quiddity, Quiksurfer772, Qxz, R. Baley, RCPayne, RUL3R, RadicalPi, Rbb1181, Rebwim76, Recognizance, Recurring dreams, RedWordSmith, Reddi, Redsxfenway, RepublicanJacobite, Reywas92, Richar4034, Rillian, Rkelly74, Rob DiLLy, Robert Merkel, RobertG, Rockero, Romanm, Ronstew, RoryLunz, Rotovia, RoyBoy, Rrburke, Rynsaha, SF007, Sadfdsf, Sahmcolorado, Salt Yeung, Sam Korn, Samuelsen, SchfiftyThree, Scottlondon, SeNeKa, SeanO, Setanta747 (locked), Sgt Pinback, Shadowjams, ShakingSpirit, Shark96z, ShaunMacPherson, Shayl, Shorne, Shreevatsa, Shrimp wong, SianMycock, Simnel, SiriusB, Sjf95948, Skarebo, Sketchmoose, Skunkbig, Skunkboy74, Smalljim, Smith03, Smsarmad, Snigbrook, Snoyes, Snufkin7, Sockerkid5, Sohailstyle, Sophroniscus, Spartan95135, Spe88, Speedoflight, SpeedyGonsales, Spiff, Splash, SpoonThief, Squix, Ssbohio, Stevenscollege, Stismail, Storm Rider, Stormie, Strandist, Struhs, SudoGhost, Suffusion of Yellow, Sumergocognito, Susan Mason, Svick, Swarm, Sweikart, TED80, THEN WHO WAS PHONE?, Tad Lincoln, Tallus, Talono, Tariqabjotu, Tarquin, Tav2244, Tckl91, Technopat, Tempshill, Tesseran, Thatguyflint, Thatha, The Evil Spartan, The Mad Echidna, The Rambling Man, The Thing That Should Not Be, Theis101, Themat21III, ThomasPusch, ThompsBenon, Thumperward, Tide rolls, Tiemannl, TigerShark, Tiggerjay, Tildeathdouspart, Tiles, Timmeh, Timwi, Tinmanic, Tintenfischlein, Tjoneslo, Tkinias, Tktru, Tohd8BohaithuGh1, Tom, Tomas e, Tommy Herbert, TommyBoy, Tony Sidaway, Tonywiki, TotoBaggins, Tpbradbury, Trackerwiki, Treisijs, Trevor MacInnis, Trusilver, TubularWorld, Tullyjoe, Tunes, Tupac13th, Twistablecorn, Tye, UW, Ucscottb4u, Ugur Basak, Ungtss, Uriber, Useight, User2004, Usien6, Valermos, Vanished895703, Vanka5, Vapour, Vary, Vedek Dukat, Vegetator, Vexorg, Vicki Rosenzweig, Vipinhari, Vivio Testarossa, Vzbs34, Waffletchnlgy, Wagino 20100516, Wally, Warling, Wavelength, Wayne Slam, Wereon, Whatamldoing, WhisperToMe, Who then was a gentleman?, WikiRN, Wikibofh, Wikimancer, Wikipeterproject, Will Beback, Wimt, WindRunner, Wittylama, Wmahan, X!, Xaoivs, Xtopher, XxDrakexD, Y, Yankees67678, YawnJan, Yfan, Yilloslime, Yinandjang, Yoberalf, Youandme, Youssefsan, Yrodro, Zalgo, Zapvet, Zdravko mk, Zenohockey, Zerak-Tul, Zntrip, Zscout370, Zzuuzz, Ævar Arnfjörð Bjarmason, Алексаньдр, ვიკა, 1304 anonymous edits

Chechen people *Source*: http://en.wikipedia.org/w/index.php?title=Chechen_people *Contributors*: 7, AAhmed, AI, Aaandrew, Adilwaris, Aelfthrytha, Alansohn, Alex Bakharev, Alex.muller, AlexPU, Alexander Domanda, Alma Pater, Altenmann, Aminullah, Amoruso, Andreany, Andynapso, Aranel, Atomicdor, Azalea pomp, Barastert, Barefact, Behemoth, Belligero, Betalgiry, Big Adamsky, Bigaufe, Bobo192, CJLL Wright, Captain Obvious and his crime-fighting dog, Cautious, Chris the speller, CommonsDelinker, Cornface, CumbiaDude, D.Papuashvili, D6, DanKeshet, Darwinek, David Gerard, Dbachmann, Deliriousandlost, DuncanHill, Elvis214, Erkhesod, Eteru, Fisenko, Folantin, Freakingchic, Fritz Saalfeld, Gadfium, Green Giant, Gurch, HamburgerRadio, HanzoHattori, Hellerick, Heshamatak, Hmains, Hodja Nasreddin, Huangdi, Huon, Ingushetia, Itai, Itdepends, Izzedine, JDarkins, JTBX, Jagged 85, Jan1nad, John Cho, Johnelwaq, Joyson Noel, K1Bond007, Kaisershatner, Kbdank71, Khiram, Khoikhoi, KillaShark, Kingturtle, Kiore, Koavf, Kocoum, Kuban kazak, Labnoor, Lamanborz, Ldingley, Levi300, Liberatium, Loman-Az,

MacTire02, Mack2, Mahhag, Mandarax, Mansmokingacigar, Maturion, Mazdakabedi, Mild Bill Hiccup, Misza13, Mjr Edit, Mo-Al, Monty845, Mr Tan, Multihunter Tame, Nakh, Nicke L, Nitzalavar, Nop684, Noxchiy, Nv8200p, Omicronpersei8, Ostateczny Krach Systemu Korporacji, PANONIAN, PakistaniNisar, Papa November, Paradplanet, Particip, Paxse, Peter Karlsen, PeterPredator, PeterSymonds, Peyre, PlatonPskov, Poeticbent, Polyhister, Polylerus, Post Falls Man, Qurqa, Qwerty Binary, R'n'B, RafaAzevedo, RamboKadyrov, RexNL, Rich Farmbrough, Rjwilmsi, Rose Garden, Ruslanbek, STUTTGART, Saf kan, Samian, Sango123, Sasha l, SeNeKa, SeanMD80, Seb az86556, Selfworm, Serein (renamed because of SUL), Shagmaestro, Shawnc, Shell Kinney, Shi Hou, Sir192, Skinsmoke, Sl1982, Sosomk, Spoon!, Stainz, Stevenmitchell, Syush, The chavi, TheoloJ, Tim1357, Tullie, User1864, Utcursch, VMORO, Valentinejoesmith, VillemVillemVillem, Vmrgrsergr, Vonones, Vuvar1, WALTHAM2, Whisperednumber, Woohookitty, Wtmitchell, Yalens, Yst, Yulia Romero, Zenit4ever, Јованвб, صلاح الدين, 386 anonymous edits

Amnesty International *Source*: http://en.wikipedia.org/w/index.php?title=Amnesty_International *Contributors*: AJMW, AMuseo, AV3000, AZylman, Aarktica, Aaron, Aaron Brenneman, Academic Challenger, Acanalez, Achmelvic, Ad Nauseam, Adam McMaster, Adambro, Addicted, Admrboltz, Agamemnon2, Ainlina, Ajbpearce, Alansohn, Alberuni, Alec - U.K., Alerante, Alex Bakharev, Altenmann, Andonic, Andre Engels, Andrej86, Andres, Andrew Merry, Andromeda466, Andy Marchbanks, AngChenrui, Angela, AnonMoos, Anskas, Antandrus, Antidotto, Araeburns1, Aremith, Argyriou, Arkuat, Arniep, Arz1969, Ashadeofgrey, Ashmoo, Astudent, Attraho, Avia, Avraham, Awesomebitch, Axon, BD2412, BabuBhatt, Bambuway, Bardwell, Bart133, BeatlesJPGR1964, Beeswaxcandle, Ben-Zin, Bencampo, Bender235, Benedingo07, Bensin, Bernd.Brincken, Betacommand, Beyond My Ken, Bkell, Blahmos, Blakkandekka, Bobak, Bobblewik, Bobrayner, Bolivian Unicyclist, Bootstoots, BorgQueen, Boud, Bozonz, BrckoGOS, Briaboru, BrokenSegue, Bubbleboys, CIreland, CSWarren, Cadr, Cajetan da kid, Can't sleep, clown will eat me, Canadian Monkey, CanadianCaesar, CapitalSasha, Captain-n00dle, Carbuncle, CarlKenner, Carltonwilliams, Carnildo, Casiraghitrio, Certes, Cheesy Yeast, Chemturion, Chensiyuan, ChrisZ, Chrisdsn, Chuck Smith, Chwyatt, Chzz, Ckincaid77, Clytie, Colonies Chris, Comandante, Cometstyles, Comte0, Coneslayer, Confusedmiked, Conversion script, Cooldude1, Corti, CountCash, CrisCris84, Crotalus horridus, Ctande, Ctyr, CyberateoShe, Cyp, D prime, DCkevin, DJ Clayworth, DLand, Da Vynci, Dacfrazer, Daffy2, Dalillama, Dark Shikari, Darkildor, DasIstRicht, Daspostloch, David.Monniaux, Davidpatrick, Davshul, Daxdigital, Derwar, Disneyfreak96, Dl2000, Dlohcierekim's sock, Dominus, Donalds, Donnachadelong, Donreed, Doug kwan, Dr.Sorcerer, Dr.enh, Draco Emendator, Dragon2Zero, Drogetti, Drrll, Dsdukcy, Dumbledore, ESkog, Editingbill, EdwinHJ, Edwinstearns, Eedwa 01, Eisfbnore, El C, Elder Kibwe, Elinnea, Eloise wiki, Emerson7, Enchanter, Engelsam, Enviroboy, Epeefleche, Equinox137, Erolos, Esaborio, Esperant, Eugenechh, EverSince, Everyking, Excelsior Deo, Exteray, FJM, FWBOarticle, Favonian, Feto34, FiggyBee, Fowler Pierre, Fran Cowan, Francis Tyers, Freakofnurture, FreedomByDesign, FriendOfPanda, Frymaster, Fuseau, Fvw, G913, Gabbe, Gaius Cornelius, Galar71, Gaurav1146, Gfoley4, Glane23, Gondola, Grace Note, Graham87, GreenReaper, Greenshed, Grim23, GrizzledOldMan, Gump Stump, Gurch, Guy Montag, Gwernol, H2g2bob, Habeshawoman, HaeB, Hajhouse, Hajor, HamburgerRadio, Handbook3, HanzoHattori, Harryboyles, Hdc-en, Headbomb, Headhitter, Hellomoto1020, Henrik, Historicist, Hjr, Hkelkar, Homer Landskirty, Horace528, Hoserjoe, Humus sapiens, Hurdygurley, Husond, Hypnosadist, I386freak, ICSR - KCL, II MusLiM HyBRiD II, IdiotSavant, Ifuneedmeillbe, Ignatzmice, Infrogmation, Iridescent, IronDuke, Ivanakralova, J.delanoy, JForget, JYi, Jackol, Jacob.jose, JamesAM, JamesPassiton, Janu86, Jatkins, JayJasper, JayW, Jayjg, Jbd107, Jcampozano, Jcw69, Jessjeffers, Jetermans, Jeus, Jiang, Jidanni, JillandJack, Joao Xavier, JoaoPl, Joel7687, Joey80, John K, Jonik, Jonkerz, Joseph Solis in Australia, Jpeob, Jqstar77, Jschnur, Jtkiefer, Jumpmanlounge, K. Lastochka, KGasso, Kaal, Kaisershatner, Kaliz, Keilana, Kellen`, Keverich1, Kevin W., Khazaei.mr, Kidesena, Killeymouski, Kingpin13, Kingturtle, Kintetsubuffalo, Kitty1983, Kjfletcher, Klassobanieras, Klehti, Knare, Koavf, Korny O'Near, Kotiwalo, Kpjas, Krukouski, Kurieeto, Kuru, Kusma, L Kensington, LOTRrules, Lacrimosus, Ladybugldsu, Lahiru k, Lakhim, Lapsed Pacifist, Lavateraguy, Law, Leandrod, LegCircus, Leonard Vertighel, Lightdarkness, Lightmouse, Lights, Little Mountain 5, Lod, Logophile, Lokal Profil, Lquilter, Luke ormerod, LukeSurl, Luna Santin, M@sk, MZMcBride, Mac, Maias, Makalp, Malcolm, Malcolm Farmer, Malepheasant, MarkGallagher, Markt3, Martin451, Mattis, Mausy5043, Mav, Maziotis, Mceder, Meakin, Meco, Megamonkeyextreme, Mehah, Mentifisto, Merbabu, Methyl, Mgw, Michael Hardy, Mindcry, MisterSpooky, Modify, Mom1123, Montanean, Morwen, MosheA, Mostlyharmless, Mr.Z-man, MrJones, Ms2ger, Msaditi, Mustafaa, Mypowercell, Mystache, NEThomasYoung, NJA, NJW494, NSH001, NSH002, Nableezy, Namorfilus, Nandesuka, Naval ship, Necrothesp, NeilN, Neutrality, Newsjunkie, Niallbh, Nirvana2013, Niteowlneils, Noctibus, Noosphere, Notinasnaid, Nrlight, Nuno Tavares, OCNative, Ohconfucius, Olegwiki, Omegatron, OrangeDog, Orangemike, Orangutan, Orionpilot, Otto Antid, OwenX, Oxymoron83, Ozkaplan, Padraic, Pakaran, Palica, Paralympic, Parcadio, Parkwells, Patxi lurra, Pauly04, Pcpcpc, Perspicacite, Petrb, Pfetky, Phi beta, Philip Cross, Philwelch, Pigsonthewing, Plasticup, Plrk, Pnowosad, Porqin, Preform, Prosfilaes, Prowikipedians, Ptah, the El Daoud, Puellanivis, Pugs Malone, Pumeleon, Quatschman, Qxz, R Lowry, R. fiend, Rad Racer, RadManCF, Rama, Ran4, Randy2063, Randywombat, Raven4x4x, Rbrwr, Rd232, Rd232 public, Rdsmith4, Redb, Redthoreau, Reenem, RexNL, Rimshot, Rjwilmsi, Rls, Robert Merkel, RobertG, Robth, Rock4rights, Ronhjones, Roscoe x, Rostz, RudyB, SFC9394, SMC, Sagi Nahor, Samsontu, Samuelgodfrey, Sango123, Sardanaphalus, Savidan, Scarian, Scarykitty, Schneelocke, Scottperry, Sean.hoyland, Septegram, Serapindal, Sethmahoney, Shaliya waya, Shamir1, SiobhanHansa, SirFrog, Skaraoke, Skinnyweed, Skysmith, Slarre, Sligahan, Smallbighorn, Smalljim, SohailKhanifar, Someguy1221, Soosim, SpNeo, Spacejam2, Spiff, Spitzl, Ssidney15, StaticGull, Sterling63, Steven Argue, Student7, Stwalkerster, SudoGhost, Sully, Sullyss73, Super nat60, Swads, THEN WHO WAS PHONE?, TJRC, TUF-KAT, Tabletop, TaerkastUA, Techdawg667, Tedneeman, Tempodivalse, Thalgas, The Baroness of Morden, The Brain, The Evil Spartan, The Land, The wub, TheClerksWell, TheParanoidOne, Themfromspace, ThinkingTwice, Threeafterthree, Thryduulf, Tibetibet, Tide rolls, TimKroenert, Timdownie, Tkn20, ToddFincannon, Todeswalzer, Tom Morris, Tony Corsini, Toussaint, Tranzid, Trewornan, Triddle, Trident13, Troy 07, Tundrabuggy, Tyronen, Ukeu, Uliv, Uncle.bungle, Unused0029, Urban011, Urdutext, Uriyan, V95micfa, Vaceituno, Val233, Vanished user 05, Vapour, Versus22, Viajero, Viriditas, Vsmith, WGee, Waggers, Walden, Wasted Time R, Webbosoft, Welsh, WhatamIdoing, Whiskey Rebellion, WhisperToMe, Whooligan, Whosasking, Whywhenwhohow, Wiki.Boy, Wikifan12345, WillT.Net, Willking1979, Winhunter, Wsamuel3, Wuzzy, Xed, Ybbor, Youssefsan, Yvwv, Zache, Zadcat, Zeno Gantner, Zero0000, Zntrip, Zodon, Zoicon5, Zzyzx11, Δ, 997 anonymous edits

Martin Ennals Award for Human Rights Defenders *Source*: http://en.wikipedia.org/w/index.php?title=Martin_Ennals_Award_for_Human_Rights_Defenders *Contributors*: A930913, Belovedfreak, Bolivian Unicyclist, Boud, Clicketyclack, Danski14, Eastlaw, Ephraim33, Hvd69, Lapsed Pacifist, Mild Bill Hiccup, MrKIA11, Sean.hoyland, SteinbDJ, Tibetibet, نرامه, 18 anonymous edits

Thorolf Rafto Memorial Prize *Source*: http://en.wikipedia.org/w/index.php?title=Thorolf_Rafto_Memorial_Prize *Contributors*: Andrwsc, Benjamin P. Holder, Buldri, Coyets, DHN, Dr.K., Espen Henriksen, Espenrh, Geschichte, Hauganm, I-330, Inga330, Inge, LarRan, Manxruler, Mirithing, Nyenyec, Rafto86, Rskoly, SE7, Samuelsen, Shanes, Stevenliuyi, Tibetibet, Tkynerd, Ufinne, Vegardb, Zuccherinodolce, 25 anonymous edits

International Federation for Human Rights *Source*: http://en.wikipedia.org/w/index.php?title=International_Federation_for_Human_Rights *Contributors*: AndrewRT, Blogfidh, Bolivian Unicyclist, Boreas74, Bridesmill, Chai drinker, Chai drinker 2, Choij, Cmdrjameson, Cybercobra, Damzin2005, El C, Funandtrvl, Fuseau, Ggenellina, Huldra, Irishtimes, Khazar, Lapicero, LilHelpa, MER-C, Qwyrxian, Retired username, Rédacteur Tibet, Sc.helm, Scanlan, Skysmith, SomeHuman, The Tuna, Tibetibet, Tim!, Tkn20, Webmasterfidh, Zodon, 26 anonymous edits

Death threat *Source*: http://en.wikipedia.org/w/index.php?title=Death_threat *Contributors*: 123Hedgehog456, Aaron Kauppi, Alidha125, Anna Lincoln, Anythingyouwant, ArglebargleIV, AznBurger, Ben Ben, Bobmack89x, Boneyard90, Businessman332211, Bwiki, C.Fred, C4blows, CalPaterson, Captainlanks, CesarB, Cherkash, Chris the speller, CrawlPeezy, Dinkytown, DoubleCross, Dreadstar, Ed Poor, Ekashp, Eric, FootballExpert101, GVOLTT, Gadfium, Gamaliel, George, George100, Giggy, Gilliam, Grazon, Gwern, InShaneee, JForget, JHunterJ, JohnOlsson, Johndburger, Kbh3rd, Ketiltrout, Knowsetfree, Kuru, LFaraone, LGF1992UK, La Pianista, MC10, Mark.murphy, Miesianiacal, Moonriddengirl, Morwen, MuZemike, Newyorkbrad, NickelShoe, Pablo-flores, Pissant, Property, PsychoJosh, RJFJR, Riana, Roswend, SGGH, Sabbut, Samuel Blanning, Secretlondon, Slowking Man, Snowolf, SoMuchStuff, Soetermans, Sommers, Stepanstas, Stevertigo, Teehee123, The C of E, Thecheesykid, Thefrontdoor, Tisane, Toussaint, Tregoweth, VernoWhitney, Vranak, Wendell, Wuhwuzdat, X42bn6, Xerxesy, YUL89YYZ, Yfgfhgfhgf, 70 anonymous edits

Image Sources, Licenses and Contributors

Image:English Bill of Rights of 1689.jpg *Source*: http://en.wikipedia.org/w/index.php?title=File:English_Bill_of_Rights_of_1689.jpg *License*: unknown *Contributors*: Parliament of the United Kingdom

File:Declaration of Human Rights.jpg *Source*: http://en.wikipedia.org/w/index.php?title=File:Declaration_of_Human_Rights.jpg *License*: unknown *Contributors*: Agrafian Hem Rarko, Anne97432, AnonMoos, Avicennasis, Bohème, Cecil, Chaemera, Consta, David.Monniaux, Erasoft24, Eugrus, Frania Wisniewska, Herbythyme, Kallerna, Maksim, Shizhao, Taketa, Thabet202, Ultimate Destiny, Unai Fdz. de Betoño, , 19 anonymous edits

File:EleanorRooseveltHumanRights.png *Source*: http://en.wikipedia.org/w/index.php?title=File:EleanorRooseveltHumanRights.png *License*: unknown *Contributors*: CommonsDelinker, Ediacara, JdH, Kbolino, Knightedg, Temporaluser, Väsk, 2 anonymous edits

Image:Original Geneva Conventions.jpg *Source*: http://en.wikipedia.org/w/index.php?title=File:Original_Geneva_Conventions.jpg *License*: unknown *Contributors*: Kevin Quinn, Ohio, US

Image:UN General Assembly hall.jpg *Source*: http://en.wikipedia.org/w/index.php?title=File:UN_General_Assembly_hall.jpg *License*: unknown *Contributors*: Patrick Gruban

Image:United Nations Human Rights Council Logo.svg *Source*: http://en.wikipedia.org/w/index.php?title=File:United_Nations_Human_Rights_Council_Logo.svg *License*: unknown *Contributors*: Fastily, Jovianeye, Sfan00 IMG

Image:White mans burden the journal detroit.JPG *Source*: http://en.wikipedia.org/w/index.php?title=File:White_mans_burden_the_journal_detroit.JPG *License*: unknown *Contributors*: Kintetsubuffalo, Ras67, Thuresson, Travb, 2 anonymous edits

Image:Fgm map.gif *Source*: http://en.wikipedia.org/w/index.php?title=File:Fgm_map.gif *License*: unknown *Contributors*: afrol News. Always cite afrol News as the source when the map is reproduced.

Image:Chechnya and Caucasus.png *Source*: http://en.wikipedia.org/w/index.php?title=File:Chechnya_and_Caucasus.png *License*: unknown *Contributors*: User:Kbh3rd

Image:RussiaChechnya.png *Source*: http://en.wikipedia.org/w/index.php?title=File:RussiaChechnya.png *License*: unknown *Contributors*: Angela, Morwen, PANONIAN, Patrick-br, Template namespace initialisation script, 6 anonymous edits

Image:Evstafiev-chechnya-iternal-praying.jpg *Source*: http://en.wikipedia.org/w/index.php?title=File:Evstafiev-chechnya-iternal-praying.jpg *License*: unknown *Contributors*: User:Evstafiev

Image:Evstafiev-chechnya-women-pray.jpg *Source*: http://en.wikipedia.org/w/index.php?title=File:Evstafiev-chechnya-women-pray.jpg *License*: unknown *Contributors*: User:Evstafiev

Image:Evstafiev-chechnya-palace-gunman.jpg *Source*: http://en.wikipedia.org/w/index.php?title=File:Evstafiev-chechnya-palace-gunman.jpg *License*: unknown *Contributors*: User:Evstafiev

Image:Evstafiev-chechnya-boy-house-burns.jpg *Source*: http://en.wikipedia.org/w/index.php?title=File:Evstafiev-chechnya-boy-house-burns.jpg *License*: unknown *Contributors*: User:Evstafiev

Image:Evstafiev-chechnya-tank-helmet.jpg *Source*: http://en.wikipedia.org/w/index.php?title=File:Evstafiev-chechnya-tank-helmet.jpg *License*: unknown *Contributors*: User:Evstafiev

Image:Evstafiev-chechnya-handshake.jpg *Source*: http://en.wikipedia.org/w/index.php?title=File:Evstafiev-chechnya-handshake.jpg *License*: unknown *Contributors*: User:Evstafiev

Image:Evstafiev-chechnya-killed-in-truck.jpg *Source*: http://en.wikipedia.org/w/index.php?title=File:Evstafiev-chechnya-killed-in-truck.jpg *License*: unknown *Contributors*: User:Evstafiev

Image:Grozny2.jpg *Source*: http://en.wikipedia.org/w/index.php?title=File:Grozny2.jpg *License*: unknown *Contributors*: Melesse, PeterPredator, Remember the dot

File:Chechnya and Caucasus.png *Source*: http://en.wikipedia.org/w/index.php?title=File:Chechnya_and_Caucasus.png *License*: unknown *Contributors*: User:Kbh3rd

File:Evstafiev-helicopter-shot-down.jpg *Source*: http://en.wikipedia.org/w/index.php?title=File:Evstafiev-helicopter-shot-down.jpg *License*: unknown *Contributors*: User:Evstafiev

File:Mass grave in Chechnya.jpg *Source*: http://en.wikipedia.org/w/index.php?title=File:Mass_grave_in_Chechnya.jpg *License*: unknown *Contributors*: Natalia Medvedeva

File:Beslan school no 1 victim photos.jpg *Source*: http://en.wikipedia.org/w/index.php?title=File:Beslan_school_no_1_victim_photos.jpg *License*: unknown *Contributors*: aaron bird

File:Dmitry Medvedev 27 March 2009-2.jpg *Source*: http://en.wikipedia.org/w/index.php?title=File:Dmitry_Medvedev_27_March_2009-2.jpg *License*: unknown *Contributors*: Presidential Press and Information Office

File:AlfredNobel adjusted.jpg *Source*: http://en.wikipedia.org/w/index.php?title=File:AlfredNobel_adjusted.jpg *License*: unknown *Contributors*: Gösta Florman (1831–1900) / The Royal Library

File:Norske nobelinstiutt 1.jpg *Source*: http://en.wikipedia.org/w/index.php?title=File:Norske_nobelinstiutt_1.jpg *License*: unknown *Contributors*: user:bep

File:Dalai Lama and Bishop Tutu. Carey Linde.jpg *Source*: http://en.wikipedia.org/w/index.php?title=File:Dalai_Lama_and_Bishop_Tutu._Carey_Linde.jpg *License*: unknown *Contributors*: Carey Linde - who took the photo in Vancouver, Canada, 2004

File:1933 Nobel Peace Prize awarded to Norman Angell.JPG *Source*: http://en.wikipedia.org/w/index.php?title=File:1933_Nobel_Peace_Prize_awarded_to_Norman_Angell.JPG *License*: unknown *Contributors*: user:Anubis3

Image:Sheikh Mansur 140-190 for collage.jpg *Source*: http://en.wikipedia.org/w/index.php?title=File:Sheikh_Mansur_140-190_for_collage.jpg *License*: unknown *Contributors*: Geagea, Machinarium, Peter593022

Image:Kunta-haji 140-190 for collage.jpg *Source*: http://en.wikipedia.org/w/index.php?title=File:Kunta-haji_140-190_for_collage.jpg *License*: unknown *Contributors*: User:Papa November

Image:Pyotr Zakharov-Chechenets 140-190 for collage.jpg *Source*: http://en.wikipedia.org/w/index.php?title=File:Pyotr_Zakharov-Chechenets_140-190_for_collage.jpg *License*: unknown *Contributors*: User:Papa November

Image:Tapa Tchermoeff 140-190 for collage.jpg *Source*: http://en.wikipedia.org/w/index.php?title=File:Tapa_Tchermoeff_140-190_for_collage.jpg *License*: unknown *Contributors*: User:Papa November

Image:Khanpasha Nuradilov 140-190 for collage.jpg *Source*: http://en.wikipedia.org/w/index.php?title=File:Khanpasha_Nuradilov_140-190_for_collage.jpg *License*: unknown *Contributors*: Peter593022

Image:Milana Terloeva 140-190 for collage.jpg *Source*: http://en.wikipedia.org/w/index.php?title=File:Milana_Terloeva_140-190_for_collage.jpg *License*: unknown *Contributors*: User:Papa November

File:Flag of Russia.svg *Source*: http://en.wikipedia.org/w/index.php?title=File:Flag_of_Russia.svg *License*: unknown *Contributors*: Anomie

File:Flag of the Chechen Republic.svg *Source*: http://en.wikipedia.org/w/index.php?title=File:Flag_of_the_Chechen_Republic.svg *License*: unknown *Contributors*: User:Lokal_Profil

File:Flag of Ingushetia.svg *Source*: http://en.wikipedia.org/w/index.php?title=File:Flag_of_Ingushetia.svg *License*: unknown *Contributors*: Alex Spade, AnonMoos, Artem Karimov, Incnis Mrsi, Mattes, Mysid, Permjak, Ratatosk, Stianbh, Thuresson

File:Flag of Dagestan.svg *Source*: http://en.wikipedia.org/w/index.php?title=File:Flag_of_Dagestan.svg *License*: unknown *Contributors*: User:Stianbh

File:Flag of Rostov Oblast.svg *Source*: http://en.wikipedia.org/w/index.php?title=File:Flag_of_Rostov_Oblast.svg *License*: unknown *Contributors*: User:Lokal Profil, User:Walden69

File:Flag of Moscow (Russia).png *Source*: http://en.wikipedia.org/w/index.php?title=File:Flag_of_Moscow_(Russia).png *License*: unknown *Contributors*: Anime Addict AA, Chesnok, Conscious, Cycn, Homo lupus, Imz, Little Savage, Oren neu dag, Panther

File:Flag of Stavropol Krai.png *Source*: http://en.wikipedia.org/w/index.php?title=File:Flag_of_Stavropol_Krai.png *License*: unknown *Contributors*: User:Conscious

File:Flag of Volgograd Oblast.png *Source*: http://en.wikipedia.org/w/index.php?title=File:Flag_of_Volgograd_Oblast.png *License*: unknown *Contributors*: vector-images.com

File:Flag of Tyumen Oblast.svg *Source*: http://en.wikipedia.org/w/index.php?title=File:Flag_of_Tyumen_Oblast.svg *License*: unknown *Contributors*: User:Conscious

File:Flag of Astrakhan Oblast.svg *Source*: http://en.wikipedia.org/w/index.php?title=File:Flag_of_Astrakhan_Oblast.svg *License*: unknown *Contributors*: User:Conscious

File:Flag of Europe.svg *Source*: http://en.wikipedia.org/w/index.php?title=File:Flag_of_Europe.svg *License*: unknown *Contributors*: User:-xfi-, User:Dbenbenn, User:Funakoshi, User:Jeltz, User:Nightstallion, User:Paddu, User:Verdy p, User:Zscout370

File:Flag of Turkey.svg *Source*: http://en.wikipedia.org/w/index.php?title=File:Flag_of_Turkey.svg *License*: unknown *Contributors*: User:Dbenbenn

File:Flag of Kazakhstan.svg *Source*: http://en.wikipedia.org/w/index.php?title=File:Flag_of_Kazakhstan.svg *License*: unknown *Contributors*: -xfi-

File:Flag of Jordan.svg *Source*: http://en.wikipedia.org/w/index.php?title=File:Flag_of_Jordan.svg *License*: unknown *Contributors*: User:SKopp

File:Flag of Azerbaijan.svg *Source*: http://en.wikipedia.org/w/index.php?title=File:Flag_of_Azerbaijan.svg *License*: unknown *Contributors*: User:SKopp

File:Flag of Egypt.svg *Source*: http://en.wikipedia.org/w/index.php?title=File:Flag_of_Egypt.svg *License*: unknown *Contributors*: Open Clip Art

File:Flag of Syria.svg *Source*: http://en.wikipedia.org/w/index.php?title=File:Flag_of_Syria.svg *License*: unknown *Contributors*: see below

File:Flag of Georgia.svg *Source*: http://en.wikipedia.org/w/index.php?title=File:Flag_of_Georgia.svg *License*: unknown *Contributors*: User:SKopp

File:Flag of Iraq.svg *Source*: http://en.wikipedia.org/w/index.php?title=File:Flag_of_Iraq.svg *License*: unknown *Contributors*: User:Hoshie, User:Militaryace

File:Flag of Iran.svg *Source*: http://en.wikipedia.org/w/index.php?title=File:Flag_of_Iran.svg *License*: unknown *Contributors*: Various

File:Flag of the United States.svg *Source*: http://en.wikipedia.org/w/index.php?title=File:Flag_of_the_United_States.svg *License*: unknown *Contributors*: Anomie

File:Flag of Canada.svg *Source*: http://en.wikipedia.org/w/index.php?title=File:Flag_of_Canada.svg *License*: unknown *Contributors*: Anomie

Image:Evstafiev-chechnya-prayer3.jpg *Source*: http://en.wikipedia.org/w/index.php?title=File:Evstafiev-chechnya-prayer3.jpg *License*: unknown *Contributors*: User:Evstafiev

File:Amnesty International logo.svg *Source*: http://en.wikipedia.org/w/index.php?title=File:Amnesty_International_logo.svg *License*: unknown *Contributors*: Avicennasis, Eastmain, Gump Stump, Melesse, 1 anonymous edits

File:Faroe stamp 132 amnesty international.jpg *Source*: http://en.wikipedia.org/w/index.php?title=File:Faroe_stamp_132_amnesty_international.jpg *License*: unknown *Contributors*: Arne List, Ephraim33, Ies, Zache

File:Amnesty International Sections 2005.svg *Source*: http://en.wikipedia.org/w/index.php?title=File:Amnesty_International_Sections_2005.svg *License*: unknown *Contributors*: User:Lokal_Profil

File:Goodwin House2.JPG *Source*: http://en.wikipedia.org/w/index.php?title=File:Goodwin_House2.JPG *License*: unknown *Contributors*: Padraic, Skeezix1000

File:Flag of the United Kingdom.svg *Source*: http://en.wikipedia.org/w/index.php?title=File:Flag_of_the_United_Kingdom.svg *License*: unknown *Contributors*: Anomie, Mifter

File:Flag of Sweden.svg *Source*: http://en.wikipedia.org/w/index.php?title=File:Flag_of_Sweden.svg *License*: unknown *Contributors*: Anomie

File:Flag of Senegal.svg *Source*: http://en.wikipedia.org/w/index.php?title=File:Flag_of_Senegal.svg *License*: unknown *Contributors*: user:Nightstallion

File:Flag of Bangladesh.svg *Source*: http://en.wikipedia.org/w/index.php?title=File:Flag_of_Bangladesh.svg *License*: unknown *Contributors*: User:SKopp

File:Flag of India.svg *Source*: http://en.wikipedia.org/w/index.php?title=File:Flag_of_India.svg *License*: unknown *Contributors*: Anomie, Mifter

File:Logo FIDH Francais.svg *Source*: http://en.wikipedia.org/w/index.php?title=File:Logo_FIDH_Francais.svg *License*: unknown *Contributors*: User:Blogfidh

MIX
Papier aus verantwortungsvollen Quellen
Paper from responsible sources
FSC® C105338

Printed by Books on Demand GmbH, Norderstedt / Germany